THE HORRID PIT

Also by Alan Axelrod

Eisenhower on Leadership
Patton: A Biography
A Political History of America's Wars
Encyclopedia of the United States Armed Forces
America's Wars
Congressional Quarterly's American Treaties and Alliances
Patton on Leadership: Strategic Lessons for Corporate Warfare

THE HORRID PIT

THE BATTLE of THE CRATER, THE CIVIL WAR'S CRUELEST MISSION

ALAN AXELROD

CARROLL & GRAF PUBLISHERS
NEW YORK

For Anita and Ian

THE HORRID PIT
The Battle of the Crater, the Civil War's Cruelest Mission

Carroll & Graf Publishers
An Imprint of Avalon Publishing Group, Inc.
245 West 17th Street, 11th Floor
New York, NY 10011

AVALON
publishing group incorporated

Copyright © 2007 by Alan Axelrod

First Carroll & Graf edition 2007

Library of Congress Cataloging-in-Publication Data

Axelrod, Alan, 1952-
The horrid pit : the Battle of the Crater, the Civil War's cruelest mission / Alan
Axelrod. -- 1st Carroll & Graf ed.
    p. cm.
includes bibliographical references and index.
ISBN-13: 978-0-7867-1811-5 (hardcover)
1. Petersburg Crater, Battle of, Va., 1864. I. Title.
E476.93.A96 2007
973.7'37--dc22

2007012250

ISBN-10: 0-7867-1811-0

9 8 7 6 5 4 3 2 1

Interior design by Maria E. Torres

Printed in the United States of America
Distributed by Publishers Group West

Contents

PROLOGUE

By Direction of the President

SPECIAL ORDERS No. 205.
    HDQRS. ARMY OF THE POTOMAC,
       August 1, 1864.

*   *   *   *   *   *   *   *   *   *

4. A board of officers will assemble at such time and place on Tuesday, the 2d instant, as the presiding officer may appoint, to examine into and report upon the facts and circumstances attending the unsuccessful assault on the enemy's position in front of Petersburg on the morning of July 30, 1864. The board will also report whether in their judgment any party or parties are censurable for the failure of the troops to carry into successful execution the orders issued for the occasion. . . .

By command of Major-General Meade:
S. WILLIAMS,
Assistant Adjutant-General[1]

As an occasion of human suffering, "the unsuccessful assault on the enemy's position in front of Petersburg on the morning of July 30, 1864" was appalling. By the hundreds, people were blown up, mangled, killed, buried alive; others were shot, stabbed, bludgeoned, trampled; the wounded were allowed to writhe in pain and want of water under a merciless summer sun; the dead were left to rot. Yet, despite what it is commonly called—the *Battle* of the Crater—this operation was merely an assault rather than a fully developed battle, and, compared with so many of the battles that had come before it (and that would follow it), the Crater produced modest casualty numbers: about 5,600 killed, wounded, or captured on both sides. Casualties resulting from the Battle of Fort Donelson (Tennessee, February 13-16, 1862) totaled 19,455; from Shiloh (Tennessee, April 6-7, 1862), 23,741; Stone's River (Tennessee, December 31, 1862), 24,645; Second Bull Run (Virginia, August 29-30, 1862), 25,251; the Wilderness (Virginia, May 5-7, 1864), 25,416; Antietam (Maryland, September 17, 1862), 26,134; Spotsylvania (Virginia, May 8-19, 1864), 27,399; Chancellorsville (Virginia, May 1-4, 1863), 30,099; Chickamauga (Georgia, September 19-20, 1863), 34,624; and from Gettysburg (Pennsylvania, July 1-3, 1863), 51,112. Nevertheless, Ulysses S. Grant himself singled out the Crater as a "stupendous failure,"[2] and Army of the Potomac commander George Gordon Meade, whose subordinate Ambrose E. Burnside had been in charge of the operation, thought it serious enough to convene an extraordinary Court of Inquiry.

Meade pushed for the Court, pushed hard, and he handpicked the presiding board—Generals Winfield Scott Hancock, Nelson A. Miles, and Romeyn B. Ayres, plus Colonel Edward Schriver. Schriver was one of Meade's own staff officers, and the others were all commanders in the Army of the Potomac. The four were subordinate and answerable to Meade, a circumstance that hardly boded well for the court's objectivity. Their relation to Meade notwithstanding, however, the board members demurred in response to their assignment, reporting themselves "embarrassed by the requirements of the order, viz, to report upon the facts and circumstances of a failure of the troops to execute certain orders on the 30th of July, and whether any one is answerable therefor." Not only did the members point out that they lacked the authority to summon witnesses and examine them under oath, they observed that "the Rules and Articles of War especially forbid the institution of a tribunal, by whatever name it may be designated, for an object like that specified in the special order, unless directed by the President of the United States, or on the demand of the accused, who in this case, although not actually known to exist, may become no less a real personage by the finding of the Board, but who will not have had the privilege of being present throughout the investigation and of confronting witnesses by whose evidence he is placed in the position of an accused party."[3]

Undaunted by this most daunting response, Meade sent a message to General Grant, "respectfully suggest[ing] the matter be referred to the President of the United States, with the request that he either confirm the powers given to the Board or constitute them into a court of inquiry. I am clearly of opinion the interest of the army and of the country are involved in having an investigation. I am desirous that my conduct, as well as that of all others concerned, should be thoroughly examined. . . . I trust you will exercise your influence to induce the President to confer upon the Board the necessary authority, and for this purpose I would suggest an officer being sent to Washington." On the same day that he sent this message, August 2, 1864, Meade ordered the relief of Ambrose Burnside and preferred two charges against him, "Disobedience of orders" and "Conduct prejudicial to good order and military discipline."[4]

President Lincoln knew Burnside well and, back in November 1862, had pressured him into accepting command of the Army of the Potomac, which Burnside led to catastrophic defeat at Fredericksburg. Despite that terrible failure, Lincoln seems to have respected Burnside and, in any case, the president surely had a reputation for giving a man a fair hearing. It is surprising, therefore, that a Court of Inquiry, presided over by Meade's chosen members, was in fact convened "By direction of the President."[5]

Could Lincoln, the savvy lawyer and politician, have really believed that Ambrose Burnside would get a fair hearing in what was, after all, Meade's courtroom? We don't know. Perhaps Lincoln actually wanted the very thing Meade wanted: a forum to clear Meade's name. Often memorialized as an unbending idealist, Abraham Lincoln was in fact a double-jointed pragmatist, who might well have been willing to sacrifice Burnside, failed former commander of the Army of the Potomac, to prevent that army's current commander from coming under a cloud. Or perhaps all that mattered to the president was that two of his principal generals, Ulysses S. Grant and George G. Meade, deemed the Union failure at the Battle of the Crater too important to let slip by unexamined.

For only now, after it had failed, was the assault on the Crater seen as a missed opportunity, an opportunity of far greater consequence than the brief duration of the action and its comparatively modest casualty figures suggested. It was regarded now as an opportunity—forever lost—to break the siege at Petersburg, Virginia, thereby crowning the costly Overland Campaign, Grant's drive for total victory in the Civil War, with sudden and final success.

Was this perception realistic?

We can do no more than speculate. The instant the assault on the Crater failed, it became one of American history's great *what ifs,* a subject of permanent speculation. For Abraham Lincoln, however, it was also yet one more heartbreak in a long war thickly sown with heartbreak, each a source of war weariness, popular disappointment, and national discontent. That it had occurred during what was of necessity the culminating campaign of the war—fought in an election year—made the heartbreak, weariness, disappointment, and discontent all the more critical. Reelecting Lincoln represented a national commitment to continuing the Civil War until the Union was restored unambiguously and without compromise. As the president himself saw it, each defeat reduced his chances for reelection. Perhaps victory at the Crater would have dramatically hastened victory in the war—or, at the very least, would have ensured reelection, which Lincoln believed vital to victory.

Perhaps.

Certain, however, was the fact that defeat at the Crater put reelection in peril and therefore imperiled the prospects for victory, whether sooner or later. This much was unalterable. His generals having lost a battle, Abraham Lincoln could do nothing to recover whatever opportunity that battle had represented. What he could do, however, was to authorize a process aimed at understanding and explaining the struggle and its failure. Such, too, is our purpose in this book.

- 1 -

The Broken Generals

Ambrose Everett Burnside loved his men, and they loved him in return. Back in 1862, when he was still a winning general, achieving victories in North Carolina—small victories, to be sure, but magnified in their apparent significance by the prevailing dearth of Union triumphs—he was famous for two things. First, the public was attracted to the striking figure he cut. Not only did he fill out a uniform admirably, but his high, balding forehead dramatically set off his exuberant mutton chops, which inspired a tonsorial style immediately dubbed *burnsides*, later inverted to *sideburns*. Second, there was his already legendary concern for his soldiers and their reciprocated affection for him. Officers and men liked to recount how, in July 1862, he personally oversaw the transfer of some of his troops to the control of General McClellan, shuttling in a launch among the steamers that transported his boys, "nosing from steamer to steamer like a border collie herding his flock,"[1] and boarding at least one ship to scold an officer for having failed to spread awnings to protect the men from the southern summer sun. It was typical, and every soldier who served with Burnside had a story to tell about the general's solicitousness—as when, after the Battle of New Bern (March 14, 1862), the general was visiting the wounded in a field hospital and encountered a man, John Hope, who had served in his artillery battery during the Mexican War. Hope had been

Ambrose Burnside (Library of Congress)

hit in the leg, and Burnside, on the spot, fished in his pocket for a ten-dollar bill, which he gave the wounded man, telling him to buy fresh fruit and vegetables because they would speed the healing process. He stopped by to see Hope again just before the wounded were evacuated. Burnside gave him another five dollars— for the journey.

Only those few who had not heard the stories marveled at Burnside's tremendous popularity, how soldiers clamored to serve under him and called to him and cheered him wherever he went. "Vociferous cheering," one officer recalled, "first heard in the distance and increasing in apparent volume as it came nearer, was recognized as the sure announcement of the coming of Burnside."[2]

But all of that was in the past, near the beginning of the war. As the months oozed into years, Burnside's celebrated solicitude remained undiminished and, perhaps far more astoundingly, his men retained warm feelings for him. Yet, more and more, General Burnside was getting them killed.

A muted, costly victory commanding the right wing of McClellan's Army of the Potomac at South Mountain (September 14, 1862) was followed days later by a performance so sluggish as left wing commander at Antietam (September 17) that it helped turn what should have been a decisive victory for McClellan into at best a bloody draw in which 12,400 (of 56,000) Union soldiers were killed or wounded.

As Abraham Lincoln saw it, Burnside's performance was no worse than that of other commanders at Antietam and was in fact superior to that of McClellan. Besides, he had (at least in the recent past) something no other Union commander in the East possessed: a winning record. Disgusted with McClellan even before Antietam, Lincoln, about July 27,

1862, offered Burnside the opportunity to replace him as commander of the Army of the Potomac. Shaking his mutton chops, the general candidly replied that McClellan was the better commander and just needed a fair chance to prove it. Weeks later, just before Antietam, Lincoln repeated his offer. This time, Burnside answered even more frankly: he was incapable of managing so large an army, whereas McClellan could.

At last, on November 5, Abraham Lincoln stopped asking. Through the War Department, he issued General Order No. 182, which was delivered to Burnside in Virginia on the 7th by General Catharinus Putnam Buckingham. The order summarily announced the relief of George Brinton McClellan from command of the Army of the Potomac and the appointment in his place of Ambrose Burnside.

To Buckingham, Burnside protested that not only was he incapable of leading 120,000 men, but that McClellan was a perfectly fine commander. Worse, he said, it was a bad mistake to change commanders in the middle of a campaign.

Buckingham had been well coached by the War Department in how to overcome what everyone knew would be Burnside's reluctance. He explained that the president was intent on relieving McClellan, and that it was Burnside he wanted in his place—but even if he declined, McClellan was still out. Buckingham went on to explain that he fully understood the general's self-doubts, but, if he did not take the job, somebody far less able just might. And then he mentioned the one colleague the almost pathologically affable Burnside was known to despise: Joe Hooker. Hooker, whose arrogance and selfish careerism ran counter to Burnside's very grain, had served under him at South Mountain, where he had proved so dilatory in executing orders that what might have been a signal triumph there became instead a narrow victory, close-run and bloody.

Buckingham had struck a nerve, found the tipping point. Burnside swept his self-doubt into a corner of his mind, accepted the order, and accompanied Buckingham to McClellan's tent. "Little Mac" could not help noting the glum faces of his visitors. After a few uncomfortable preliminaries, Buckingham handed McClellan General Order 182. He read it, looked up, fixed his eyes on Burnside—whose friendship and loyalty he cherished—and said simply, "Well, Burnside, I turn the command over to you."[3]

Even before he positioned a single soldier or ordered the firing of a single shot, Ambrose Burnside blundered. Grasping for some way to simplify the management of 120,000 men, he reorganized the Army of the Potomac into three vast two-corps "grand divisions," commanded by Generals Edwin V. Sumner, Joseph Hooker, and William B. Franklin. On paper, this gave the organization an efficiently streamlined appearance, but, in the field, the unwieldy units were clumsy, slow, and freighted with inertia.

Reluctant to take command, Burnside had nevertheless made a bold—if bad—administrative move, as if to compensate for his reluctance. So, too, he yielded to pressure from Washington, which demanded an equally bold move against Robert E. Lee, something that would exorcise the crippling caution of McClellan and deliver victory in a single stroke. Accordingly, Burnside deployed the Army of the Potomac north of the Rappahannock River at Warrenton, Virginia, thirty miles from Lee's outnumbered Army of Northern Virginia, which consisted of just two corps, commanded by Stonewall Jackson and James Longstreet. A patient general, an unpressured general, a confident general, a better general would have launched an attack between the separated wings of Lee's army. This modest approach could well have defeated Lee in detail. Instead, intent on making *the* bold move, Burnside was bent on instantly bagging all of the Army of Northern Virginia, so he decided to press his advance against Richmond and make his attack south of Warrenton, at a place called Fredericksburg.

It was a very big bite to chew, and it required quick and vigorous action. Yet when Sumner's Grand Division arrived at a position across the Rappahannock River from Fredericksburg on November 17, Burnside insisted that the general wait until six pontoon bridges were in place. Administrative bungling delayed their arrival for a month, more than enough time for Confederate general Longstreet to dig his forces into the hills south and west of Fredericksburg and for Stonewall Jackson to arrive on the scene. By December 11, when Union engineers were struggling to assemble the belated bridges under heavy sniper fire, 78,000 Confederates were entrenched on the south bank of the Rappahannock, with Fredericksburg between the Confederate positions and the river.

Lee did not vigorously contest the Union landings on December 11-12, but, rather, allowed Burnside's men to occupy Fredericksburg, which lay just below his heavily fortified hillside positions. Burnside was marching into an ambush. Worse, he had ordered an artillery barrage just before the crossing, in which 5,000 shells were lobbed against the town, visiting gratuitous destruction upon it. This was followed by looting once the bluecoats entered what was left of the city. The spectacle of devastation and pillage ignited a fire in every Confederate belly.

When the battle proper commenced on December 13, Burnside enjoyed slight success against Jackson on the Confederate left, but the Army of the Potomac began to disintegrate in a series of hopeless assaults against the impregnable hillside positions. Even as the Union dead piled up before a stone wall in front of a sunken road below the Confederates' principal position at Marye's Heights, Burnside persisted in ordering one assault after another, fourteen charges in all, each a useless suicide mission.

At dusk, openly weeping for the men he loved, he announced one final attack—which he would lead personally. But then he yielded to the persuasion of others, who bade him withdraw back across the Rappahannock.

This time, his men were silent as he rode past them. When his aide demanded three cheers, the silence remained unbroken. Of the 106,000 Union soldiers who participated in the fourteen charges against the Confederate positions at Fredericksburg, 12,700 were killed or wounded. Confederate losses were 5,300 killed or wounded out of some 72,500 engaged.

Burnside cared nothing for the cheers he failed to receive. That evening, he wrote to his superior, Henry Wager Halleck:

5

> To the brave officers and soldiers who accomplished the feat of . . .
> recrossing the river in the face of the enemy, I owe everything. For the
> failure in the attack I am responsible. . . . To the families and friends of
> the dead I can offer my heartfelt sympathies, but for the wounded I can
> offer my earnest prayers for their comfortable and final recovery.[4]

Ambrose Burnside did not seem a man spun on the wheel of tragedy.
Far from it. Dark he most certainly was not. His popularity sprang not
just from his concern for his command, but from his all-around lika-
bility. Happy-go-lucky, many called him. Born in the little town of Liberty, Indiana, in 1824, he apprenticed to a tailor until, at age nineteen,
he secured an appointment to West Point, where, during his plebe year,
he racked up demerits for his free-and-easy conduct: seating himself at
breakfast before the command was given, making unauthorized
"visits" to fellow cadets, talking while on guard, gambling, ignoring
his duties in order to celebrate his birthday—the list of disciplinary
sins went on and on. By the end of the year, he had 198 demerits in an
institution that cashiered a cadet for 200. Yet he improved year by year,
rising above the middle of his class, until his final year when, for
playing hooky with his genial roommate, future Confederate general
Henry Heth, he again earned enough demerits very nearly to get him
kicked out. Yet his academic performance, especially in mathematics,
"natural philosophy" (physics), and tactics, saved him, and he graduated in 1847, eighteen in a class of thirty-eight, with a commission in
the artillery.

Like other officers of his class, Burnside served in the Mexican War,
reaching the front, however, when the fighting was essentially over.
While sitting out the interval between Santa Anna's surrender and the
conclusion of the Treaty of Guadalupe Hidalgo, Burnside beguiled
boredom in the gambling dens of Mexico City and environs. He emerged
an inveterate gambler, a firm believer in doubling down when the cards
went against him, so that, by the time he was transferred from Mexico to
Fort Adams, Rhode Island, he owed half a year's pay.

Burnside married Mary Richmond Bishop, a Rhode Island girl, in 1851, and resigned his commission in October 1853, borrowed money, and started the Bristol Rifle Works in Rhode Island with the object of manufacturing a new breech-loading carbine he was in the process of inventing. The Burnside carbine was patented on March 25, 1856. Lighter, faster, and more durable than anything that had come before it, the weapon found a ready buyer in the United States Army, and President Buchanan's secretary of war, John B. Floyd, contracted for a huge order, prompting Burnside to borrow more money to expand his factory. No sooner was the new plant finished than a competing gun maker bribed Floyd into breaking the Burnside contract. That man sold 55,000 of the Burnside carbines to the Union Army during the Civil War, and the weapon remained in service until 1876.

On the brink of triumph, Burnside became bankrupt, but he managed to save himself and his family by finding employment as treasurer of the Illinois Central Railroad. And there he renewed his friendship with a West Point classmate, George B. McClellan, the railroad's chief engineer, who would become his commanding officer in the Civil War. Burnside entered that war not by way of McClellan, however, but at the invitation of the governor of Rhode Island, who asked him to take command of one of the state's militia regiments. This led to command of a brigade, then of IX Corps, followed by command of both I and IX Corps in the Army of the Potomac, and, at last, his replacement of McClellan as commanding general of that entire army.

After the Fredericksburg catastrophe, Burnside yielded command of the battered Army of the Potomac to—of all men—Joseph Hooker on January 26, 1863. Burnside would have been amply justified in resigning his commission, but he did not so much as consider doing so. In his *Personal Memoirs,* Ulysses S. Grant wrote of Burnside, that he "was generally liked and respected," but "was not . . . fitted to command an army. No one knew this better than himself. He always admitted his blunders," Grant wrote, "and extenuated those of officers under him beyond what they were entitled to. It was hardly his fault that he was ever assigned to a separate command."[5] Having refused army command twice and having tried to do so a third time, Burnside would not have argued with Grant's assessment. He did understand, better than anyone else, that he was not suited to the highest command, and Fredericksburg had proved that, but he also believed that he still had much to offer his country in a more subordinate position. After being relieved as leader of the Army of the Potomac, Burnside fought competently as commander of the Department of the Ohio before being assigned once again to the command of IX Corps in the Army of the Potomac under his former subordinate, George Meade.

In spilling blood, Burnside was perhaps second only to Ulysses Simpson Grant himself, whose march "On to Richmond!" was a purgatory of gore. Burnside led his IX Corps gallantly in the Battle of the Wilderness during May 5-7, 1864, a contest that cost the Union Army 17,666 killed or wounded out of 101,895 men engaged. Next came Spotsylvania, a campaign that spanned May 7 to May 20 and that produced nearly 11,000 Union casualties. Cold Harbor, May 31 to June 12, spent another 10,000 men. In the month of blood-drenched days leading to the arrival of the Army of the Potomac just outside of Petersburg, Virginia, at least 50,000 Union soldiers were killed or wounded—41 percent of Grant's original strength. Robert E. Lee's Army of Northern Virginia lost fewer men during this period—32,000 killed or wounded—but his army was much smaller, and his losses represented fully 46 percent of his original strength. Grant accepted this as the terrible calculus of war. With each battle he lost, he sidestepped Lee and continued to advance southward, as if he had won. And, paradoxically, with each battle he won, Lee lost ground and lost men. Whereas Grant could replace the men he lost, drawing on the vast population of the North, Lee fought for a South whose young manhood was dwindling, and there was no one to take the place of the fallen. Like Burnside, Grant got men killed. But whereas the terrible loss of life at Fredericksburg gained the Union nothing, the lives Grant so prodigally spent in his progress toward Richmond were so many down payments against the defeat of the Confederacy.

That was one difference between Burnside and Grant.

Another difference was that, while some condemned Grant as "the Butcher," he was, in fact, a most thoughtful tactician and strategist. He had not spent his soldiers' blood in a war of attrition alone, trading Lee man for man, but had for a month and more also fought a war of maneuver, making one turning movement after another against Lee's right flank, forcing him to stretch his lines thinner and thinner, and ultimately deceiving Lee into concentrating around Grant's obvious objective: the Confederate capital city of Richmond. Grant had played upon Lee's logical assumption and merely feinted toward that city before crossing the James River and marching not against Richmond, but Petersburg.

Grant's genius for war was to harbor no illusions of glorious conquest. The well-meaning but tragically conventional generals who had preceded him in the top Union command had all been bent on occupying this or that territory and taking one city or another. Grant, in contrast, understood that the war would be won not by capturing any place—not even Richmond itself—but by killing the enemy army. Once that army was dead, the war would be over and the places won. True, the people and politicians of the North pressed him to take Richmond, but he saw that, at the moment, Petersburg was the more valuable prize. It was large for a southern city of the time, with a population of some eighteen thousand, and it was close to the capital, lying twenty-two miles south of it. Most important of all, it was a city of factories and warehouses located on the Appomattox River and at the junction of major rail lines: the Richmond & Petersburg Railroad, which ran directly to Richmond; the Southside Railroad, which ran west; the City Point Railroad, running northeast to City Point on the James River; the Weldon Railroad, bound due south; and the Norfolk & Petersburg, which ran southeast to the coast. Good wagon roads—rare in the South—ran through Petersburg as well: the Boydton Plank Road to the southwest; the Halifax Road, south;

the Jerusalem Plank Road, southeast; the Stage Road, due east; and there were also major roads running northeast, north (to Richmond), and northwest. Petersburg was critical to the supply of Richmond, and it was even more critical to the supply of the Army of Northern Virginia. Take Petersburg, and Richmond would weaken. Take Petersburg, and Lee's army would hunger and thirst and exhaust its ammunition. Take Petersburg, and the Army of Northern Virginia would start to die.

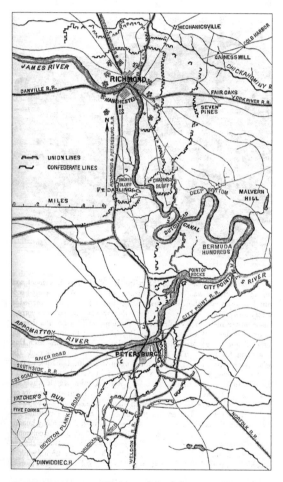

Contemporary map of Union and Confederate positions at the time of the Petersburg siege. (*Harper's Pictorial History of the Civil War,* 1866)

Misled by Grant's long, bloody, turning march, Lee had apportioned most of his meager resources to cover Richmond. Petersburg, therefore, was vulnerable in June 1864—but it had not been left entirely undefended.

One year into the war, the Confederate high command finally recognized that a city of strategic and logistical importance like Petersburg should not be left unfortified. On August 4, 1862, Colonel A. L. Long, military secretary to Robert E. Lee, transmitted an order to Major General D. H. Hill, commander of the Department of North Carolina, whose headquarters was in Petersburg:

> GENERAL: General Lee desires me to inform you that Lieutenant Colonel Stevens, Engineer Corps, has been ordered to Petersburg to make an examination of the country and establish a line of works for the defense of that position.[6]

Lieutenant Colonel Walter Stevens recommended encircling the "Cockade City" (as Virginians called Petersburg) with a ring of forts, partially enclosed and connected by trenches. It was a major project, which required the labor of more than 4,000 soldiers (drawn from three brigades) augmented by about 1,000 slaves conscripted from Virginia and North Carolina. Stevens drew up the initial plan along with Colonel J. F. Gilmer, but the massive project was completed under the supervision of Captain Charles Dimmock. Originally assigned to the Petersburg area to build obstacles on the Appomattox River, Dimmock was a sixty-two-year-old engineer with a great deal of experience. He was a Northerner by birth, a native of Massachusetts, and had graduated from West Point with the class of 1821. He served briefly as assistant professor of engineering at the academy, then became an artillery instructor. During 1831-1833, he supervised construction of the Delaware breakwater. Promoted to captain on August 6, 1836, he resigned at the end of September and moved to the South, where he worked as a civil engineer, building railroads and, in 1837-1838, advising on the location of a U.S.

military road to Fort Smith, Arkansas. From 1843 to 1847, Dimmock was director of the James River and Kanawha Canal and also served during this period as an officer in the Virginia state militia, rising to the post of superintendent of the state armory in 1843, an office he held at the outbreak of the Civil War. Dimmock enjoyed prominence among his fellow citizens of Richmond, serving on the city council in 1850, 1854, and 1858. He entered the Confederate service at the outbreak of the war.

With the Army of the Potomac uncomfortably close by, at Harrison's Landing on the Virginia Peninsula, work on the Petersburg fortifications at first moved rapidly, but when the Federals withdrew to northern Virginia, progress slowed considerably, and Dimmock was still requisitioning both slave conscripts and free blacks to work on the line as late as March 1863. After Dimmock died on October 27, 1863, the fortifications were named in his honor. The Dimmock Line was a system of fifty-five artillery batteries—small forts—deployed in an irregular ten-mile semicircle around Petersburg, both ends of the semicircle, east and west, anchored on the bank of Appomattox River. The batteries were tied together by trenches, the walls of which were built up as high earthen parapets, reinforced with logs. At various strong points, the parapets were reinforced by elaborate gabion revetments.[7]

Producing the basket-like gabions required highly labor-intensive hand work, as did excavating trenches, mounding up great earthen parapets, and building revetments of logs. The labor called for was even greater than the ten-mile extent of the Dimmock Line implied. For the "works" (as fortifications of the period were called) were not designed as a simple straight line of trench, but zigzagged and included numerous structures, such as bomb-proofs and covered ways. The zigzag plan of the trenches—more accurately a crenellated layout, resembling a row of teeth—was intended to provide fields of crossfire and also to defend against a disastrous flanking attack. In a straight trench, all an enemy had to do was overrun the trench, turn 90 degrees, and fire down the length of the trench, very easily rolling up the defender's flank. In a zigzag or crenellated trench, however, the enemy would not have a clear line of fire down the length of the trench; on the contrary, he would be exposed to fire and crossfire from the various projecting points of the crenellated layout. Structures such as

A Union photographer took this picture of an intact portion of the Confederate fortifications at Petersburg after the lines had been captured. The maze-like complexity of the trench layout is vividly apparent. Note the heavy log reinforcements throughout and, in the right foreground, the use of gabions (woven basketlike anti-blast reinforcements). In the distance, to the left, chevaux-de-frise are visible. Union works on the Petersburg front were similarly constructed. (Library of Congress)

bomb-proofs and covered ways provided considerable protection against artillery and siege mortar attacks.[8]

In addition there were any number of obstacles in front of the Line. These ranged from simple felled trees to elaborately constructed chevaux-de-frise.[9]

As impressive as the Dimmock Line was, it had notable weaknesses. Between Battery 24 and Battery 25, a short distance east of the important Jerusalem Plank Road, there was a significant gap in the line.

This half of a stereograph superbly illustrates a cheval-de-frise, a defensive obstacle traditionally used to thwart attacks on fortifications. The obstacles shown here lay before the Confederate lines, but both sides employed them. (Library of Congress)

Moreover, at some places in the irregular line, salients projected far enough out to expose them unduly. This was especially true precisely where the Union might be expected to advance from the James River. Also vulnerable were a number of the guns, many of which were exposed too far above the protecting parapets. Dimmock had devoted little attention to clearing fields of fire directly in front of the line, which compromised the effectiveness of defensive fire. It was also the case that not a single one of the fifty-five batteries/forts in the Dimmock Line was entirely enclosed. Covered to varying degrees, all were completely open at the rear. If an attacker managed to penetrate the line, he could easily enter a fort from the rear, capture it, and turn its fire against the defenders. When General Pierre Gustave Toutant Beauregard inherited the mission of defending the Dimmock Line in June 1864, he was highly critical of the design, complaining especially that Petersburg would have been better served by a set of completely enclosed forts connected by simple entrenchments rather than an elaborate set of trenches joining partially enclosed forts.

As Grant saw it, despite the Dimmock Line, thinly defended Petersburg was ripe for capture. Yet his decision to move against it while merely feinting toward Richmond had been motivated in part by a stroke of strategic genius and in part by the failure of Ben Butler and his Army of the James to take Petersburg earlier.

Portly, crude Benjamin Franklin Butler was the very archetype of the "political general," a man of no military experience or aptitude who nevertheless had been assigned high command because of his prewar political pull. Before the war, Butler had been a brilliant criminal lawyer and politician. Assigned to command the District of Annapolis at the start of the war, he had the good fortune to occupy Baltimore on May 13, 1861 without opposition. In August, he captured two more easy objectives, Forts Hatteras and Clark in North Carolina, which conferred upon him an undeserved reputation as a master tactician. This was amplified when he occupied New Orleans on May 1, 1862—an objective David Farragut's fleet had effectively handed to him by reducing all of its river defenses.

Butler commanded the military government of New Orleans with a touch infamous for its ungracious, unfeeling, and even brutal cloddishness. After one William Mumford took it upon himself to tear down the American flag that had been raised by one of Farragut's naval officers over the New Orleans mint on April 26, 1862, Butler ordered the unfortunate man hanged. The execution was carried out on June 7, just before noon, in the courtyard of the mint itself. Seeking to teach the city a lesson, Butler invited the public and even allowed Mumford to speak before he swung. The condemned man expressed no regrets, but spoke only of his devotion to the Confederacy. Butler had created a martyr.

The hanging came shortly after Butler's equally infamous "Woman Order," promulgated on May 15 and authorizing a unique retribution against New Orleans ladies who had been so impertinent as to hurl insults at the Union occupiers. "It is ordered, that hereafter, when any female shall, by word, gesture, or movement, insult or show contempt for any officer or soldier of the United States, she shall be regarded and held liable to be treated as a woman of the town plying her avocation."[10] As if these actions were not bad enough, Butler "confiscated" $800,000 from the Dutch consulate in New Orleans on his sole assertion that the money had been given to the consul with the understanding that he was to use it to purchase war materiel for the Confederacy. It was an act that solidified Butler's reputation for highhanded corruption so thoroughgoing that he was dubbed "Spoons" because he allegedly made it a habit to purloin silverware from the city's wealthier houses.

Butler was recalled from New Orleans on December 16, 1862, and, late in 1863 was given command of what soon became the Army of the James. It was upon this sorry excuse for a general that Grant relied to capture Petersburg as he and the Army of the Potomac continued to fight their way toward Richmond. Butler planted his small army at Bermuda Hundred, between Richmond and Petersburg at the confluence of the Appomattox and James Rivers. This positioned him to attack Petersburg from both the north and the east, but, by putting his back against the rivers, it also rendered him vulnerable to entrapment. He failed to take advantage of the position, at first dithering and then half-heartedly jabbing at Petersburg from one direction and then the other instead of making a coordinated simultaneous thrust from both available directions. Butler's inability or unwillingness to strike hard and decisively prompted Beauregard to exploit the vulnerability of the Army of the James's position at Bermuda Hundred by sending a few thousand soldiers to tie off the space between the two rivers. With this, he bagged most of the small army in a tidy cul-de-sac. Butler had not been defeated, but, except for a single corps, simply and utterly neutralized.

Perhaps admonishing himself for ever having been so foolish as to assume that the likes of Benjamin Butler could capture Petersburg, Grant decided to cross the James and take the vulnerable city himself. He appropriated from Butler his one free corps, the XVIII under William Smith, ordering it to attack that portion of the Dimmock Line northeast of Petersburg. Unlike Ben Butler, "Baldy" Smith was not a political general. He had in fact graduated from West Point in 1845 so far up in his class—fourth of forty-one—that he was assigned to the prestigious Corps of Engineers. This meant, however, that, by the outbreak of the Civil War, he had little field experience, having spent much of his career as a surveyor and a teacher of mathematics at the academy. While serving in Florida, Smith contracted malaria, from which he never fully recovered. For the rest of his life, he struggled with bouts of depression, fatigue, and bodily weakness. Despite this, Smith managed to serve ably and, during the Chattanooga Campaign, he even performed with distinction. But by June 15, 1864, when he and XVIII Corps were called on to attack Petersburg, Baldy Smith was sick and tired. He managed to capture Battery No. 5 and the adjacent sections of the Dimmock Line, thereby making an auspicious beginning in the Union assault against Petersburg,

Half of a stereograph view of a "Redoubt near Dunn's house in outer line of Confederate fortifications captured June 14, 1864, by Gen. William F. Smith." Had "Baldy" Smith acted with greater vigor, the Union would likely have succeeded in taking Petersburg without a protracted siege. (Library of Congress)

but these gains were quickly dissipated by fatigue and an excess of caution. Like Butler, Smith now dithered, giving Lee the time he needed to begin transferring men to the Petersburg front.

The momentum of the Union assault was lost and could not be regained. Winfield Scott Hancock led II Corps into the fray late on the afternoon of June 15, rested, then resumed the attack on the morning of the 16th. Between June 16 and 18, three more Union corps—the V Corps under Gouverneur K. Warren, the VI under Horatio G. Wright, and the IX under Burnside—hit the Dimmock Line, pushing the Confederates back by feet and yards. Absorbing each thrust, the defenders of Petersburg extended their trenches and exacted a price in Union lives.

Even with forces combined, the Union generals could not seem to make their attacks stick. Maybe this was because, like Baldy Smith, they were mostly tired men, worn out by war. In the past, Hancock had been a brilliant and fiery commander, but he was grievously wounded at Gettysburg and never really recovered. In place of his former fire was a mixture of fatigue and most unsoldierly testiness. As for General Warren, the weeks of concentrated slaughter preceding the attack on Petersburg had quite undone him. Grant never called him a coward—he never called any officer that—but, in his *Personal Memoirs,* while conceding him to be a "man of fine intelligence, great earnestness, [and] quick perception," Grant wrote that Warren suffered from "a defect which was beyond his control . . . . He could see every danger at a glance before he had encountered it. He would not only make preparations to meet the danger which might occur, but he would inform his commanding officer what others should do while he was executing his move."[11]

As for Burnside, his IX Corps performed more effectively than any of the other units engaged from June 15 through June 18, yet by the time he arrived at the front, the moment in which a relatively easy breakthrough was possible had vanished. The Confederate lines were now too well fortified. Had the Army of the Potomac and its commanders been fresh instead of all but bled white by the cumulative impact of the Wilderness, Spotsylvania, and Cold Harbor, doubtless they could have broken through. But such was not the case. As worn out as any of his commanders, Grant, who still burned with remorse for having uselessly sent men to their deaths at Cold Harbor ("I have always regretted that the last assault at Cold Harbor was ever made," he confessed in his *Personal Memoirs*. "[N]o advantage whatever was gained to compensate for the heavy loss we sustained."),[12] called off the frontal assaults against Petersburg on June 19 and decided to settle in for a siege.

Of all the worn-out, wounded, dispirited, overly cautious, and nearly broken generals gathered in the Union lines at Petersburg, Ambrose Burnside had the most reasons for being nearest the brink. He was a failure. He believed that of himself, and, what is more, he was keenly aware that others believed this of him as well—especially his commander, the general in charge of the Army of the Potomac, George Meade. Yet what saved Burnside from the abyss was a character capable of absorbing, it seemed, almost limitless heartbreak. Instead of bitterness, he felt sympathy for Meade, for Grant, and certainly most of all for the men of the IX Corps and the entire Army of the Potomac. In calling off the direct assault on Petersburg, Grant sent a message to Meade: "Now we will rest the men, and use the spade for their protection until a new vein can be struck."[13]

Rest the men. Siege duty, Burnside knew, would not bring rest. In addition to the back-breaking labor of "the spade"—for the Union would now have to dig in—there would be the siege itself, a nerve-destroying misery and boredom punctuated only by the short, sharp terror of snipers' bullets and the more prolonged agony of artillery bombardment. In a siege, such torture, he knew, might go on for a very long time. Could anything be done to bring it all to a quicker end? Perhaps more than anyone else—more than Meade, more than Grant, even—Ambrose Burnside, contemplating the prospect of languishing under fire and under the Virginia sun, longed for the war to end.

- 2 -

The Engineer and the Lawyer

W ar is death's feast" runs a seventeenth-century English proverb. It is one of many ways of stating the obvious: war is destruction itself. Less obvious yet no less true is the amount of *construction* war also occasions: the assembly of armies, the making of weapons, the sewing of uniforms, the building of forts and fortifications. To his staff, on the evening of June 18, after the failure of the final frontal assault on Petersburg, Ulysses Grant declared:

> Lee's whole army has now arrived, and the topography of the country about Petersburg has been well taken advantage of by the enemy in the location of strong works. I will make no more assaults on that portion of the line, but will give the men a rest, and then look to extensions toward our left, with a view to destroying Lee's communications on the south and confining him to a close siege.[1]

Within Grant's innocuous sounding phrase "then look to extensions toward our left" was a whole world of hard labor. His plan was to dig his own entrenchments parallel to the Confederate line. By extending these trenches to the left—to the south and the east—Grant hoped to envelop Lee's lines. To prevent this from happening, Lee had to outdig Grant, extending his own lines to prevent the Union forces from cutting across his flank. As Grant saw it, he might or might not be able to flank the Confederate line, "destroying Lee's communications on the south and confining him to a close siege," but even if he could not, by forcing Lee to commit his men to extending their lines, he was compelling the Confederate commander to stretch his severely limited manpower thinner and thinner.

Immediately, then, both sides working, as it were in tandem, soldiers began gouging the rich Virginia farmland into twenty-six miles of trenches, a double line that crossed two large rivers and traversed no fewer than four counties. The labor was as simple as it was backbreaking. The men began by digging a ditch, taking care to throw the earth out in the direction of the enemy, so that a defensive rampart rose on what was termed the "engaged side" of the ditch—which, once deepened to six to eight feet and widened to about ten, merited redesignation as a trench.

Alfred R. Waud (1828-1891) was one of many artists who sketched scenes of battle and camp life during the Civil War. This sketch, titled "Making parrallels" (the misspelling is the artist's), shows Union soldiers digging trenches. A version of the sketch was subsequently published in *Harper's Weekly*, August 6, 1864. (Library of Congress)

Wherever possible, logs were laid on the engaged side of the trench, and the rampart mound was reinforced with these.

As with the original Dimmock Line—which the Union works paralleled and from which the Confederates extended their works to keep pace with the Union's entrenchments—the new trenches required far more than straightforward digging. They zigzagged or were laid out in a crenellated pattern, always with an eye toward preventing an "enfilade"—gunfire directed along the length of the trench by an infiltrating enemy. This pattern meant that twenty-six miles of trench required something more like fifty miles of digging.

Both sides devoted much time and effort to improving their works. Officers on both sides had learned the art of field fortification at the same place, West Point, and what the United States Military Academy taught was a tradition of fortification rooted in medieval siege craft. The result might be ugly and filthy—it always was—but it was not crude or haphazard. Not only were the trenches protected by carefully shaped earthen parapets, often reinforced with logs, the inside of the trench was equipped with a laboriously sculpted firing step, a shelf of mounded earth on which soldiers stepped to raise themselves up just above the level of the parapet so that they could deliver fire. After discharging his musket, a soldier would step down and, under cover of the parapet, reload. When he was ready to take his next shot, he would mount the firing step again.

As with the Dimmock Line, soldiers took time to prepare earth-filled gabions to revet, or reinforce, the inner walls of the trenches. In places, they modified the parapet with logs or sandbags to provide more cover for sustained shooting. At specified intervals, the laborers enlarged the trench into a specially fortified strong point or fort, which might shelter one or more cannon. Bomb-proofs and covered ways were strategically placed, as were separate pits to hold trench mortars—short, thick-barreled artillery designed to lob very heavy projectiles at a steep trajectory that sent them over even the highest parapet and landed them even in the deepest trench.

Soldiers who were not engaged in digging or in fitting log revetments or weaving gabions were put to work building chevaux-de-frise and the

Fighting at Petersburg ranged from the atavistic hand-to-hand brutality of the bayonet and rifle butt to the newly developed sophistication of very heavy artillery. "The Dictator" was built for the Union's seacoast defense, but was mounted on a railroad flat car for use in the Petersburg siege. It fired a 218-pound, 13-inch-diameter shell about 2.5 miles on a charge of 20 pounds of powder. (Library of Congress)

Alfred Waud depicted men of "Jackson's Connecticut battery" aiming a mortar. Mortars varied in size from such giants as the 13-inch "Dictator" to modest pieces of artillery such as this one. Whether large or small, the mortar hurled a projectile at a high trajectory, which was ideal for penetrating trenches and other defensive works. (Library of Congress)

At Petersburg, some soldiers killed and others were killed, but *everybody* dug—tunnels, trenches, and—as depicted here—water wells. (Library of Congress)

abatis—the latter nothing more than felled trees stripped of leaves and smaller branches, the remaining larger branches having been sharpened to points. These obstacles were placed side by side, then staked into the earth, ensuring that the sharpened branches pointed toward the enemy. No one had any illusion that either the chevaux-de-frise or the abatis would prevent or stop an attack, but it would surely slow one down, breaking up the assaulting formation of troops, reducing their momentum, and holding them close under the musket fire of the defenders. Work on the obstacles in front of the trenches was especially dangerous, since the labor detail was exposed to enemy fire.

On both sides, all enlisted men were liable for service on the labor detail, but both sides always gave the hardest work to black men. The Confederates used free blacks as well as slaves. The Union employed freemen as well as fugitive slaves, in addition to "colored" troops.

Even before there had been a United States, black men served in American militia companies. They were freely enlisted in the North, and even the South sometimes conscripted slaves in times of emergency. During the American Revolution, black men served in many northern militia companies, but they were initially barred from service in the

Continental Army by resolution of the Continental Congress, which was sensitive to southern wariness of arming any African Americans, free or slave. George Washington himself, the slave-owning commander in chief of the Continental Army, defied the congressional resolution and began to enlist African Americans in 1776. Congress never repealed its ban, but Washington's stature was such that it never enforced it, either, and by the end of the War for Independence, about five thousand African Americans had served in the Continental Army—and many, many more had served in the various militias.

After the revolution, the Continental Army was almost completely disbanded, but when a small national army was again formed, black troops were recruited for it and fully integrated with white soldiers, serving in various Indian wars as well as the War of 1812. In 1820, how-ever, Secretary of War John C. Calhoun, a South Carolinian, ordered an absolute end to African American enlistments. As soon as the enlistment term of the last serving African American soldier had expired, the U.S. Army became, for the first time in its history, an all-white force.

This was the situation that prevailed at the outbreak of the Civil War.

As early as August 1861, the nation's most famous African American abolitionist, Frederick Douglass, had earnestly advocated the enlistment of black soldiers in the Union army, but resistance throughout the North was almost universally unyielding. Even President Lincoln and a majority of Congress opposed the enlistment of African Americans. Some generals, however, acted on their own initiative. In the spring of 1862, a contingent of free blacks who had formed a never-activated Confederate regiment in 1861 called on Union general Benjamin Butler when he became head of the martial government of New Orleans. Butler initially declined their offer of enlistment in the Union cause, but when his forces were threatened by a Confederate counterattack in August, he quickly raised three black regiments as the Louisiana Native Guard, or *Corps d'Afrique*. The troops took to the field in November 1862, even though the War Department refused to muster them in officially.

In the meantime, to the east, also during spring 1862, Major General

David Hunter raised a black regiment on the Union-held Sea Islands of South Carolina and Georgia. The unit was made up of volunteers as well as men Hunter conscripted. The War Department testily refused to sanction the regiment, and Hunter dissolved all but a single company by August.

In Kansas at about this time, militia major general James H. Lane raised two regiments of fugitive slaves and free blacks. They actually saw action before the War Department grudgingly recognized them in 1863.

"Grudgingly" is the adverb that generally applies to the beginning of black enlistment. Congress and President Lincoln did not boldly adopt a policy of recruiting African Americans, but backed into it. On July 17, 1862, Congress passed the Confiscation Act, which authorized the president to "employ as many persons of African descent as he may deem necessary and proper for the suppression of this rebellion." On the same day, Congress repealed a 1792 law (which had never been enforced in any case) barring African Americans from military service, and the legislative body explicitly authorized the recruitment of free blacks and freedmen. Pursuant to this, on August 25, 1862, the War Department authorized the military governor of the South Carolina Sea Islands to raise five regiments of black troops. In the beginning, volunteers trickled in, but by autumn the trickle became a flood, and the first regiment was mustered in on November 7 as the 1st South Carolina Volunteers.

Following the Emancipation Proclamation of January 1, 1863, President Lincoln himself called for the raising of four black regiments. Service was always in segregated regiments under the command of white officers. Nevertheless, Lincoln's call opened the floodgates of African American enlistment, so that, by the end of the Civil War, some 178,985 black troops had served in 166 segregated regiments. This was about 10 percent of the U.S. Army.

Most of the reasons for the resistance to black recruitment were, of course, racist. Many officers as well as politicians believed that blacks were inferior, difficult if not impossible to train, and, by heritage of race, cowards. A white missionary serving black parishioners on the Sea Islands of South Carolina remarked in the spring 1862: "I don't

Civil War photographers rarely turned their lenses on African Americans. This unusual stereo-graph half shows a cook at work at City Point, Virginia, headquarters of the Army of the Potomac. (Library of Congress)

believe you could make soldiers of these men at all,—they are afraid, and they know it. Negroes—plantation negroes, at least—will never make soldiers in one generation. Five white men could put a regiment to flight."[2]

Others simply could not bring themselves to trust black men with firearms, while still others simply could not come to terms with putting a blue uniform over a black skin.

There were other reasons for objection to African American recruit-ment. Lincoln feared that enlisting them would turn the tenuous Border States—the slaveholding states that had not seceded—against the Union. "To arm the negroes," the president said in the late summer of 1862, "would turn 50,000 bayonets from the loyal Border States against us that were for us. . . . if we were to arm [the blacks], I fear that in a few weeks the arms would be in the hands of the Rebels." Many military officers sin-cerely believed that the presence of black soldiers in the Union army would boost Confederate morale as well as incite Southern soldiers to acts of retribution fueled by outrage. As it turned out, their fears were well founded. On May 1, 1863, the Confederate Congress authorized President Jefferson Davis to "put to death or . . . otherwise" punish any black soldiers taken as prisoners of war. Later, the order was extended to white officers commanding black troops. On July 30, President Lincoln responded to the Confederate legislation by warning that "for every soldier of the United States killed in violation of the laws of war, a Rebel soldier shall be executed; and for every one enslaved by the enemy or sold into Slavery, a Rebel soldier shall be placed at hard labor on public works."[3]

Many black men, including two of Frederick Douglass's own sons, who joined the 54th Massachusetts, were proud to serve in the Union army, but most white enlisted men and officers failed to greet them enthusiastically. Black troops were segregated in all-black regiments commanded by white officers. They were exposed to physical abuse and verbal insult, and they were always the last in line to receive equipment and proper uniforms. For a time, they were even paid less than white soldiers.

The field and staff officers of 39th U.S. Colored infantry. Virtually all the officers of "colored" regiments were white. A few enlisted men are seen in the background. (Library of Congress)

Worst of all, as many African American soldiers saw it, they were often kept out of the fighting. Most black regiments were initially assigned fatigue duty (common labor) and garrison duty (minding the fort). Despite the prevailing policy of using black troops as laborers, black units did ultimately fight in more than four hundred engagements, including thirty-nine major battles, and seventeen African American soldiers received the Medal of Honor. A very small number of black men— fewer than one hundred—were even commissioned as officers. Among these, eight—all surgeons—achieved the rank of major.

Grant resigned himself to a siege, and much of the labor involved fell to black troops. It was obvious that the army would not be moving for a while. But if Grant found that he could readily reconcile himself to a siege, there were some officers for whom the prospect was nearly intolerable. Ambrose Burnside was one, and Henry Pleasants, one of Burnside's regimental commanders, was another.

Pleasants had never planned on being a soldier, but by June 1864, he certainly looked the part of a veteran lieutenant colonel in the Union army. At thirty-one, he trimmed his well-waxed mustaches and tapered his slender goatee in the style favored by French officers in homage to their emperor, Napoleon III, a fashion widely imitated by American warriors. But his jaunty "Imperial," as the look was called, could not disguise the melancholy etched deeply into his face.

Pleasants had gone to war neither for glory nor even out of a conviction that slavery was evil and the Union had to be saved. It was loss, terrible loss, that propelled him onto the stage of combat. The death of his bride from a virulent fever had, in the span of a single day, drained all meaning from his life, leaving him nothing to do but follow his young wife into a place where, he thought, death was inevitable.

Born in Buenos Aires in 1833, Pleasants was the son of a Pennsylvania engineer who moved his family back to his home state, where the boy grew up. He studied to become a designer of railroads, but found himself increasingly interested in coal mining, which was the chief occupation of his region.

It was an era in which men were transforming the American land- ⌐
scape, reshaping it above and probing it below, extracting from the earth
the stuff of energy itself. Pleasants possessed a quiet genius for these
consuming enterprises of his age. He saw how coal was being mined, the
miners barely scratching the surface, hauling out only what they found
right away, then moving on. Pleasants believed that, on any given acre
of land, there was much more coal to be had, deeper down. He concluded
that, so far, the nation's coal fields were being exploited for only a small
fraction of their value. He meant to get that deeper ore.

Henry Pleasants set about boldly developing a set of revolutionary
techniques for digging deeper. Deep-shaft mining, he called it, and he
was just beginning to reap the financial rewards of his first successes
with it when the love of his life died.

After that, the work no longer spoke to him, and so he packed his
belongings and marched to war with the 6th Pennsylvania Infantry as a
second lieutenant. When his regiment mustered out from under him in
July 1861, he joined the 48th Pennsylvania, this time as a captain, and
fought alongside Ambrose Burnside in North Carolina, then at the
Second Battle of Bull Run and at bloody Antietam. Most intelligent,
highly capable young men are keenly aware of their value. They believe
they have a future, and, naturally, they behave in ways that tend to preserve and protect that future. Bereft of his bride, Henry Pleasants was
now a rarity among intelligent, highly capable young men. He was convinced that he had no future, and, for this reason, he fought with
unusual boldness. Accordingly, in September of that year, he was promoted to lieutenant colonel and given command of the 48th.

The regiment had been recruited by order of Pennsylvania Governor
Andrew Gregg Curtin, in response to Lincoln's July 1861 call for one
hundred thousand men to serve for three years or the duration of the
war. Colonel James Nagle, of Pottsville, raised the regiment exclusively
from local Schuylkill County men. Henry Pleasants was among his first
officers and did a good part of the recruiting. Companies B, D, G, and H,
were recruited in Pottsville, Company A in Port Clinton and Tamaqua,

Company E in Silver Creek and New Philadelphia, Company F in Minersville, Company I in Middleport and Schuylkill Valley, and Company K, in Cressona and Schuylkill Haven. A handful of the men had already served in the 6th, 14th, 16th, 25th, and other Pennsylvania regiments, but the overwhelming majority were green recruits. That did not mean they had been accustomed to the typical fat-and-happy life of a civilian. Most of the volunteers had been hardscrabble coal miners—then as now a hard and hazardous vocation.

On September 20, 1861, at Camp Curtin, the governor presented the regiment with two stands of colors, one from the state, the other the gift of a Pottsville patriot. Upon the latter's blue field was the motto adopted by the 48th: "In the cause of the Union we know no such word as fail."

Issued uniforms and "Harper's Ferry muskets" on the 22nd, the companies were drilled in light infantry tactics, and in the ensuing three years saw a great deal of action. Initially posted to Fortress Monroe, Virginia, from September 24 to November 11, 1861, the regiment was then attached to Williams's Brigade in Burnside's North Carolina Expedition and fought at New Bern before joining General John Pope in Virginia, fighting at Groveton (August 29, 1862), at Second Bull Run (August 30), and Chantilly (September 1). In Maryland, the 48th fought under Burnside at South Mountain (September 14) and at Antietam (September 16–17). Most of the regiment managed to live through the Battle of Fredericksburg (December 12–15), before being transferred to the Kentucky front, serving variously there, including at the Siege of Knoxville (November 17–December 5, 1863) and in the pursuit of Longstreet (December 5–29). After being granted "veteran furlough" till March 1864, the regiment fought at the Wilderness (May 5–7), Spotsylvania (May 8–12), and Cold Harbor (June 1–12).

By the time Lieutenant Colonel Pleasants and his command reached Petersburg, only about a hundred of the eight hundred or so miners who had originally signed on with the 48th were still with the regiment. Nearly three hundred had been killed in action or had succumbed to the diseases endemic to armies in the field. (In all, 11 officers and 145 enlisted men would be killed in action before the 48th mustered out on

July 17, 1865. Three officers and 142 enlisted men would die of disease by this date.) Yet more of the original members were wounded severely enough to be invalided out of the service.

The hundred or so miners who survived to reach Petersburg had been rough-hewn when they joined the regiment: Irish immigrants mostly, lungs black with anthracite, many of them Molly Maguires, veterans of bare-knuckle labor wars against the hired thugs of the mining companies. Three years of war against the Confederates only hardened them more. As for Pleasants, he was as tough as his men, and even more implacable than at the start of the war. For him, always at the head of the growing roll of the regimental dead was the name of his own sweet bride.

Henry Pleasants by no means hated war, but he could not endure siege warfare. Being on the move, marching, maneuvering, thrusting forward, even falling back were infinitely preferable to the prospect of hours and days and weeks of peering over a parapet, dodging snipers, enduring bombardment and boredom, passing the time, waiting for one side or the other to break, ever so slightly, so that movement could begin again. The waiting only gave him more unwelcome time to think, to brood, to grieve all over again.

Edwin Forbes (1839-1895) made this on-the-spot sketch of the Union lines. The inscription below the image reads: "Figures standing and sitting near guns, and in the foreground looking toward Richmond, June 16th. '64." They were, in fact, looking toward Petersburg. (Library of Congress)

The 48th had fought as hard as any regiment during the several days before Grant called off the frontal assault against Petersburg. The regiment had crossed Chickahominy Creek on the morning of June 14 and the James River on the evening of the 15th. The following afternoon, outside of Petersburg, it charged under heavy artillery fire, taking and occupying a position close to the Dimmock Line. Before daybreak, June 17, together with the 36th Massachusetts, the 48th stealthily made its way across a marsh, marching single file and in perfect silence, to assume a new attack position. As part of a line that included men of the First and Second Brigades, the regiment made a bold and sudden dash against the Dimmock Line, capturing a section of it and driving the Confederates at this point back a half mile. Four cannon, fifteen hundred muskets, and six hundred rebel prisoners were taken. Sergeant Patrick Honaghan, of Company F, and Private Robert A. Reid, Company G, captured the flag of the 44th Tennessee Regiment, on which the legend *Shiloh* had been emblazoned, and also recaptured the colors of the 7th New York Heavy Artillery. Both men received Medals of Honor for the exploit. The 48th Regiment lost seventy-five killed and wounded.

Shortly after sunrise, the 48th and the entire division moved forward and hastily dug entrenchments. The Confederates responded by shelling the Union line, but they did not attempt to overrun it. That night, the rebel forces in this sector quietly pulled back to the outskirts of Petersburg and dug in. A new assault was made against this position on June 18, but failed—although the 48th participated in the successful capture of the Norfolk and Petersburg rail line here and was instrumental in extending the Union line closer to that of the enemy.

Thus it was on June 19, stinging with the disappointment of Grant's failed attack, facing the grim, anxious certainty of a prolonged siege, that Lieutenant Colonel Pleasants contemplated the fresh red clay of the newly dug trenches in his sector. He mounted the firing step and peeked over the parapet.

He thought: *How close we are to the Confederate lines.*

Leslie's Illustrated published "The war in Virginia—the 18th Army Corps storming a fort on the right of the Rebel line before Petersburg, June 15 / sketched by our special artist, E. Forbes" on July 9, 1864. (Library of Congress)

They were no more than 130 yards away, he calculated. Certainly no more than that.

A Confederate redoubt, a small fort slapped together with nothing stronger than earth, packed and reinforced with logs and grandiosely dubbed "Elliott's Salient," was built into that rebel trench little more than a hundred yards away. Surveying this strongpoint, Pleasants imagined what would occur if the lightly held salient could be overcome or destroyed completely. A major gap would be opened in the Confederate line, which could be flanked, even gotten around, both to the left and the right. Kick this door open, and Petersburg lay beyond, ripe and waiting.

Henry Pleasants suddenly felt a rush of something he had not known in years, not since those happy days when he was pioneering deep-shaft mining in the coalfields of Pennsylvania. It was the excitement of invention, a eureka moment, the rush of a problem met and a solution suddenly found.

He turned from the trench wall and jogged the quarter mile to the tent of his CO, Brigadier General Robert Potter, commanding the Second Division, of which the 48th Pennsylvania was a part. He caught his breath.

"We could blow that damned fort out of existence if we could run a mine shaft under it," he told the general.[4]

To Potter these words must have seemed nothing less than prophetic. His rise from private soldier to general officer had been meteoric, and now that uncanny trajectory had delivered him *here*, to *this* place and *this* moment, to hear the words of an expert, a mining engineer. What else could it be but destiny? For earlier that very day, Potter had also looked over the trench, had gazed at Elliott's Salient, and had thought, sure enough, about a tunnel, a *mine*—the military term for a tunnel dug under an enemy emplacement either as a route of attack or as a means of laying explosives.

Potter had pondered: *Dig a mine beneath the redoubt, blow it up, then mount a major assault through the gap blasted into the Confederate line.* With Elliott's Salient destroyed, the line would be fatally vulnerable at this point. Vigorously exploited, such a breach would allow an attack on the enemy's flanks as well as his rear. Lee wouldn't stand a chance.

But Robert Potter was a lawyer by profession, not an engineer. His thoughts that morning had focused on a tactical wish rather than a practical method of accomplishing his goal. Yet that was just the point: palpable—probative—evidence of destiny. Here *was* an engineer, standing before him, and giving words to his very own thoughts.

Robert Potter was a New Yorker. Born in 1829, he had attended some classes at Schenectady's Union College before the war, but left without graduating and, gaining admission to the New York bar, set himself up as an attorney. Like Pleasants, he had not been born to the military, but in a remarkably brief span, the Civil War would make him a very good officer.

It is not clear why the outbreak of the war found the young attorney so eager to taste battle. But this was the case with many young men. In

1861, thousands dropped the tools of their trade wherever they stood and rushed to war in search of—what, exactly? An opportunity to do their duty, to fulfill a patriotic debt, to win glory, or perhaps to test themselves in the one arena where the contest could not be feigned or rigged. Of course, many of Potter's fellow professionals actively sought to avoid service. Unlike them, Potter looked for no strings to pull or arms to twist in order to wangle high rank and a comfortable berth. Instead, he rushed to the recruiting office and enlisted as a buck private. He did not linger long in this lowly rank, but quickly fought his way to a field commission as a second lieutenant and, by October 1861, was promoted to major in the 51st New York Infantry. No more than a month later, he was jumped to lieutenant colonel, at which rank he distinguished himself under the command of Burnside in North Carolina, receiving a none-too-grievous but entirely honorable wound at New Bern in March 1862. By March of the following year, he had been promoted to brigadier general of volunteers.

As Potter rose in rank, he began to emulate the tonsorial style of his commanding general, growing a magnificent set of mutton-chop sideburns, although he distinguished himself from his model by maintaining his mustache separately from the side whiskers rather than allowing it to flow into them, as Burnside did. Now, thrilled by his conversation with Pleasants, he dashed off the idea of a mine in a brief memorandum to Burnside.

To Potter's dismay, the missive struck no spark with the IX Corps commander. He decided therefore to renew his assault, and he called on Pleasants to turn the idea into a detailed proposal. Pleasants responded by making a hazardous personal reconnaissance of the ground in front of the Union works. The divisional

Robert Potter (Library of Congress)

staff officer who accompanied him on this mission took a sniper's bullet in the face for his effort. But the reconnaissance confirmed in Pleasants's mind that the idea was sound. He talked it over with other engineers and asked his regimental officers to prepare an exact list of all those with mining experience in the 48th. Armed with this data, he returned to Potter on June 24 with a plan, assuring him that, given just a few simple implements—picks, shovels, wheelbarrows, and a theodolite (an early version of the modern surveyor's transit)—he and the miners of the 48th Pennsylvania could tunnel twenty-five, maybe even fifty feet a day, reaching Elliott's Salient in two or three weeks at most. And, he told Potter, he had already spoken to the miners. They were eager and excited, absolutely confident that it could be done.

Potter accepted Pleasants's report, devoured it, then quickly digested it in a message sent that day to Major General John G. Parke, Burnside's chief of staff:

GENERAL: Lieutenant-Colonel Pleasants, of the Forty-eighth Pennsylvania Veteran Volunteers, commanding First Brigade, has called upon me to express his opinion of the feasibility of mining the enemy's work in my front. Colonel Pleasants is a mining engineer and has charge of some of the principal mining works of Schuylkill County, Pa. He has in his command upward of eighty-five enlisted men and fourteen non-commissioned officers, who are professional miners, besides four officers. The distance from inside of our work, where the mine would have to be started, to inside of enemy's work, does not exceed 100 yards. He is of the opinion that they could run a mine forward at the rate of from twenty-five to fifty feet per day, including supports, ventilation, and so on. It would be a double mine, for as we cannot ventilate by shafts from the top, we would have to run parallel tunnels and connect them every short distance by lateral ones, to secure a circulation of air, absolutely essential here, as these soils are full of mephitic vapors. A few miner's picks, which I am informed could be made by any blacksmith from the ordinary ones; a few hand-barrows, easily constructed; one or two mathematical instruments, which could be supplied by the engineer department, and our ordinary intrenching tools, are all that are required. The men themselves have been talking about it for some days, and are quite desirous, seemingly, of trying it. If there is a prospect of our remaining here a few days longer I would like to undertake it. If you desire to see Colonel Pleasants I will ride over with him or send him up to you. I think, perhaps, we might do something, and in no event could we lose more men than we do every time we feel the enemy.[5]

This time, Burnside took notice. That very evening, amid the murmuring buzz of soldiers' conversation and the occasional crack of a sniper's rifle, the commander of IX Corps summoned both Robert Potter and Henry Pleasants to his tent. He wanted to talk to them right away.

CHAPTER

- 3 -

The Tunnel

There is no detailed record of the meeting between Ambrose Burnside, Robert Potter, and Henry Pleasants that evening of June 24. We know, however, that Burnside was sufficiently concerned about the issue of ventilation that he asked several questions about it. Potter's own message to General Parke had raised the issue, specifying that "It would be a double mine, for as we cannot ventilate by shafts from the top, we would have to run parallel tunnels and connect them every short distance by lateral ones, to secure a circulation of air, absolutely essential here, as these soils are full of mephitic vapors."[1]

The issue of ventilation was indeed critical and, for two reasons, should have given Burnside pause. First, there was the identification of "mephitic"—poisonous, noxious—vapors arising from the local soils. Was this the analysis of Henry Pleasants, mining engineer, or Robert Potter, attorney at law? Doubtless, Pleasants was familiar with the dangers of methane gas found in coal mines. Also called coal-seam gas, methane in coal mines is a byproduct of coalification—the long geological process in which heat and pressure transform underground organic debris into coal. During this process, methane (as well as carbon dioxide, nitrogen, and water) is trapped within the coal bed. When the bed is disturbed by mining, the methane is released, and unless the shaft is well ventilated, the results can be fatal to miners. But, as any mining engineer would well know, neither methane nor any other "mephitic vapor" was a problem inherent in digging a long, relatively shallow tunnel that was not a coal mine. The ventilation problem was certainly real, but it had nothing to do with poison gas. In a horizontal shaft longer than about four hundred feet, the pressure of the surface atmosphere is inadequate to circulate the air essential to the exchange of oxygen for carbon dioxide that surface-dwelling humanity takes for granted. In all history, no military tunnel had ever exceeded four hundred feet in length, because it is at this distance that the circulation of air stops. It is not that the air is poisonous, but that it is of a volume insufficient to support life. And Pleasants calculated that *his* tunnel would have to be just over five hundred feet long.

Perhaps Burnside questioned the faulty analysis of the circulation problem, its attribution to "mephitic vapors" rather than to inadequate air pressure. Perhaps the mephitic explanation was entirely Potter's idea, and perhaps, that evening in Burnside's tent, Pleasants even corrected it. Or perhaps Burnside did not question the basis of the ventilation problem, but merely its solution. We don't know. All we do know is that the only written record of the original Petersburg mine proposal was based on utterly erroneous science.

As for the solution proposed to the ventilation problem, it was the second item that should have given Burnside doubt as to the feasibility of the plan. Potter's message proposed a "double mine," consisting of "parallel tunnels" connected "every short distance by lateral [shafts] to secure a circulation of air."

If digging a five hundred-foot tunnel through the no-man's land separating the Union and Confederate lines, running this tunnel under the enemy's fortifications, and doing all of this secretly, even as the two sides continually traded fire, was a formidable proposition, how much more daunting was the prospect of digging *two* of these tunnels, in parallel, and connecting them with transverse shafts?

In the event, Pleasants did not dig two parallel tunnels, but found another solution. As the historian of the 48th Pennsylvania later explained:

Ventilation was accomplished in a very simple way—after a method quite common in the anthracite coal mines. A perpendicular shaft or hole was made from the mine to the surface at a point inside of the Union rifle pits. A small furnace, or fire-place, was built at the bottom of this hole, or shaft, for the purpose of heating the air, and the fire was kept constantly burning, thus creating a draft. The door made of canvas was placed in the gallery, a little outside of this fire-place, thus shutting it in and shielding it from the outside air at the mouth of the mine. Wooden pipes, extending from the outside of his canvas door, along the gallery to the inner end thereof, conducted the fresh air to the point of operations, which, after supplying the miners with pure air, returned along the gallery towards the entrance of the mine, and, being stopped by the canvas door, the vitiated air moved into the furnace and up the shaft to the surface. By this means a constant current of air circulated through the gallery. As the work advanced, the inside end of the wooden pipe was extended so as to carry good air up to the face of the workings.[2]

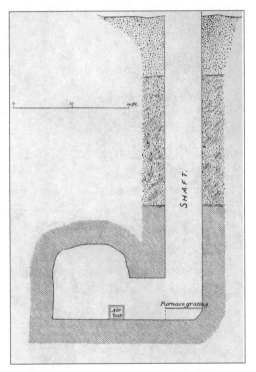

Of particular significance is the observation that this method of ventilation was "quite common in the anthracite coal mine," which was, of course, the venue of engineer Pleasants. Again, we are left to wonder why

This diagram of the ventilation system Pleasants engineered into his long mine was published in the U.S. War Department's *War of the Rebellion: A Compilation of the Official Records of the Union and Confederate Armies* (1880-1901).

Pleasants's expertise was not evident in Potter's message to Burnside's chief of staff, General Parke. Why was the unwieldy parallel-shaft plan ever proposed, a plan so labor-intensive as to be unfeasible? It is hard to believe that Pleasants didn't know better, and that the "quite common" simple shaft ventilation system only occurred to him later.

If Burnside approved the plan as presented in Potter's message, he was clearly authorizing a seriously flawed proposal, based on incorrect science. If this was the case, one is tempted to conclude that, desperate to make a bold stroke that might redeem a career wrecked at Fredericksburg, Ambrose Burnside was grasping at the thinnest of straws. But it is also possible that, in talking the plan out that evening of June 24, Pleasants not only clarified the ventilation problem beyond the nonsense about "mephitic vapors," but also replaced the double mine proposal with the much more practical single mine vertically ventilated. We do not know. In any case, if Burnside's testimony to the army Court of Inquiry held in August 1864, is to be trusted as both accurate and truthful, his response to the proposal was neither desperately enthusiastic nor even wholehearted:

Soon after this army arrived before Petersburg I received a note from General Potter, stating that if it was desirable the fort in front of his position could, in his opinion, be mined, and that he would, at my request, make a statement of the matter or would come to my headquarters with Colonel Pleasants, of the Forty-eighth Pennsylvania, and lay the matter before me verbally. I sent him word that I would be glad to take the matter into consideration; and accordingly he and Colonel Pleasants came to my headquarters and laid before me a plan for running a mine to that position. In the course of the conversation Colonel Pleasants remarked to me that this thing had first been suggested by the men of his regiment who, I think, were stationed in the advance line and pretty much all of whom were miners from Schuylkill County, Pa. The matter was fully discussed, and I authorized General Potter to commence the work, *making the remark, if I remember right, that it could certainly do no harm to commence it, and it was probably better that the men should be occupied in that way,* and I would lay the matter before General Meade at my earliest opportunity. We parted with that understanding, and the work was commenced.[3]

It appears, then, that Burnside's initial response to the mine proposal was at best tepid. Based on what he told the Court of Inquiry, it would seem that Burnside had little faith in the project, but believed "it could certainly do no harm" and would keep the men occupied. To be sure, this was no small consideration in a siege, during which discipline could easily disintegrate among idle soldiers, but if Burnside presented the proposal to his commanding officer, George Gordon Meade, in this same half-hearted manner, the commanding officer of the Army of the Potomac could hardly be blamed for his own absence of enthusiasm. "I did communicate the substance of this conversation [with Pleasants and Potter] to the commanding general of the army of the Potomac," Burnside testified on December 17, 1864, before the congressional Joint Committee on the Conduct of the War, "and received from him his assent, rather than his approval of the work." In fact, Meade told Burnside that he had no authority over siege operations and would have to pass the mine proposal on to General Grant.[4]

In the meantime, however, Major James Duane, Meade's chief engineer, weighed in. In his testimony before the Joint Committee, Pleasants reported that "General Burnside told me that General Meade and Major Duane, chief engineer of the army of the Potomac, said the thing could not be done; that it was all clap-trap and nonsense; that such a length of mine had never been excavated in military operations, and could not be; that I should either get the men smothered for want of air or crushed by the falling of the earth, or the enemy would find it out, and it would amount to nothing."[5] Despite claiming that he had to defer to Grant, and despite Duane's condemnation of the plan, Meade ended his meeting with Burnside by telling him that he would not raise any immediate objection if he wanted to start building the tunnel.

Inscribed by the artist, Edwin Forbes: "The tired soldier—a sketch from life at Petersburg during the siege." (Library of Congress)

Actually, as Pleasants testified to Congress, the digging had already begun before Burnside sought approval from Meade: "The work was commenced at 12 o'clock, noon, on the 25th of June, 1864. I saw General Burnside the night previous, and commenced the mine right off—the next day." Burnside had given his permission; indeed, he "was very favorable to" the operation.[6] There is no hint in Pleasants's testimony that Burnside was lukewarm to the tunnel.

"Was General Burnside the only officer who seemed to favor the mine?" a Congressman asked.

"The only officer of high rank, so far as I learned. General Burnside, the corps commander, and General Potter, the division commander, seemed to be the only high officers who believed in it," Pleasants answered.[7]

Those who have written about the "Petersburg mine" invariably condemn Meade and Duane for letting their low estimation of Burnside unduly influence their assessment of the Pleasants mine; and it is undeniable that Burnside and Meade did have a history, as did Burnside and Duane.

In truth, many Union army officers had a history with George Gordon Meade, a notoriously difficult personality with the pinched, ascetic features of a Protestant preacher. Observed one of his staff officers: "I don't know any thin old gentleman with a hooked nose and cold blue eye, who, when he is wrathy, exercises less of Christian charity than my well-beloved Chief." Grant said he was "brave and conscientious," yet also cautious, dull, and quarrelsome—"of a temper that would get beyond his control . . . and make him speak to officers of high rank in the most offensive manner." Like Robert E. Lee, he had been trained at West Point as an engineer. In sharp contrast to Lee, he was void of charisma and deficient in heart, but always meticulous. Learning that he would face Meade at Gettysburg, Lee, who had served with him in the prewar army, remarked: "General Meade will commit no blunder on my front, and if I make one he will make haste to take advantage of it."[8] That was Meade— competent, vigilant, unimaginative, and mean, mean-spirited, ready to pounce, whether the enemy wore a uniform of gray or of blue. General Meade regarded not a few subordinates with contempt, but of no officer was he more contemptuous than Ambrose Burnside, to whom he himself had once been subordinate and over whom he now

wielded command. Burnside's disastrous failure at Fredericksburg seemed ample to confirm Meade's low opinion of him. Yet even in his contempt there was a vein of the old envy and resentment he had felt over Burnside's rapid elevation, earlier in the war, above him.

The relationship between Major James C. Duane and Ambrose Burnside was even more intense. Meade's chief engineer was the author of a West Point manual on military tunnels and, as recently as 1863, had published with the New York publishing firm

George Gordon Meade, commander of the Army of the Potomac (Library of Congress)

of D. Van Nostrand the second edition of his *Manual for Engineer Troops*. Whereas Meade was tepidly dismissive of the Pleasants proposal, Duane flatly denied that the tunnel could be dug at all. Recent historians have pointed out that Duane had served as Burnside's engineer, and that Duane had twice failed him, once at Antietam and once at Fredericksburg. He misled Burnside by identifying the wrong place to ford Antietam Creek, which delayed the capture of "Burnside's Bridge," exposing the twelve thousand men of Burnside's corps to the lethal action of a mere 450 Georgia sharpshooters from about 9:30 in the morning until 1:00 p.m. Not only costly in itself, the delay helped transform what might have been a magnificent Union triumph into the bloodiest single day of combat in the Civil War, one that yielded only the narrowest of victories for the North. At Fredericksburg, Duane was responsible for another fatal delay when he failed to make timely delivery of pontoons to bridge the Rappahannock. This gave the Confederates ample time to dig into the high ground above the town, from which cover they delivered a storm of lethal fire. Those who did not know Ambrose Burnside well were astonished by his refusal to place any official or even unofficial blame on James Duane. Those who knew Burnside, however, understood that he was magnanimous to a fault. Indeed, Burnside freely accepted sole and absolute responsibility for the problem at Antietam and the defeat at Fredericksburg. Yet his generosity of spirit earned neither Duane's gratitude nor loyalty. Instead, it seemed only to intensify the contempt Duane manifested for Burnside and, perhaps, for the tunneling plan he presented.

Doubtless, Meade's and Duane's dismal estimation of Ambrose Burnside colored their assessment of the Pleasants mine, but this does not justify overlooking the fact that both Meade and Duane were well-trained military engineers—Duane a published authority on military tunnels, an art with a written history stretching back to the ancient world—and if they had been presented with the identical plan Potter transmitted to Burnside's chief of staff, they would have been fully justified in rejecting it out of hand as embodying faulty science and proposing an unfeasible solution.

The plot line of the Petersburg mine saga would surely be more straightforward in its tragic drama if it were simply this: A mining engineer presents a brilliant plan for radically shortening the war. He proposes to burrow a mine under the formidable Confederate fortifications defending Petersburg, pack the mine with tons of blasting powder, then touch off an explosion of unprecedented magnitude, powerful enough to blast through the rebel lines and instantly end the stalemated siege of Petersburg. In a single stroke, the Army of Northern Virginia and the city of Richmond would be cut off from their major sources of supply. Total victory might come to the Union almost instantly, in July of 1864. What would that have meant? Consider: Most of the approximately 1,150,000 killed or wounded in the Civil War fell in seventy-six major battles between April 1861 and April 1865. As of July 1864, eight of those seventy-six battles had yet to be fought and some 150,000 of those men were still alive and well. But (so the straightforward version of the saga goes) the petty jealousies of George Gordon Meade and James C. Duane sabotaged the plan from the beginning, the operation failed, the resulting battle was an unmitigated disaster—"the saddest affair I have witnessed in the War," Grant would famously call it[9]—and the killing continued for another nine months.

Dramatic, tragic, and sudden the failure of the assault on Petersburg was, but its trajectory was not nearly as stark as some have portrayed it. Pleasants had an idea. He sold it to the like-minded Potter, who presented it to Burnside. All were eager to find a way of avoiding a long siege at Petersburg. But Burnside had questions, Meade had doubts, and Duane—like his commanding officer, an engineer—flatly believed the project could not succeed. Based on the only extant record of the original mine proposal as presented by Potter, the idea was indeed shoddy— though we do not know if Burnside, Meade, and Duane were responding to the Potter version or to the design of the mine as actually excavated. If we knew this, we could determine with a reasonable degree of certainty whether the operation was crippled from the start by deliberate acts of sabotage on the part of both Meade and Duane or whether it was hobbled by genuine doubt.

Based on the extant record—Potter's message to Major General Parke—doubt rather than willful sabotage seems the more likely engine of disaster. The saddest affair, Grant called it, not the most tragic. Tragedy is the product of will pitted against forces beyond the power of will to shape, bend, and control. Sadness is a circumstance that prevails in the absence of will, when command yields to drift. No more potentially momentous military operation has ever been born amid such drift, such abandonment of will and abrogation of command. Burnside testified that he saw no harm in the busywork of digging a mine, so he approved it. Meade, according to Burnside, gave "his assent, rather than his approval of the work." In a letter written at the request of the army's Court of Inquiry, Meade went even further into drift, virtually removing himself from the entire picture of command. He did not even mention his meeting with Burnside, but instead emphasized that he had learned of the mine only after it had been started:

> Soon after occupying our present lines Major-General Burnside, commanding Ninth Corps, at the suggestion of Lieutenant-Colonel Pleasants, Forty-eighth Pennsylvania volunteers, commenced the running of a gallery from his line to a battery occupied by the enemy with a view of placing a mine under this battery. *When my attention was called to this work* I sanctioned its prosecution, though at the time, from the reports of the engineers, and my own examination, I was satisfied the location of the mine was such that its explosion would not be likely to be followed by any important result, as the battery to be destroyed was in a reentering part of the enemy's line exposed to an enfilading and reverse fire from points both on the right and left.[10]

To Burnside, Meade had said that he must defer judgment on the mine to the Union commander in chief, General Grant. Like Meade, Grant did not so much approve the operation as he assented to it, doing so, curiously enough, on the same grounds as those Burnside asserted in his own testimony: the work was harmless and would keep the soldiers busy.

No victorious army is commanded by assent, by officers who merely refrain from opposing what their subordinates propose. In classical tragedy, the high and the mighty, in the exercise of their will, fall to the gods or to destiny itself. At Petersburg, the high and the mighty exercised nothing of will at all, yielding instead to drift. It was, rather, the lower actors, the subordinates, Lieutenant Colonel Henry Pleasants and the officers and men of his 48th Pennsylvania Infantry, who struggled to work *their* will—not in the face of the gods or destiny, but amid the peculiar indifference of those who should have boldly led and firmly commanded them.

Meade may have been disingenuous in his letter to the Court of Inquiry, but he was not lying outright. The digging, as Pleasants himself testified, had begun on June 25, sometime before Burnside met with Meade. But while Meade did not halt the work, neither he nor Duane provided even the most rudimentary support for it.

Pleasants began his mine a full hundred feet behind the Union's own breastworks. That meant more digging, but—and this was the key—it put the entrance to the mine far enough back to hide from Confederate eyes all the activity of digging and then carrying out and dumping the excavated earth. The countryside on the outskirts of Petersburg consisted of a series of parallel ridgelines, which ascended from the Union toward the Confederate position, thus giving all the advantages to the defenders. The Union lines lay on the lower end of a ravine through which Taylor's Creek (also called Poor Creek) flowed, and the Confederate lines were located upslope from this ravine. Thus Pleasants knew that he had to dig an ascending tunnel, or gallery, to match the upward slope. That would add appreciably to the labor of excavation, but it would make carrying away the excavated material easier, since gravity would lend a hand.

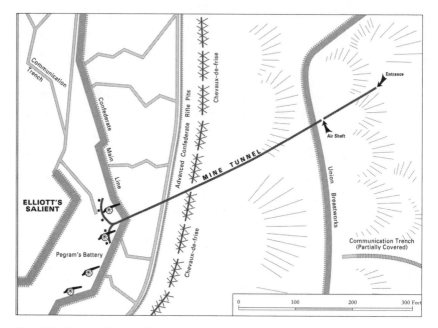

Plan of the Pleasants Mine. Credit: Kat Bennett.

Eager to save work as well as shoring lumber, Pleasants designed the cross-section of the main gallery as a small shaft in the shape of a truncated pyramid. The base of the pyramid—the floor of the shaft—was about four feet wide, and the top was only two feet wide. The height of the shaft was about four and a half feet, on average. It is not known precisely when Pleasants decided on sinking a vertical ventilation shaft, but he dug it as close behind the Union picket line as he dared rather than attempt to set men digging in the exposed no-man's land between the Union and Confederate lines.

Once the work began in earnest, Meade's policy became somewhat more than passive indifference. In addition to basic surveying equipment, James Duane's own manual on military mines listed about forty pieces of equipment required for tunneling. Duane refused to provide any of this equipment, even the most basic, to Pleasants and his men.

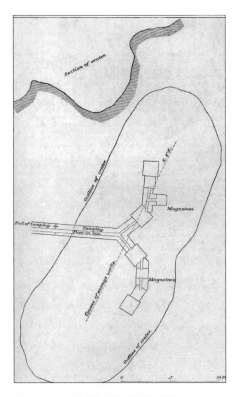

These two diagrams of the Pleasants mine were published in the U.S. War Department's *War of the Rebellion: A Compilation of the Official Records of the Union and Confederate Armies* (1880-1901). In the cross-section view, note the upward detour Pleasants was forced to make in order to avoid a vein of slippery marl (clay). (Author's collection)

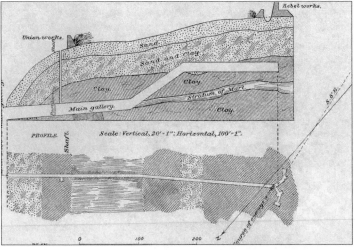

There is no evidence that Meade ordered him to withhold the equipment, but neither did the commander of the Army of the Potomac order him to supply it. The tunnel, Pleasants reported to the Court of Inquiry, "was commenced at 12 m. the 25th of June, 1864, without tools, lumber, or any of the materials requisite for such work. The mining picks were made out of those used by our pioneers [soldiers who clear the way for an advancing column]; plank I obtained, at first, by tearing down a rebel bridge, and afterward by sending to a saw-mill, five or six miles distant. The material excavated was carried out in hand barrows made out of cracker-boxes."[11] In his testimony to the congressional Committee on the Conduct of the War, Pleasants provided more detail:

> The great difficulty I had was to dispose of the material got out of the mine. I found it impossible to get any assistance from anybody; I had to do all the work myself. I had to remove all the earth in old cracker boxes. I got pieces of hickory and nailed on the boxes in which we received our crackers, and then iron-cladded them with hoops of iron taken from old beef and pork barrels.

> Question: Why were you not able to get better instruments with which to construct so important a work?

> Answer: I do not know. Whenever I made application I could not get anything, although General Burnside was very favorable to it. The most important thing was to ascertain how far I had to mine, because if I fell short of or went beyond the proper place the explosion would have no practical effect. Therefore, I wanted an accurate instrument with which to make the necessary triangulations. I had to make them on the furthest front line, where the enemy's sharpshooters could reach me. I could not get the instrument I wanted, although there was one at army headquarters; and General Burnside had to send to Washington and get an old-fashioned theodolite, which was given to me.

Question: Do you know any reason why you could not have had the better instrument which was at army headquarters?

Answer: I do not. I know this: that General Burnside told me that General Meade and Major Duane, chief engineer of the army of the Potomac, said the thing could not be done; that it was all clap-trap and nonsense . . . . I could get no boards and lumber supplied to me for my operations. I had to get a pass, and send two companies of my own regiment with wagons outside of our lines to rebel saw-mills and get lumber in that way, after having previously got what lumber I could by tearing down an old bridge. I had no mining picks furnished me, but had to take common picks and have them straightened for my mining picks. . . .

Question: How long from the time you commenced the mine did it take you to finish it?

Answer: I finished the whole thing, lateral galleries and all, ready to put the powder in, on the 23d of July.

Question: How long would it have taken you had you been supplied with the proper tools and instruments?

Answer: I could have done it in one-third or one-fourth of the time. The greatest cause of the delay was taking the material out.[12]

Each day of delay was, of course, another day of war. It was also another day in which the enemy improved his works, and another day in which the enemy might discover the mine. To compensate for the lack of proper tools and to make up for lost time, Pleasants steadily increased the number of miners dedicated to the dig. "About how many men did you employ in the work?" one member of the congressional committee asked. "My regiment was only about four hundred strong," Pleasants answered. "At first I employed but a few men at a time, but the number was increased as the work progressed, until at last I had to use the whole regiment, non-commissioned officers and all." Pleasants had been more specific about this in his answer to a July 7, 1864, query from Brigadier General J. G. Barnard, Chief Engineer, U.S. Armies in the Field: "There are 210 men employed every twenty-four hours, but only two can mine at a time at the extremity of the work."[13] Of course, the more men Pleasants put to work on the mine, the more conspicuous the activity became, and the greater the likelihood of discovery.

Aside from the sniper fire, the siege of Petersburg promised to be especially hard—on Union and Confederate troops as well as on the townsfolk, who were cut off from the outside—because the summer of 1864 was uncommonly hot and droughty. Between the Union and Confederate lines, the vegetation had been burned brown and sere. Working in the tunnel gave some relief from the sun, but the confines of the shaft were so close that the heat was stifling nonetheless. The large kerosene lanterns used to light the gallery contributed to the heat, like so many little iron stoves. The monotonous labor of digging was paced to the equally monotonous labor of removing the earth from the tunnel. Instead of wheeled handbarrows—which were not supplied—the men hauled the earth out using their improvised cracker boxes. The boxes, reinforced with discarded barrel hoops, were nailed atop a pair of parallel hickory poles. Each box could hold perhaps four cubic feet of earth, which would then be carried out by two men, one grasping the hickory poles at the front, the other at the rear, as if they were transporting a wounded comrade on a stretcher. The four-and-a-half-foot height of the shaft meant that both men had to crouch low all the way—and the way became longer with each day's digging—straining backs and knees, each man struggling to remain steady on his feet, to keep from jostling himself or the other "stretcher bearer." The average width of a man's head is perhaps seven inches, and it is, say, nine inches from back to front. In the tunnel, that head was thrust into the upper space of the truncated pyramid of the shaft, which was no more than twenty-four inches wide, leaving a clearance of about eight and a half inches on either side of the head—an inch less back and front, if he turned his head. Crouching while trundling perhaps eighty pounds of earth between them, moving downhill over uneven ground, in the dark, it was a struggle to avoid scraping and dragging nose, ears, and forehead across a timber or the rough walls or ceiling of the narrow shaft.

Nor could the men simply dump the earth at the entrance to the mine. Each load had to be carried somewhere behind the Union lines to a place that needed filling, lest it pile up and become visible to the Confederate pickets, who, seeing rising mounds of fresh earth, would instantly assume that a mining operation was under way. Sometimes the bearers would have to walk a long way with their burden to find a likely spot before finally dumping it. That done, they trotted back into the mine for another load. In the dwindling light of dusk, some of Pleasants's men would go about in search of brush, which they would use to cover the mounds of new soil, the better to disguise them.

Lieutenant Colonel Pleasants detailed one of his most experienced coal miners, Sergeant Henry Reese, a burly Welshman from Minersville, Pennsylvania, to oversee the labor. For most of what was nearly a month of digging, acting either on his own initiative or under orders from Pleasants, Reese limited each man to no more than three hours in the tunnel per day—although this was increased in the final days, as fears of detection mounted. Shifts were continuous, round the clock, day and night. Working with improvised implements and moving in postures between a crawl and a crouch, the men moved eighteen thousand cubic feet of earth, about forty-five hundred full cracker-box loads. Although the enemy eventually began to suspect that a mine was being dug, the Confederates never spotted the removal of all this earth.

It is hard to guess what the other soldiers thought of the men of the 48th Pennsylvania. The labor radically transformed their appearance. The miners emerged at the end of their shift, stooped and caked with cracked clay, hands blistered, perhaps bleeding, heads doubtless scraped and bruised. The regiment's assistant surgeon treated a host of abrasions and, some fifty years after the siege, recalled that digging the mine had

Alfred Waud sketched this for an engraving published in *Harper's Weekly* on August 6, 1864. He described the scene: "Bivouac of the 5th corps in the rifle pits. The men in the trenches were not only exposed to shot & shell but had scant protection from the elements. They stretched their shelter tents across the pit formed by the outer work and a second embankment in the rear; or they built bough houses over the space. [A]nd there they cooked and ate, and slept and fought. In front of the ditch a strong abbatis [sic] and beyond a line of pickets in separate pits & shelters." (Library of Congress)

left the entire regiment all "used up."[14] Yet the soldiers of the 48th enjoyed two special privileges. One was a gill of whisky at the end of the day, and the other was a degree of protection from the ubiquitous danger of sniper fire. Nevertheless, one officer and a private of the 48th were picked off by snipers during the course of the digging, and two other enlisted members of the regiment were wounded seriously enough to be invalided home. In exchange for these privileges, the miners endured the agonies of their suffocating, close-quarters labor as well as the daily danger of imminent cave-in or even falling victim to a Confederate countermine.

Each of these Pennsylvania miners was on intimate terms with the prospect of sudden suffocating death under tons of earth. The possibility of such a fate was part and parcel of the profession of mining. Fortunately, most of the earth in the neighborhood of Petersburg made for easy digging and presented few rocks or other obstacles—although the miners did bring out what at least one regimental officer believed was the fossilized thighbone of a mastodon. Indeed, Pleasants reported to the army's Court of Inquiry that work on the mine "progressed rapidly until the 2nd of July, when it reached all extremely wet ground; the timbers gave way and the gallery nearly closed, the roof and floor of the mine nearly meeting." Despite the sun-baked drought above, the tunnel had hit "a stratum of marl," in part soft and slippery, undermining the footing of the timbers, and in part of a "consistency . . . like putty," so that, Pleasants explained to the court, "our progress . . . necessarily slow[ed]." In some parts of the tunnel, timber props were spaced as much as thirty feet apart. In other parts, they were as close as three feet. To prevent a collapse, Sergeant Reese hauled in more timber to shore up the sagging shaft. He also planked over the shaft floor in order to distribute the weight of the shoring timbers and the miners' feet more evenly over the slippery clay. For his part, Pleasants redirected the course of the mine upward to avoid the marl vein: "I started an incline plane, and in about 100 feet rose thirteen and a half feet perpendicularly."[15] This incline took the shaft above the marl vein, but not before many of the miners carried out wet clumps of the clay, passing their off-shift time by shaping these into dolls, miniature sculptures, and, most of all, pipes. The objects were baked in the Virginia sun and sometimes retained by the troops and sometimes sent home to friends and family as souvenirs of the front.

It was one thing to decide to redirect the tunnel on an upward incline, and another to determine just how far up to go. This was one of three factors Pleasants could not afford to guess about. He needed to *know* how far to elevate the shaft, as well as how long to make it and in what horizontal direction the shaft should run. If he brought the shaft too near the surface, it would surely cave in. If he stopped digging too soon or kept digging too long, he would not be able to place the explosives where they would have any tactical effect. The same was true if the tunnel veered too far left or right. As Pleasants had testified to Congress, accurate measurement required using the best theodolite that could be obtained. A theodolite is a precision instrument that measures both horizontal and vertical angles. The precursor of the modern surveyor's transit, it was essential for surveying projects—such as tunnel work—that required coordination in more than two dimensions. If anyone knew this even better than Henry Pleasants, it was Meade's engineer James Duane, who personally possessed a state-of-the-art theodolite. Not only would his modern instrument ensure accurate measurement, its design was such that Pleasants could make his surveys quickly—a boon when surveying the course of the mine required exposing oneself to enemy fire. Yet Duane refused Pleasants the use of his theodolite, protesting that it was too important an instrument to release from headquarters. Even against Burnside's pleas, he remained adamant, and, clearly, Meade did nothing to change his mind. Burnside therefore called on a friend in Washington, who was able to send down what Pleasants described to his congressional interrogators as an "old-fashioned" theodolite, which was both less reliable and less efficient than a modern instrument. Because he could not absolutely depend on the instrument, Pleasants lived in an agony of second guessing, repeatedly exposing himself to fire to confirm and reconfirm his measurements.

It is a testament to Pleasants's skill, endurance, and courage that, "on the 17th of July," when "the main gallery was completed, being 510.8 feet in length," the end of the tunnel was precisely where it was supposed to be, under Richard G. Pegram's artillery battery in Elliott's Salient. Against all the odds, it was a masterpiece of subterranean navigation.

There is evidence that, even if he was lukewarm at the commencement of the project, Ambrose Burnside became increasingly enthusiastic as the tunnel approached its end. He praised and congratulated the miners personally, and also personally inspected the mine, on one occasion showing it off to Senator William Sprague of Rhode Island and David Tod, former governor of Ohio, who were visiting the front. Good naturedly, one of the politicians chided the miners that they were willing to do *anything* for a drop of whiskey.

The men needed such morale lifting. Burnside, Potter, and Pleasants might have been encouraging, but the rank and file of the 48th could not have avoided sensing that the prevailing sentiment elsewhere was that the mine was a fool's errand, destined to fail. Worse, word had just reached the 48th that their native Schuylkill County was being menaced by Confederates, principally under Jubal Early. Pleasants took pains to assure his men that their families were in no danger, that Early would be stopped well before he reached their homes. The regimental commander wanted his troops to maintain their focus on the mine, and he was doubtless greatly relieved when he was able to read them newspaper stories of how Early and the other Confederates, having penetrated into Maryland as well as Pennsylvania, had finally withdrawn into Virginia.

The lack of decent tools and instruments was the product of command by benign neglect. The near collapse of the mine was the result of a change in the prevailing soil. The third threat, a countermine, came directly from enemy action.

In 1864, there was hardly anything new about the idea of a military mine. The Greek historian Polybius (c. 203 BC–120 BC) wrote of both mining and countermining during the Roman siege of Ambracia in 189 BC. After the Aetolians "offered a gallant resistance to the assault of the siege artillery," Polybius wrote, the Romans "in despair had recourse to mines and underground tunnels." The historian described how the Romans worked "in relays . . . unceasingly day and night" to dig a two hundred-foot shaft, its entrance concealed from the enemy with wattle screens.

> For a considerable number of days the besieged did not discover them carrying the earth away through the shaft; but when the heap of earth thus brought out became too high to be concealed from those inside the

city, the commanders of the besieged garrison set to work vigorously digging a trench inside, parallel to the wall and to the stoa which faced the towers. When the trench was made to the required depth, they next placed in a row along the side of the trench nearest the wall a number of brazen vessels made very thin; and, as they walked along the bottom of the trench past these, they listened for the noise of the digging outside. Having marked the spot indicated by any of these brazen vessels, which were extraordinarily sensitive and vibrated to the sound outside, they began digging from within, at right angles to the trench, another underground tunnel leading under the wall, so calculated as to exactly hit the enemy's tunnel. This was soon accomplished, for the Romans had not only brought their mine up to the wall, but had under-pinned a considerable length of it on either side of their mine; and thus the two parties found themselves face to face.[16]

Mining and countermining were practiced throughout the Middle Ages, and, in 1863, General Grant himself had ordered a mine to be run under the Confederate trenches at the siege of Vicksburg, digging under what Andrew Hickenlooper, chief engineer of Major General James B. McPherson's XVII Corps, characterized as the "most formidable redoubt" of the 3rd Louisiana, a veteran regiment. Indeed, to dig the Vicksburg tunnel, Hickenlooper had put out a call "for all men in the corps having a practical knowledge of coal-mining."

Thirty-six of the strongest and most experienced were selected and divided into two shifts for day and night duty, and each shift was divided into three reliefs. On the night of the 22d these men, properly equipped with drills, short-handled picks, shovels, etc., under the immediate command of Lieutenant Russell of the 7th Missouri and Sergeant Morris of the 32d Ohio commenced the mining operations by driving a gallery, four feet in width by five feet in height, in at right angles to the face of the parapet of the fort. Each relief worked an hour at a time, two picking, two shoveling, and two handing back the grain sacks filled with earth, which were deposited in the ditch until they could be carried back. The main gallery was carried in 45 feet, and then a smaller gallery extended in on the same line 15 feet, while from the end of the main gallery two others were run out on either side at angles of 45 degrees for a distance of 15 feet. The soil through which this gallery was driven was a reddish clay of remarkable tenacity, easily cut and requiring but little bracing. So rapidly was this work executed that on the morning of the 25th the miners commenced depositing the powder, 800 pounds at the extreme end of the main gallery and 700 pounds at the end of each of the lateral galleries, making a total of 2200 pounds. From each of these [three] deposits there were laid two strands of safety fuse,—obtained, as was the powder, from the navy,—this duplication being made to cover the possible contingency of one failing to burn with the desired regularity and speed. These six strands were cut to exactly the same length, and having been carefully laid, the earth, which had been previously removed in grain-sacks, was carried back and deposited in the most compact manner possible, and well braced by heavy timbers, beyond the junction point of the three galleries. From this point out to the entrance it was more loosely packed in.[17]

Discovering the mine, the Confederates "countermined in hopes of tapping the gallery. So near were they to the attainment of this object that during the last day the miners could distinctly hear the conversation and orders given in the counter-mine." However, by that time it was too late for the defenders.

The powder was brought up in barrels and . . . placed in grain-sacks, each one of which contained about 25 pounds. These were taken up on the backs of the miners, who made the run over the exposed ground during the intervals between the explosion of the enemy's shells; and so well timed were these movements that, although it required nearly one hundred trips with the dangerous loads, all were landed in the mine without a single accident.

The commanding general having been advised on the day previous that the work would be completed before 3 P. M. of the 25th, general orders were issued directing each corps commander to order up the reserves and fully man the trenches, and immediately following the explosion to open with both artillery and musketry along the entire twelve miles of investing line; under cover of which the assaulting columns, composed of volunteers from the 31st and 45th Illinois, preceded by ten picked men from the pioneer corps under charge of the chief engineer, were to move forward and take possession of the [Confederate] fort. . . .[18]

"Every eye was riveted upon that huge redoubt standing high above the adjoining works" as the mine was detonated.

At the appointed moment it appeared as though the whole fort and connecting outworks commenced an upward movement, gradually breaking into fragments and growing less bulky in appearance, until it looked like an immense fountain of finely pulverized earth, mingled with flashes of fire and clouds of smoke, through which could occasionally be caught a glimpse of some dark objects,—men, gun-carriages, shelters, etc. Fire along the entire line instantly opened with great fury, and amidst the din and roar of 150 cannon and the rattle of 50,000 muskets the charging column moved forward to the assault. But little difficulty was experienced in entering the crater, but the moment the assaulting forces attempted to mount the artificial parapet, which had been formed by the falling debris about midway across the fort, completely commanded by the Confederate artillery and infantry in the rear, they were met by a withering fire so severe that to show a head above the crest was certain death. . . .[19]

After a bloody struggle, the resulting crater was secured, and, from here, yet another mine was dug, this one "under the left wing of the fort. This mine was exploded on the 1st of July, leaving the fort a total wreck."[20]

Despite gaining a foothold in the Confederate line, the Union forces were ultimately beaten back—though, by this time, the defenders were generally reeling, and the city fell on July 4.

The radical innovation of the Petersburg mine lay not in the ancient concept of a military mine, but in its unprecedented length. Pleasants and his men took elaborate measures to conceal the masses of earth moved out of the mine, and for several days their activities remained undetected by the enemy. Soon, however, some Confederate observers began to suspect that something was going on in the Union works, and at least one commander, Brigadier General E. Porter Alexander, artillery chief of the Army of Northern Virginia's I Corps, guessed that a mine was in progress.

In 1857, Alexander had graduated third in his West Point class of thirty-eight and, like all of the most promising graduates, was commissioned in the engineers. His academy coursework had taught him about the mine Polybius described, and he had studied at the academy the art of military mining from the Middle Ages onward. He was well aware that Grant had already employed a mine at Vicksburg. So it required no great leap of imagination for him to draw certain conclusions from what he observed as a gap in the otherwise continuous fusillade of Union musket fire coming from just opposite Elliott's Salient. At first, he assumed that the Yankees were digging a trench approaching the salient, from which they would try to knock it out. But as the hours and days passed, Alexander saw no such trench and therefore concluded it was a tunnel that was being dug.

On the very day that he drew this conclusion, June 30, Alexander's curiosity got the better of him, and he incautiously peered above the parapet once too often. Hit by sniper fire, he was sent to the rear to recover from his wound. En route, he visited Robert E. Lee's headquarters to report to the chief himself his observations and conclusion. A correspondent for the *Times* of London attached to Lee's headquarters happened to overhear the conversation and interrupted. Much as Meade's engineer, Major Duane, had done, the *Times* man scoffed at the very idea that anyone could dig a five hundred-plus-foot tunnel in the first place, much less do so undetected and without suffocating. Alexander did not dispute the difficulties, but he countered that the Federal forces at Petersburg included in their number Pennsylvania coal miners who probably had experience ventilating shafts even longer than five hundred feet.

Even if Lee and the *Times* correspondent were skeptical, back at the Petersburg front lines others by this time had also become suspicious. A captain of Virginia engineers, Hugh Douglas, was so certain that a mine was in progress that he began sinking "listening shafts," short, narrow wells, in an effort to detect the sounds of digging. When he believed he heard something, Douglas had his men dig horizontal galleries to the right and left of his vertical listening shaft. They were much larger than Pleasants's galleries—six feet high by three feet wide—and Douglas descended into them, boring into the floor with an inch-wide augur, in search of soft spots that would betray the enemy shaft. Douglas excavated several galleries, like his Union counterparts taking elaborate pains to conceal his digging from enemy observers. But at least one of Douglas's

"Sharpshooters 18th corps," by Alfred Waud. (Library of Congress)

men deserted to the Yankee lines and told his captors that countermining operations were under way.[21]

The Pennsylvanians had begun to suspect as much, and, for the last several days of digging, a deadly tense game of cat and mouse ensued, a game that had been played and replayed for as long as armies had practiced siege warfare. Attackers dug a tunnel to undermine the enemy's fortifications. Detecting evidence of an approaching mine, the defenders dug a countermine with the object of tunneling parallel to the attackers, not so close as to be heard by them, but close enough to set off an explosive charge that would collapse the enemy mine—and, in so doing, bury the miners alive. The stakes of this game could not have been higher.

Douglas was coming very close to detecting the Union mine. He had been shorthanded, so he could not dig as many listening shafts and galleries as he had wanted, but by about July 17, the very day Pleasants announced that the main gallery, at precisely 510.8 feet in length, had reached its target, Douglas received a contingent of more than a hundred diggers, who rapidly pushed his galleries farther out.

Throughout the digging of the Union mine, Lieutenant Colonel Pleasants had urged his men on, encouraged them, had told them that what they did with their picks and spades was, for a fact, far more important than what the others were doing with their rifles. Often, he longed to join his men in the shaft, but it would have been unseemly for an officer to labor alongside troops, and, in the Union army of 1864, officers were bound by even more rules than enlisted soldiers. However, on July 17, when the main shaft was completed, reports were coming in that the miners were hearing "digging noises." In his report to the army's Court of Inquiry, Pleasants noted that, "The enemy having obtained some knowledge of the mine, and having commenced searching for it, I was ordered to stop mining" on the 17th.[22] In fact, Pleasants responded to this order by laying aside military propriety, and descending into the shaft to investigate personally.

The last thing Henry Pleasants wanted was to abandon the tunnel, but he well knew that, under interrogation, one or more Confederate deserters had been full of talk about countermines. Pleasants ordered complete silence, and, in the flickering candlelight, he strained to hear.

There it was, unmistakable: the muffled, rhythmic cadence of enemy implements biting into Virginia clay.

After an eternity of breathless minutes, Pleasants turned to his men and quietly pronounced the sounds to be nothing more than evidence of routine construction along the Confederate lines. No countermine was drawing near, he assured them.

Accordingly, on the next day, digging began on one of two galleries, which would extend in broad arcs from the left and right of the main shaft, like the curved top of a letter T. "The left gallery, being thirty seven feet long, was stopped at midnight on Friday, July 22; the right gallery, being thirty-eight feet long, was stopped at 6 p.m. July 23," Pleasants reported to the Court of Inquiry. Although "the mine could have been charged and exploded at this time," Pleasants took extra care to ensure an effective explosion by employing "the men . . . in draining, timbering, and placing in position eight magazines, four in each lateral gallery."[23]

The lateral galleries with their eight magazine rooms were intended to ensure that the maximum amount of powder could be packed in and that the force of the explosion would go where it was intended—out and up, rather than back through the main tunnel. Excavating these galleries was critically important work, and although Pleasants had persuaded his miners as well as his superiors that they need have no fear of being detected, let alone blown up by a Confederate countermine, he either did not realize how close Douglas was to finding his mine or chose not to admit it.

With the last-minute addition of new laborers, Douglas had been able very rapidly to push his listening galleries far enough out to intercept the Pleasants mine. The reason he failed actually to intercept it was that he had started the galleries at an insufficient depth. Douglas's deepest tunnel was just ten feet below grade. His augur would push through a gallery floor no more than another five feet. As it entered the Confederate lines and neared Elliott's Salient, the Union tunnel was at least twenty feet below grade, perhaps more. After a hot, hazardous

month of epic labor, in which military engineering history had quietly—
oh so quietly—been made with the completion of the longest military
tunnel in more than two thousand years of siege warfare, the great work
escaped detection and destruction by a matter of no more than five vertical feet. Now Henry Pleasants awaited the order to "charge the mine"
with the six tons of black powder he had ordered from Army of the
Potomac stores.

- 4 -

Men of War

The left gallery, being thirty seven feet long, was stopped at midnight on Friday, July 22; the right gallery, being thirty-eight feet long, was stopped at 6 p.m. July 23. The mine could have been charged and exploded at this time. I employed the men, from that time, in draining, timbering, and placing in position eight magazines, four in each lateral gallery."[1] Such were the facts Henry Pleasants reported to the army's Court of Inquiry. Their bland expression belies what must have been a fury of frustration seething within the lieutenant colonel.

The mine could have been charged and exploded at this time. But it was not. Meade, Duane, Grant, all of whom had greeted the dangerous labor of the Petersburg mine with vaguely obstructive indifference, now dithered over when to "spring"—detonate—the mine, or even whether to detonate it all.

And while they dithered, *I employed the men . . . in draining, timbering, and placing in position eight magazines.* What went unspoken is the critical situation the miners encountered here, at the very end of their work. The ground in which the lateral galleries and the magazines branching from them were being dug was extremely wet. On July 20, Pleasants had written to Robert Potter to explain: "The ground is full of springs where I am now mining, but I could have made better progress in the last three days if I had not stopped the work

Officers of the 114th Pennsylvania Volunteer Infantry (Collis's Zouaves) pass the time with cards. Note the Zouave uniform worn by the officer on the left. (Library of Congress)

frequently to prop it securely, and in order to listen and ascertain if the enemy was mining near us."[2] After relatively easy digging—once that vein of slippery marl had been circumvented—the men had uncovered a series of underground springs, which may have been swollen by the heavy rains that had suddenly broken the prevailing drought. These had to be drained off, and the lateral galleries as well as the powder magazines had to be shored up with extra timbers to prevent collapse. Each day the mine remained unexploded was another day in which Pleasants's miners were obliged to continue draining and shoring. The draining was necessary to maintain a dry place to accommodate the powder. The shoring was required because there was so much Confederate activity above, especially the incessant firing of Pegram's artillery, that the ceiling was in danger of imminent collapse. Each thud produced by the recoil of cannon sent a shower of clods and dust on the miners below. Unnerving? It must have been the most exquisite torture.

Like a great ocean-going steamship, an army cannot be stopped, started, or turned on a dime. The will, no matter how passionate, of any individual officer is blunted and damped by the ineluctable chain of command. Thus it was at Petersburg. Pleasants communicated with Potter—and sometimes directly with Burnside—and Burnside communicated with Meade, though almost always through the mediation of a staff officer. The result was a trail of paper that survives to this day, a trail gone cold insofar as it betrays almost none of the agonized frustration that must have motivated so many of the messages.

Did Pleasants communicate to Potter the urgency of exploding the mine as soon as possible? If he did, did Potter in turn convey the urgency to Burnside? There is nothing in the paper trail to indicate this. All we know for certain is that, on July 26, three days after "the mine could have been charged and exploded," Ambrose Burnside wrote to Meade's chief of staff, not on his own initiative, but in response to "your notes of this morning by Captains Jay and Bache also of a telegram from the commanding general."[3]

It is altogether probable that the enemy are cognizant of the fact that we are mining, because it has been mentioned in their newspapers and they have been heard to work on what are supposed to be shafts in close proximity to our galleries, but the rain of night before last no doubt filled their shafts and much retarded their work. We have heard no sounds of work in them either yesterday or to-day, and nothing is heard by us in the mine but the usual sounds of work on the surface above. This morning we had some apprehension that the left lateral gallery was in danger of caving in from the weight of the batteries above it and the shock of their firing, but all possible precautions have been taken to strengthen it and we hope to preserve it intact.[4]

What is striking about this communication is its bland nonchalance. Was this a product of Burnside's notion of proper military decorum? Or did it flow from the obtuse sensibility of the IX Corps commander? Whatever the source of its tone, Burnside had drained his message of every trace of the momentum of urgency, even as Pleasants and his men struggled to drain their galleries and magazine of spring water.

Burnside backed into the most important subject, the urgency of detonating the mine:

> The placing of the charges in the mine will not involve the necessity of making a noise. It is therefore probable that we will escape discovery if the mine is to be used within two or three days. It is nevertheless highly important, in my opinion, that the mine should be exploded at the earliest possible moment consistent with the general interests of the campaign.[5]

There is a reticence about this communication, perhaps resulting from Burnside's keen awareness that Meade and Grant were keeping him out of the strategic loop:

> I state to you the facts as nearly as I can, *and in the absence of any knowledge as to the meditated movements of the army I must leave you to judge the proper time to make use of the mine.* But it may not be improper for me to say that the advantages reaped from the work would be but small if it were exploded without any cooperative movement.[6]

The tunnel was completed on July 23. Burnside's communication to Meade's chief of staff was written on July 26. Yet, even at this late date, it is apparent from what he said next that Burnside had yet to discuss with his superiors his plan for exploiting the mine's detonation. That is, based on the written record, Burnside's letter to Meade—a response to multiple queries from Grant as well as Meade—was the very first time the IX Corps commander outlined how he proposed to assault the Petersburg line.

My plan would be to explode the mine just before daylight in the morning or about 5 o'clock in the afternoon, mass the two brigades of the colored division in rear of my line in column of divisions, double column closed in mass, the head of each brigade resting on the front line, and as soon as the explosion has taken place move them forward with instructions for the division to take half distance, and as soon as the leading regiments of the two brigades pass through the gap in the enemy's line, the leading regiment of the right brigade to come into line perpendicular to the enemy's line by the right companies, on the right into line wheel, the left companies on the right into line, and proceed at once down the line of the enemy's works as rapidly as possible, the leading regiment of the left brigade to execute the reverse movement to the left, moving up the enemy's line. The remainders of the two columns to move directly toward the crest in front as rapidly as possible, diverging in such a way as to enable them to deploy into columns of regiments, the right column making as nearly as may be for Cemetery Hill. These columns to be followed by the other divisions of this corps as soon as they can be thrown in.[7]

Viewed through a stereopticon, stereographs approximated a three-dimensional view of their subjects. This one shows the Blandford Church and Graveyard, adjacent to Cemetery Hill, the all-important high ground just behind the Confederate line at Petersburg. The Union's failure to occupy Cemetery Hill doomed the assault that followed the explosion of the Crater. (Library of Congress)

Two things are remarkable about this plan. The first is the intricacy of the troop movements proposed—a subject to which we will return shortly. The second is the fact that this complicated plan was being proposed only now, three days *after* the Petersburg mine had been dug and in response to apparently unrelated queries from Burnside's commanding officers.

After devoting several more sentences to the plan of assault, Burnside turned back to answering what must have been the substance of the queries sent him: just how the mine should be detonated. We know that, by July 23, Pleasants had completed the main shaft as well as the two lateral galleries and had excavated from these eight powder magazines. Yet, three days later, Burnside presented these accomplished facts as if they were mere proposals:

> My suggestion is that eight magazines be placed in the lateral galleries, two at each end, say a few feet apart, in branches at right angles to the side galleries, and two more in each of the side galleries similarly placed, situated by pairs equidistant from each other and the ends of the galleries. . . .[8]

We could speculate endlessly on what this deception says about Burnside's relationship with George Gordon Meade, but suffice it to recognize that a subordinate lying to his CO in an official communication suggests a profound crisis of command.

After the lie, Burnside returned to the truth. For the magazines, although already completed, were empty. He proposed a method for charging them with powder:

> Tamping beginning at the termination of the main gallery for, say, 100 feet, leaving all the air space in the side galleries. Run out some five or six fuses and two wires to render the ignition of the charges certain. I propose to put in each of the eight magazines from 1,200 to 1,400 pounds of powder, the magazines to be connected by a trough of

powder instead of a fuse. I beg to inclose a copy of a statement from General Potter on the subject.

. . .

I beg also to request that General Benham be instructed to send us at once 8,000 sand-bags to be used for tamping and other purposes.[9]

Henry Pleasants had requisitioned six tons, 12,000 pounds, of powder for the mine. Burnside's communication to Meade's chief of staff calls for sufficient powder to pack eight magazines with 1,200 to 1,400 pounds each, or roughly a total of 9,600 to 11,200 pounds of powder: 4.8 to 5.6 tons. The 8,000 sand-bags would be used primarily for "tamping"—what modern demolition experts would call *shaping* the charge in order to direct the explosion. Most of the bags were carefully stacked to plug the mouth of each magazine and also to plug the end of the main shaft itself. It would take the miners twenty hours to haul in sufficient sandbags to make up more than a thousand cubic feet of "tamping" in order to direct the blast upward, against the enemy works, rather than back out the open end of the mine. Empty sandbags were used to transport the powder itself into the mine. Two powder kegs were loaded into each bag, which was slung over the shoulder of a miner, one keg hanging over his chest, the other over his shoulder blade. Burnside's remarks on the fuse are also significant, both for what they say and what they fail to say. They say much about the degree to which Pleasants wanted to "over-engineer" the detonation and ignition process: in the main shaft, the use of "some five or six fuses and two wires to render the ignition of the charges certain" and "a trough of powder instead of a fuse" in the lateral galleries to interconnect the magazines. Yet Burnside failed to specify the type of fuse required—a matter that was highly important to Pleasants, who wanted to use nothing but long, continuous lengths of safety fuse, the kind employed in coal mines, a fuse virtually impervious to moisture, which had become, especially of late, a major issue in the mine.[10]

On July 27, Pleasants was issued the order to begin charging the

It is not known whether artist Alfred Waud ventured into the Petersburg mine to witness the scene depicted here or if he drew it from imagination. The relative spaciousness of the shaft—which we know to have been claustrophobically cramped—strongly suggests the latter. The sketch was captioned by the artist: "Carrying powder into the mine. The soldiers detailed for this duty carried the power—a keg in either end of a grain bag thrown across the shoulder. A portion of the covered way along which they had to pass, was exposed to the enemies [sic] fire. At the dangerous points they would watch their opportunity and dash over the exposed ground into comparative safety." The sketch was used to create an illustration for *Harper's Weekly*, August 20, 1864. (Library of Congress)

mine. Delivered to him, however, were four tons of powder—eight thousand pounds—instead of the six he had requested. In his report to the army Court of Inquiry, Burnside detailed a dispute (he termed it a set of "ordinary conversations") he had with General Meade "with reference to the charge which was to be placed in the mine."

> I myself from a long experience in experiments with gunpowder, having been a manufacturer of arms several years before the war commenced and in constant practice with fire-arms, had a particular view with reference to the mode in which the mine should be charged, and the amount of charge to be placed in it. It was not in accordance with the methods

laid down in scientific works upon the subject of military mining, but entirely in accordance with all experience in mining and blasting by civil engineers within the last two or three years since the method of heavy tamping had been abandoned. It is not worth while for me to enter here into an explanation of my theory, because I can present the report of the officer who built the mine, and that will explain the matter fully. It is sufficient to say that the mine was charged partially upon my theory and partially upon the theory of the old established plan of military mining. In the theory which I decided to be adopted large charges could be used without detriment, in my opinion, to persons in the immediate proximity of the mine, but persons who were not of my opinion felt that the effect of this mine at great distances, with the charge which I proposed to place in it, would be very great, and it became, from some cause or other, known to my troops, both officers and men, that a difference of opinion of that kind had arisen, and to such an extent that I have had general officers come to me and ask me if I did not think the charge I was putting in the mine was too large.[11]

Burnside studiously avoided naming names, but it is sufficiently evident that it was Meade and his chief engineer, James C. Duane, who challenged his knowledge of explosives. For someone who had invented a widely adopted carbine, that was sufficiently insulting, but Burnside went on to make it clear that Meade and Duane had undermined him in the eyes of his troops and fellow officers, to the point that they lost confidence in him, asking, presumably with fear and trembling, if he "did not think the charge [he] was putting in the mine was too large."

Little wonder, then, that those modern historians who have commented on the Petersburg mine and the disastrous battle that followed point to Meade's contempt for Burnside and see in it the seeds of deliberate sabotage. The record suggests that this was all too true: Meade and his chief engineer were indeed contemptuous of Burnside, and that contempt prompted them to undercut his effectiveness as a commander—

not just by publicly questioning his decisions, but by reducing the quantity of powder delivered to Pleasants by one-third.

Burnside explained further to the Court of Inquiry:

> I did not think the charge [I had specified] so large that there was danger of injuring our own men. This feeling among the men had a certain effect which I will leave for the Court to decide, and if they request it I will send them the names of witnesses who have mentioned to me that impression on the subject long before the mine was exploded, so that there can be no mistake as to the impression that prevailed at the time. I myself was satisfied, without knowing definitely, that the charge which I desired to place in the mine could be placed there with safety. I witnessed this anxiety among the troops with a good deal of concern, but that it did not prevail in the division which it was supposed would make the assault (it not being then upon our lines) was a source of gratification to me.[12]

He went on to testify that "General Meade . . . directed [him] to keep the amount of powder placed in the chambers within the limits of rules prescribed by military works upon that subject." Despite this, Burnside pointed out to the court, "in several verbal communications with General Meade, [I] insisted upon the other method; and it was finally decided that we should place in the mine 8,000 pounds of powder instead of 12,000 pounds."[13] That is, Meade and (presumably) Duane got their way, despite what Burnside had argued:

> that . . . the greater the explosion the greater the crater radius, and less inclination would be given the sides of the crater, and the greater breach on the right and left of the charges would be made, thereby giving a greater space for the troops to pass over, and a less inclination for them to pass up and down in the line.[14]

Burnside's argument notwithstanding, it was "determined that 8,000 pounds of powder should be put in instead of 12,000, and the mine was accordingly exploded with that charge."[15]

In his later testimony before the congressional Committee on the Conduct of the War, Burnside was initially less circumspect in recounting the dispute over the quantity of powder, stating forthrightly: "In my opinion it should have been a charge of 12,000 pounds of powder, and I so expressed myself. It was finally decided that the charge should be 8,000 pounds." In his next sentence, however, he took a step back, observing, "I do not mention this as anything material, but it happens to be a fact." Yet he went on to attribute the steepness of the crater that resulted from the blast to insufficient powder: "The enemy's works were blown up with the 8,000 pounds, but the declivity of the crater would not have been so great had it been done with 12,000."[16]

The steepness of the crater's sides—the "declivity of the crater"— would be a critical issue in the assault on the Petersburg line; for hundreds of Union soldiers would be trapped in the "horrid pit," unable, under fire, to scale its steep walls. Reading this testimony, it is easy to blame Meade and Duane for the disaster to come. Yet we must also return to Burnside's July 26 message to Meade's chief of staff, in which Burnside himself had asked for as little as 4.8 tons of powder. Whatever Meade's attitude, it was Ambrose Burnside who failed to advocate the Pleasants plan thoroughly and forcefully. Yes, Meade sent less powder than either Burnside or Pleasants specified, but Burnside had asked for less than Pleasants had wanted.

A shortage of powder was not the only way in which Henry Hunt, Meade's chief of artillery, shorted Pleasants. Instead of standard mining safety fuse, essentially waterproof and shipped in lengths of one hundred feet, Hunt sent Pleasants common blasting fuse, apparently in whatever odd lengths he could obtain from stocks at Fort Monroe. Some lengths were as short as ten feet. Had Hunt deliberately sabotaged Pleasants? Probably not. But his failure to trouble himself sufficiently to obtain safety fuse suggests how little he thought of the chances of the mine's success. His judgment of the matter notwithstanding, perhaps Hunt would have furnished the proper fuse had *Burnside* emphasized the need for such in his communication of July 26. Of course, by that time, it might have been too late to obtain the fuse. Hunt had placed the original fuse order with Fort Monroe on June 29. This suggests either that Hunt, in contrast to the likes of Meade and Duane, had responded in a timely and efficient manner to Pleasants's requisition, or it reflects Hunt's understanding that ordering large amounts of fuse simply required a long lead time.

In any case, Pleasants resigned himself to make do with what he was given. He set his miners to work meticulously splicing the short lengths of fuse. In his July 26 letter, Burnside had specified laying five or six runs of fuse to ensure multiple redundancy. Pleasants actually laid only three—still sound redundant engineering, but, with all the splicing necessary, far less time-consuming than laying five or six runs. He did take the super-redundant step, however, of laying all three lengths in an open trough of powder for the full run of the fuse—about ninety-eight feet—whereas, in his July 26 communication, Burnside had specified interconnecting only the magazines with "a trough of powder *instead of* a fuse."[17]

The process of hauling in the powder, carried in kegs within burlap sacks slung over miners' shoulders, began "at 4 p.m. [on July 27], and finished at 10 p.m."[18] Labor-intensive, the work was also extremely hazardous. The powder of the era was notoriously unstable and might have been detonated by the mere friction of the shoulder-borne jostling of the burlap and the agitation of the powder. Moreover, the illumination of the mine's interior consisted of enclosed target lanterns as well as simple candles, their flames open to the atmosphere of the mine, which, doubtless, became increasingly thick with blasting powder dust as more and more of the explosive was trundled and bounced into the shaft.

As soon as the powder was in place—"at 10 p.m. July 27"—tamping was begun. This required the miners to haul some eight thousand sandbags into the mine to tamp (seal off) "Thirty-four feet of

main gallery . . . and ten feet of the entrance of each of the side galleries" as well as the mouths of each of the eight powder magazines."
Pleasants wanted to ensure that the force of the blast would be
directed upward, against the enemy, and not outward, along the
length of the tunnel. The tamping operation was "completed at 6 p.m.
July 28."[19]

During these final operations, Pleasants set aside military propriety
entirely. He descended into the mine to personally supervise the fuse
splicing, and it was he, at about six o'clock in the evening of July 28,
who was the last to crawl out of the shaft to notify General Potter that
the mine was charged and ready to be sprung.

For little more than a month, the Petersburg mine had consumed Henry
Pleasants and the men of the 48th Pennsylvania Infantry—almost literally; as the regiment's assistant surgeon had observed, the men were
"used up" after the mine had been completed.[20] But elsewhere along the
Union's Petersburg line, especially at the highest levels of command,
little note was taken of the project.

Very little. Ambrose Burnside testified to Congress, "On the 3d day of
July General Meade sent me a letter requesting an opinion as to the probability of success of an attack upon the enemy from our front." He
offered the letter in evidence:

> 12 m., July 3, 1864
> The lieutenant general commanding [U. S. Grant] has inquired of me
> whether an assault on the enemy's works is practicable and feasible at
> any part of the line held by this army. In order to enable me to reply to
> this inquiry, I desire, at your earliest convenience, your views as to the
> practicability of an assault at any point in your front, to be made by the
> 2d and 6th corps in conjunction with yours.[21]

The brief missive made no mention of the mine then very much in
progress. Burnside replied to it later that day:

I have delayed answering your despatch until I could get the opinion of
my division commanders, and have another reconnaissance of the lines
made by one of my staff. If my opinion is required as to whether now is
the best time to make an assault, it being understood that if not made the
siege is to continue, I should unhesitatingly say, wait until the mine is
finished.[22]

Had Burnside ended his reply here, it would have been his strongest
endorsement on record of the Pleasants mine. But he had more to say: "If
the question is between making the assault now and a change of plan
looking to operations in other quarters, I should unhesitatingly say,
assault now." Then he went on to refine the basis of his opinion:

If the assault be delayed until the completion of the mine, I think we
should have a more than even chance of success. If the assault be made
now, I think we have a fair chance of success, provided my corps can
make the attack, and it is left to me to say when and how the other two
corps shall come in to my support.[23]

It was both a considered reply and yet a maddeningly vague one. What,
after all, was the difference between a "more than even chance" and a
"fair chance"? It also reiterated the endorsement of the tunnel, even as
it diluted that endorsement. Burnside suggested that waiting until the
mine could be detonated would improve the chances of a successful
assault on the Confederate lines—somewhat—but he also denied that the
mine was indispensable to the assault.

Meade's response to Burnside consisted of three significant parts.
First, he seemed to ignore—or try to cut through—Burnside's vagueness:
"As you are of the opinion there is a reasonable degree of probability of
success from an assault on your front, I shall so report to the lieutenant
general commanding, and await his instructions." Meade reduced "more
than even chance" and "fair chance" to "reasonable degree of probability
of success." In the second part of what he had to say, Meade exhibited

Waud made several sketches of the U.S. XVIII Corps. This one is inscribed, "Right section, Comp[any] E 3rd N.Y. Arty. [Artillery] Capt. Ashby. 20 pounder parrots." The Parrott Gun was named for its inventor, Robert P. Parrott (1805-1877), a U.S. Army ordnance and artillery officer. It was a muzzle-loading cannon featuring a rifled bore, which, by imparting a spin to the projectile, produced more accurate fire than conventional smoothbore artillery. Parrott reinforced the breach of his gun with a heat-shrunk wrought-iron band, which enabled the gun to withstand the higher pressures produced by the large powder charges rifled artillery required. (Library of Congress)

his characteristic proclivity for taking offense, even where no offense was intended:

> Should it . . . be determined to employ the army under my command in offensive operations on your front, I shall exercise the prerogative of my position to control and direct the same, receiving gladly at all times suggestions as you may think proper to make. I consider these remarks necessary in consequence of certain conditions which you have thought proper to attach to your opinion, acceding to which in advance would not, in my judgment, be consistent with my position as commanding general of this army.[24]

In his testimony to Congress, Burnside admitted that he had put his foot in his mouth: "It would seem that the language I employed in my letter was unfortunate, for it was entirely misunderstood, as will appear from the reply of General Meade . . ." No general likes to feel that a subordinate is attempting to usurp the "prerogative of [his] position," and Meade chose to interpret Burnside's message precisely in this way. Worse, he was being challenged by Ambrose Burnside, of all people—an officer who had once been his senior, who had stumbled notoriously at Antietam, and who had brought outright disaster at Fredericksburg. Meade therefore continued: "I consider these remarks necessary in consequence of certain conditions which you have thought proper to attach to your opinion, acceding to which in advance would not, in my judgment, be consistent with my position as commanding general of this army." This said, he announced that he had "directed Major Duane, chief engineer, and Brigadier General Hunt, chief of artillery, to make an examination of your lines, and to confer with you as to the operations to be carried on, the running of the mine now in progress, and the posting of artillery."[25]

Under ordinary circumstances, it was quite reasonable for Meade to have sent his artillery chief to inspect the lines prior to an assault; however, given the toxic relations between Burnside and Meade, either man or both might have seen this as a vote of no-confidence against Burnside.

It is tempting to conclude that this entire exchange was a prime example of how Meade's ill-tempered meddling, testily undercutting a key subordinate, wrecked the Petersburg assault. Indeed, there can be no question but that George Meade was irascible, unlikable, and often downright obnoxious. At the very least, he failed to be an inspiring leader of men. Yet he himself was in a most unenviable position, heavily freighted with ambiguity. As commander of the Army of the Potomac, Meade was now senior over his former commanding officer, Ambrose Burnside. Although Burnside seemed to have no difficulty accepting this reversal of his fortunes—perhaps, he even welcomed it—Meade apparently believed that Burnside continually questioned his command authority. Possibly this was because Meade's authority was very much open to question. Although he commanded the Army of the Potomac, he was subordinate to Ulysses S. Grant, general in chief of the Union armies, of which the Army of the Potomac was the principal constituent. Because Grant commanded the Richmond campaign and the Petersburg front, he effectively commanded the Army of the Potomac—a situation that left Meade precious little autonomy.

But while it is helpful to try to understand Meade's state of mind, there is no need to excuse or even explain his response to Burnside entirely on the basis of emotion. The fact is that, given Burnside's record, there was ample reason for Meade to question his judgment. Up to this point, Meade had treated the mine with indifference and neglect. Now— belatedly to be sure—he was taking a more responsible interest in it by sending key subordinates to survey the front. It might well be argued that Meade should have made a personal inspection, but the step he did take was by no means simply the result of his own bad temper and insecurity. It was a reasonable command decision. For that matter, Meade's reply to Burnside concluded not only by agreeing with Burnside, but by actually coming closer to unequivocally endorsing the mine than Burnside himself had come:

> I agree with you in opinion that the assault should be deferred till the mine is completed, provided that can be done within a reasonably short period—say a week. Roads should be opened to the rear to facilitate the movements of the other corps sent to take part in the action, and all the preliminary arrangements possible should be made. Upon the reports of my engineer and artillery officers the necessary orders will be given.[26]

This final note of concord should have patched matters up between Meade and Burnside. Certainly, that is the way the commander of IX Corps wanted it. On July 4, he sent an extravagantly conciliatory message to Meade:

I have the honor to acknowledge the receipt of your letter of last evening, and am very sorry that I should have been so unfortunate in expressing myself in my letter. It was written in haste, just after receiving the necessary data upon which to strengthen an opinion already pretty well formed. I assure you, in all candor, that I never dreamed of implying any lack of confidence in your ability to do all that is necessary in any grand movement which may be undertaken by your army. Were you to personally direct an attack from my front I would feel the utmost confidence; and were I called upon to support an attack from the front of the 2d or 6th corps, directed by yourself, or by either of the commanders of those corps, I would do it with confidence and cheerfulness. It is hardly necessary for me to say that I have had the utmost faith in your ability to handle troops ever since my acquaintance with you in the army of the Potomac, and certainly accord to you a much higher position in the art of war than I possess; and I at the same time entertain the greatest respect for the skill of the two gentlemen commanding the 2d and 6th corps; so that my duty to my country, to you, and to myself, forbids that I should for a moment assume to embarrass you, or them, by an assumption of position or authority. I simply desired to ask the privilege of calling upon them for support at such times, and at such points, as I thought advisable. . . . My desire is to support you, and in doing that I am serving the country.[27]

Meade replied not only gratefully, but even with a plea for Burnside's understanding of his own "trying position"—presumably a reference to the painful ambiguity of authority created by his role as Grant's subordinate:

Your letter of this date is received. I am glad to find that there was no intention on your part to ask for any more authority and command than you have a perfect right to expect under existing circumstances. I did not infer from your letter that you had any want of confidence in me. I rather thought you were anticipating interference from others, and thought it best to reply as I did. . . .

I am very grateful to you for your good opinion, as expressed, and shall earnestly try to merit its continuance. In the trying position I am placed in, hardly to be appreciated by any one not in my place, it is my great desire to be on terms of harmony and good feeling with all, superiors and subordinates; and I try to adjust the little jars that will always exist in large bodies to the satisfaction of each one. I have no doubt, by frankness and full explanations, such as have now taken place between us, all misapprehensions will be removed. You may rest assured, all the respect due to your rank and position will be paid you while under my command.[28]

Ambrose Burnside must have been relieved by Meade's note. Certainly, he had every reason to believe that his apology had been accepted, and that he could now go on to plan an assault coordinated with the springing of the mine—a plan that would gain the endorsement and support of his commanding officer. In this assumption, he was mistaken.

As Burnside mentioned in his communication of July 26 to Meade's chief of staff, his plan was to mass two brigades and move them forward "as soon as the explosion ha[d] taken place." When "the leading regiments of the two brigades" had passed "through the gap in the enemy's line" created by the explosion and were headed for Cemetery Hill (also called Cemetery Ridge), the high ground behind Elliott's Salient, a portion of the attacking force would peel off on either side of the main thrust and assume positions perpendicular to the principal attack in order to sweep the defenders from the Confederate trenches on either side. Elliott's Salient, the object of the mine detonation, bowed outward toward the Union lines; however, the explosion would take place just behind this outward projection—that is, behind the Confederate lines, so that on either side of the gap created by the explosion, intact portions of Confederate trench would be angled toward the point of Union attack and could therefore "enfilade" the attackers, catching them in a deadly crossfire. Burnside intended to use the peeling-off maneuver to neutralize the defenders in these portions of the trenches. It was, therefore, a critically important movement with very high stakes. Moreover, under combat conditions, with a large body of attackers pressing forward, it was also quite intricate.

Intricate does not mean unfeasible, let alone impossible. Burnside planned to use the time required for the completion of the mine to train and drill a division especially for the initial phase of the assault. He chose the Fourth Division under Brigadier General Edward Ferrero, consisting of nine regiments, all of them "colored."

In its obituary for Ferrero, published on December 13, 1899, the *New York Times* led off with what its readers would surely have deemed the most remarkable fact about the man: "Gen. Ferrero enjoyed the distinction of having achieved success in at least two walks of life, so widely dissimilar as to be popularly considered antitheses—those of dancing master and soldier." He had been born in Grenada, Spain, in 1831, to Italian parents. A month after his first birthday, the family moved to New York City, where the elder Ferrero opened a dancing school at the corner of 14th Street and Sixth Avenue, which, in the judgment of the

Times, soon became the most famous dance school in the nation. While the Ferrero school attracted the "boys and girls of the wealthiest families of New York," the Ferrero "house . . . was frequented by Italian political refugees," including Garibaldi himself.

The *Times* obituary did not speculate as to how childhood intimacy with the founders of Italian nationalism affected Edward Ferrero, but it did observe that the boy "was reared practically on the floors of the dancing academy" and therefore "developed into

Edward Ferrero (Library of Congress)   a master of the Terpsichorean art." The son assumed leadership of the school after his parents retired in the early 1850s and "originated many dancing figures which became popular throughout this country and Europe." Ferrero "also found time to teach dancing at the Military Academy at West Point," for "he always had a taste for military life." When the Civil War broke out, Ferrero "promptly left the polished floors of the dancing halls for the field of sterner action."[29] He raised the 51st New York Regiment (the "Shepard Rifles"), serving as its colonel and seeing first blood with Burnside at Roanoke Island, where his regiment had the distinction of capturing the first fortified redoubt in the war. He next commanded a brigade at New Bern, North Carolina, and served under John Pope in Virginia. Under Burnside again, Ferrero fought at South Mountain and Antietam, leading the brigade that, at long last, captured the infamous "Burnside Bridge." Ferrero fought at Fredericksburg, and commanded a division in east Tennessee during the siege of Knoxville.

Over the years, Burnside's many detractors have pointed with derision to his choice of a "dancing master" to lead the assault on Petersburg. A dancing master Edward Ferrero undeniably had been, but, during the years and months before Petersburg, he had also compiled a record of creditable if not brilliant military service. He was no worse than the run of Union officers and better as well as more experienced than many.

If Burnside's choice of Ferrero was, then, unremarkable, his choice of "colored" troops was more interesting, thoughtful, and, as it turned out, controversial.

He did not choose the Fourth Division because it was black. Unlike any number of New England reformers, Burnside had no social, political, or philosophical point to prove about the "worthiness" of the "colored race." Nor did he choose the division because of its battle experience. In fact, whereas Ferrero was a seasoned commander, his troops were new to combat. None had joined the army before November 1863 and most had mustered in even later, in the spring, just months before Petersburg. Assembled as a division at Annapolis, Maryland, in April, they were attached from the beginning to Burnside's IX Corps, but, until the arrival of the corps at the Petersburg front, they had been kept out of battle and were used instead to guard the ammunition train. This was standard practice in the employment of "colored" troops. Generally, they were the last chosen for combat and were instead committed to fatigue details as laborers, rear-echelon guards, and the like.

It was this very lack of combat experience that appealed to Ambrose Burnside. By the time they had reached Petersburg, most of the units of the Army of the Potomac were worn out. Ostensibly, Grant had settled into a siege at Petersburg because he decided that repeated frontal assaults against the heavily fortified Confederate line were futile. That was true enough, doubtless; but Grant knew enough about men under arms to recognize that the fight had mostly gone out of his army. His soldiers needed an interval at least approaching rest.

What was generally true of the Army of the Potomac was especially the case with IX Corps. It had fought well and hard during the initial assaults on Petersburg, and, in the siege, it was positioned closer to the Confederate line than any other corps. This put IX Corps men under continual sniper fire, a situation that took a toll on nerves even more than on bodies. The terms "shell shock" and "battle fatigue," much less "posttraumatic stress disorder," were altogether unknown in 1864, but the more perspicacious military surgeons had already begun to identify something they called "nostalgia," a complex of depression, anxiety, and general nervous exhaustion brought on by continuous combat. It was not cowardice or weakness of will, the doctors said, but an emotional wound as real as anything caused by shot and shell. In the best of circumstances, Ambrose Burnside possessed a great capacity for empathy with his men. It was a quality that had made him a popular commander. Now, when circumstances were hardly at their best, he must have experienced even stronger fellow feeling with his soldiers. If they were worn out, suffering from "nostalgia," so was he. Thus afflicted, Burnside understood that his men were not simply too tired to fight or unwilling to fight, but that they were, at present, all but incapable of fighting—or at least fighting well.

That, at least, was the condition of the white troops, who had borne the brunt of combat. In contrast, the blacks of the Fourth Division, having seen no front-line fighting, were unshaken and unthreatened by the cold grip of "nostalgia." Their freshness alone promised to make these men more effective in an offensive operation. But there was more. Although many white officers said that "the negro" made for an inherently inferior soldier, Burnside believed that the black men of Ferrero's Fourth Division burned with a hunger to fight and were eager to learn to fight well. Whereas the white soldiers craved a rest, the black troops wanted nothing more than to prove themselves. They seemed to Burnside the obvious choice to make the assault.

When Burnside transmitted Ferrero's orders to him, the Fourth Division commander responded that most of his troops were attached to various work details for various Army of the Potomac units. Burnside ordered his inspector general to file a report on the disposition of the Fourth Division, in an effort to reclaim its men for IX Corps. The Army's bureaucracy moved surprisingly quickly, and all Fourth Division men were instantly released from fatigue duty outside of IX Corps. With his soldiers reclaimed, Burnside now consulted directly with the division's two brigade commanders, Colonels Joshua Sigfried and Henry G. Thomas. He warned them not to rely on the maps they had been issued; they were inadequate for the intricate assault that was planned. Instead, he advised the officers to reconnoiter for themselves. This was accomplished by moving up to the front line of Union trench works and peeking judiciously over the parapet. It was unwise to risk more than a few glimpses. To try for a sustained view invited a sniper's bullet between the eyes. Yet, as the colonels knew, an accurate picture of the ground was essential to the success of the planned assault, and both Sigfried and Thomas steeled themselves to survey the enemy's lines and the ground that lay before it.

The colored regiments had the advantage of fighting spirits undulled by continuous combat. However, they also suffered the disadvantage of their second-class status. Because they had been used for so long as laborers, they were rarely called upon to act in a large unit on the battalion level. The typical work gang was a company or even a platoon. Now they had to relearn basic large-formation battalion drill, from marching to maneuver. This done, they began rehearsing for the specific wheeling movement required in the assault. As the main body of the division was to advance straight ahead, skirt the crater blasted out by the detonation of the mine, then take Cemetery Hill behind the Confederate lines, so the flanking regiments were to wheel—the left regiments to the left, the right regiments to the right—in order to suppress counter fire coming from the surviving wings of Confederate trench works. These massive wheeling movements had to be executed in good order and with great speed. It was not merely a question of getting x number of men to peel off left and right, but to get x number of rifles effectively pointed at the enemy. That meant ensuring that everyone in the flanking regiments had a clear field of fire—no easy feat in a crowd, on a field thick with smoke, and heavy with flying lead. Moreover, the effective lines of fire had to be fully in place before the defenders could reinforce the wings of their trenches. If such reinforcement were allowed to occur, there was very little chance of avoiding deadly enfilading fire against the main Union assault.

As they drilled, improved, then perfected a choreography far more demanding than the most elegant dance Edward Ferrero had ever taught, the black soldiers of the Fourth Division swelled with pride and enthusiasm. Soon, these emotions spilled over in song. Everyone along this stretch of the Petersburg line heard the tune and the words, Union and Confederate alike.

"We looks like men a marchin' on," the soldiers sang. "We looks like men er war."[30]

- 5 -

Battle's Eve

July 26, 1864. Although the Petersburg mine had been completed three days earlier, the miners labored round the clock to shore up the lateral galleries and their eight branching powder magazines, while also scrambling to keep them dry. On this day, too, Ambrose Burnside received an almost frantic series of messages.

The first was from General Grant himself, expressing sudden concern about Confederate countermining. The next note, from Grant's headquarters, asked Burnside if the mine could be maintained in readiness for an unspecified number of days. The author of the message, Grant's chief of staff, casually noted that the commanding general had no plans to launch an assault in conjunction with the detonation of the mine, but apparently the general wanted the information just in case he should decide that the detonation of the mine could be usefully coordinated with an attack. We don't know how this query affected Burnside, because he did not reply until after two more messages arrived, these from Meade's headquarters. The first announced that Grant had changed his mind and had now definitely decided to coordinate an assault with the mine detonation. The second asked Burnside to furnish a plan for the detonation. It was the latter request that occasioned the letter discussed in the previous chapter, in which Burnside detailed the disposition of the magazines, the use of multiple fuses, and so on. Although Meade had

Ulysses S. Grant commanded the siege of Petersburg from his headquarters at City Point, Virginia, which also served as the principal supply depot for the Army of the Potomac during this prolonged operation. (Library of Congress)

asked only for plans relating to the detonation, Burnside decided also to outline his plan for the accompanying assault, specifying his intention to use "the two brigades of the colored division."[1]

It was a fateful revelation.

Ambrose Burnside was driven by an intense desire to oblige and to be liked. It was a drive that endeared him to his men—at least until he started getting them killed—and it was a drive that had compelled him finally to accept command of the Army of the Potomac, even though he was thoroughly convinced of his inadequacy for that command. The need to please also moved him to make elaborately detailed replies even to the simplest and most straightforward requests. A good salesman knows that persuasion— the art of making a sale—depends on giving just enough information and not a bit more. Ambrose Burnside was not a good salesman. He habitually told his superiors much more than they needed to know.

On July 27, Burnside and Pleasants were ordered to "charge" the mine. On Thursday the 28th this process was completed, with just two-thirds of the powder specified and inadequate fuse. Informed of the completion, Burnside rode to Meade's headquarters to tell the general and to make final preparations for the detonation and the assault. "He informed me," Burnside testified to Congress, "that that portion of my plan which contemplated putting the colored troops in the advance did not meet with his approval."[2]

That alone was a blow to Burnside's solar plexus. But there was more: "also . . . he did not approve of the formation proposed, because he was satisfied that we would not be able, in the face of the enemy, to make the movements which I contemplated, to the right and left; and that he was of the opinion that the troops should move directly to the crest [of Cemetery Hill, behind the Petersburg line] without attempting these side movements."[3]

The "side movements" were integral to Burnside's plan. Without them, the main assaulting force would have to pass through enfilading fire. Meade not only understood this, he accepted it. To the army's Court of Inquiry, Meade spoke of his desire "to impress upon Major-General Burnside (which I did do in conversations, of which I have plenty of witnesses to evidence, and in every way I could) that this operation was to be a *coup de main;* that his assaulting column was to be as a forlorn hope, such as are put into breaches, and that he should assault with his best troops."[4] By "*coup de main*" Meade meant that he intended the assault as a sudden attack; presumably, he believed that the wheeling movements, right and left, of the advancing Union force would alert the enemy and thereby compromise the shock of its suddenness. Since the distance between the Union and Confederate lines was little more than a hundred yards and the contemplated wheeling movements were to be performed simultaneously with the principal advance, the basis of Meade's implied argument is at least questionable. Given such a short distance and the simultaneous nature of the movements contemplated, there was little reason to anticipate that the shock of the attack would somehow be diminished. Even more revealing of Meade's expectation for the attack was his observation that the assaulting column "was to be a forlorn hope." This was traditional military parlance for an advance unit of troops sent on a hazardous mission, but by the time of the Civil War it was a rather archaic expression, and its connotation was unmistakable. A *forlorn* hope is a *lost* hope. Meade expected that most of the initial assaulting force—shock troops, as it were—would be killed, sacrificed to make way for others.

And that was the sticking point. Like Grant, George Meade was perfectly willing to sacrifice soldiers to gain an objective. He was, however, unwilling to sacrifice black soldiers.

Meade testified to the Court of Inquiry that he told Burnside "that he should assault with his best troops":

"The war in Virginia—the 22nd Colored Regiment, Duncan's brigade, carrying the first line of Rebel works before Petersburg / from a sketch by our special artist, Edwin Forbes." The 22nd United States Colored Troops, part of a "colored division" attached to XVIII Corps, had been used in combat operations at Petersburg earlier in the siege, weeks before the Pleasants mine was sprung. Published in *Leslie's Illustrated,* July 9, 1864. (Library of Congress)

. . . not that I had any intention to insinuate that the colored troops were inferior to his best troops, but that I understood that they had never been under fire; not that they should not be taken for such a critical operation as this, but that he should take such troops as from previous service could be depended upon as being perfectly reliable.[5]

For Burnside, Meade's veto of the "colored" division in the initial assault was such a blow that (based on Burnside's testimony) he did not even address with Meade the issue of the wheeling movements. Instead, he attempted to counter Meade's expressed objection, that the black unit was inexperienced:

A long conversation ensued [Burnside told Congress], in which I pointed out to General Meade the condition of the three white divisions, and urged upon him the importance, in my opinion, of placing the colored division in the advance, because I thought it would make a better charge at that time than either of the white divisions. I reminded him of the fact that the three white divisions had for forty days been in the trenches in the immediate presence of the enemy, and at no point of the line could a man raise his head above the parapet without being fired at by the enemy.[6]

In a word, the white soldiers were gun shy: "they had been in the habit, during the whole of that time, of approaching the main line by covered ways, and using every possible means of protecting themselves from the fire of the enemy. . . . their losses had been continuous . . . amounting to from thirty to sixty men daily."[7] And they were exhausted, utterly spent:

. . . the men had had no opportunity of cooking upon the main line— everything having been cooked in the rear, and carried up to them. . . . they had had very few, if any, opportunities of washing; and . . . in my opinion, they were not in condition to make a vigorous charge.[8]

Clearly recognizing that General Meade had little regard for his judgment in such matters, Burnside sought to bolster his "opinion, which had been formed from personal observation, by the report of my inspector general, who had taken occasion to look at the troops with a view to making up his mind as to their effectiveness for a work of that kind."[9]

Perhaps based on the inspector general's assessment, Meade relented—somewhat—by taking refuge in the ambiguity of his command authority. He "still insisted that the black troops should not lead; that he could not trust them, because they were untried, and probably gave other reasons which do not occur to me at this moment," Burnside testified. "But he said that, inasmuch as I was so urgent in the matter, he would refer it to General Grant, whom he expected to visit that afternoon, and his decision of course would be final." Burnside replied to Meade that he "would cheerfully abide by any decision that either one of them would make," but he still "urge[d] upon him that [he] thought it of the utmost importance that the colored troops should lead."[10]

"General Meade did go to see General Grant that day, and I think returned the same afternoon, but I did not hear from him," Burnside testified to Congress. Assuming that no news was good news, Burnside, during "the next forenoon, Friday," met with Orlando Bolivar Willcox and Robert Potter, "commanding two of my white divisions," to discuss the attack, "which it was understood would be made the next morning."[11]

> I told them I had been very much exercised the day before lest that portion of my plan which contemplated putting the colored division in advance should be changed by General Meade, but that I was pretty well satisfied he had given it up, because I had heard nothing further from him about it. While in the midst of this conversation . . . [about 11 a.m.], General Meade [with General Edward O. C. Ord] came to my headquarters, and there told me that General Grant agreed with him as to the disposition of the troops, and that I would not be allowed to put the colored division in the advance.[12]

In his meeting with General Grant, Meade had presented a different objection to using the black troops from the one he had offered Burnside. Grant testified to Congress:

> General Burnside wanted to put his colored division in front, and I believe if he had done so it would have been a success. Still I agreed with General Meade in his objection to that plan. General Meade said that if we put the colored troops in front, (we had only that one division,) and it should prove a failure, it would then be said, and very properly, that we were shoving those people ahead to get killed because we did not care anything about them. But that could not be said if we put white troops in front.[13]

In his second meeting with Burnside, Meade added this political dimension to the objection against using the black troops, but he did not tell Burnside that this new angle originated with him rather than with Grant. In any case, Burnside remained unconvinced. Usually so willing to oblige, he uncharacteristically refused simply to yield—at least at first. He responded by asking Meade "if that decision could not be reconsidered."

"No, general, the order is final; you must detail one of your white divisions to take the advance."

It was now the more familiar Ambrose Burnside who spoke: "Very well, general, I will carry out this plan to the best of my ability."[14]

After Meade left Burnside's tent, the IX Corps commander sent for Brigadier General James Ledlie, First Division commander, to join Potter (commanding Second Division) and Willcox (Third Division), who were already in the tent. Brigadier General Edward Ferrero, who commanded the Fourth Division (Colored Troops), was not summoned, but he and his division were nevertheless much talked about, as Burnside testified:

> Each of the division commanders, as well as every officer in the command, who had given his attention to the subject in the least degree, was

fully aware of the condition of the white troops, as I had previously stated it to General Meade, and were firmly impressed with the conviction that the colored troops were in much better condition to lead the attack, and of the wisdom of using the white troops as supports.[15]

To his commanders of the white divisions, Burnside laid out the dilemma:

There is a reason why either General Wil[l]cox's or General Potter's division should lead the assault, and that is, that they are nearer to the point of assault, and it would require less time to get them into position for the work. But there is also a reason why General Ledlie's division should lead, which is, that his men have not been in such close proximity to the enemy as those of the other two divisions, and in fact have not had to do quite as hard work for the last thirty or forty days.[16]

Throughout the debate among them, which consumed about three hours, the generals repeatedly agreed on one thing and one thing only: that Ferrero and the Fourth Division should lead the assault. But Meade and Grant, who had for weeks avoided making any bona-fide command decisions regarding the Petersburg mine, finally issued an order, an order that made it impossible for the one division that was thoroughly prepared and motivated for the assault to take on the mission.

As for Burnside, he now found himself incapable of deciding which white division should lead the assault. Nor were his three generals of much help. None volunteered.

"There was no time to be lost," he told the congressional Joint Committee, "as the hour for springing the mine had been fixed for half past three o'clock the next morning, and it was now afternoon." Burnside's decision? An abrogation of decision itself: "I finally decided that I would allow the leading division to be designated by lot."[17]

Ambrose Burnside passed a hat, from which James Ledlie drew the short straw.

I am the "unlucky victim," Ledlie grumbled.[18]

*   *   *

Not nearly as unlucky as the men of his First Division—and those who would follow them into the "horrid pit."

Ironically, up to the moment he drew the short straw, James Hewett Ledlie may actually have been the luckiest commander in the Civil War. As with all too many officers of high rank, Ledlie enjoyed sufficient political influence to gain him a command for which he had neither experience, qualifications, nor temperament. Appointed major of the 19th New York Infantry (later renamed the 3rd New York Artillery) at the outbreak of the war, Ledlie not only escaped censure when the regiment mutinied at the expiration of its original term of service, he achieved promotion to colonel in December 1861. A year later, he became brigadier general of volunteers and commanded the Artillery Brigade of the Department of North Carolina. His appointment in this post expired in March 1863 because the Senate, apparently thinking little of his qualifications, failed to confirm him. He was nevertheless reappointed in October 1863 and, partly through the intervention of Ambrose Burnside, was later confirmed by the Senate.

Ledlie served for the next eighteen months as a commander of North

This photograph of James H. Ledlie was taken using a three-lens camera. Daguerreotypes could not be duplicated; multiple-lens cameras were a means of producing multiple copies. (Library of Congress)

Carolina garrisons, mostly manning the coastal artillery. Throughout his military career, up to this point, he had seen no real action. And therein lay his remarkable good fortune. For while he had not led men in battle, he had performed his other duties competently, neither making complaint nor earning censure. As far as his military superiors were concerned, this passed for flawless performance and, shortly after Grant commenced his Overland Campaign in 1864, Ledlie was transferred to the Army of the Potomac as a brigade commander in IX Corps. On June 9, 1864, he was bumped up to command of the First Division.

Ambrose Burnside knew Potter and Willcox to be excellent division commanders. Ledlie he hardly knew at all but was under the impression that, as a brigade commander in what had been Thomas L. Crittenden's division, he had acquitted himself well at Cold Harbor in a spirited attack on the Confederate position at Ox Ford on May 26.

The facts of that action were quite different from Burnside's understanding of them. On May 26, 1864, Ledlie sent out the 35th Massachusetts to skirmish with a small detachment of Confederate sharpshooters. After the regiment pushed the enemy back, Ledlie stumbled upon a portion of Robert E. Lee's defensive line near Ox Ford. Here was no clutch of sharpshooters, but a segment of formidable fortifications well situated on high ground and covered by a line of rifle pits. No one in his right mind would assault this impregnable position. But Ledlie was drunk—that seemed to be his normal condition as a commander—and, as the 35th Massachusetts traded shots with the men in the rifle pits, Ledlie recklessly sent in the 56th, 57th, and 59th Massachusetts.

They didn't have a chance.

Charging the Confederate works in complete disarray, the men of these regiments were mowed down by artillery firing grape and canister shot. As a heavy thunderstorm burst upon the battlefield, the Confederates sortied out in a full counterattack, capturing 150 Bay State men and sending the rest of the survivors into headlong retreat.

Ledlie, who had remained cozily enough in the rear with a bottle, did not reap censure and relief from command, but, on the contrary, received the praise of General Crittenden, who recommended him to Burnside as his replacement when he stepped down as division commander two weeks after the Ox Ford battle. Not only did Burnside give Ledlie the division, he also wrote to Grant on June 5, 1864, to enlist the aid of the general-in-chief in securing Senate confirmation of Ledlie's reappointment as a brigadier.

By the time the First Division took up its position on the Petersburg line, most of Ledlie's fellow officers were well aware that he was a drinker. To be sure, many joined him from time to time in a glass of cheer. Perhaps Ledlie took to the bottle because he sensed that his good luck was about to run out as he increasingly faced the test of actual combat. Perhaps he drank to smother a growing awareness of his own inadequacies. Or maybe he was simply scared. Whatever his reasons, he was so drunk during the Petersburg assault on June 17 that he was all but unconscious and left his division to fend for itself. No one reported this to Burnside, however, who was led to believe that Ledlie had turned in yet another "spirited" performance—an adjective that the waggish among those who knew Ledlie might well have taken as a pun. Was the silence of his subordinates and colleagues the product of loyalty to a brother officer? Perhaps.

In any case, having made his choice of leader—or, rather, having left that choice to chance—Ambrose Burnside outlined for Ledlie and the other two division commanders the plan. Presumably, by this time, all four generals were impatient to be done with the conference. None had confidence in the impending assault. And, almost surely, Ledlie was drunk, maybe even too drunk to take in much of what Burnside had to say.

The IX Corps commander—wearily, we may suppose—explained that Ledlie's division was to charge around the crater that had been blasted in the Confederate works and attempt to take Cemetery Hill. Willcox's Third Division would follow Ledlie's advance, moving to the left of Ledlie's line to occupy the Jerusalem Plank Road, which lay to the west of Cemetery Hill, roughly paralleling that high ground. That is, Cemetery Hill lay directly behind (and parallel with) the Confederate entrenchments, and the Jerusalem Plank Road was located behind Cemetery Hill. Willcox's division would suppress any counterattack from the road. Potter would also lead his Second Division against the Jerusalem Plank Road, but to the right.

In this initial phase of the assault, Burnside proposed for the three white divisions something like a large-scale version of what he had originally envisioned for Ferrero's Fourth Division alone: a main thrust straight ahead, toward the high ground behind the Confederate entrenchments, with flanking movements to the left and right. There were, however, two critical differences between the new plan and the original one.

First, the new plan lacked the simultaneity of the original. Ferrero's "colored troops" had been slated for an advance in which the left and right flanks peeled off as the main body pressed forward. The objective of this movement, risky in its complexity, had been to suppress enfilading fire that would otherwise hammer the flanks of the initial assaulting force. Presumably in obedience to Meade's orders—that the initial attack be launched in one direction only, straight ahead—Burnside confined the flanking movements to the Third and Second Divisions, and these would be made not simultaneously with the advance of the First Division, but serially, one after the other. The First Division would, for better or worse, advance straight ahead only. The Third Division would follow to the left, and then the Second Division would follow the Third, to the right. This sequence would take time, of course, during which the Confederates would be re-forming their defenses, presumably firing on the First Division from the left and right.

The second difference between the original plan and the new one was that the white divisions were wholly unprepared to make the assault. Unlike the black division and its officers, they had not trained for it. They had not drilled for it. Their officers had not even examined the ground they were to traverse. Moreover, the white troops still suffered from the exhaustion—the "nostalgia," the gun shyness, call it what you will—that had motivated Burnside to choose the "colored troops" in the first place. The soldiers of the white divisions were unready and unmotivated. Worse, they were even less than willing.

Assuming that the three white divisions achieved their objectives, in effect having opened a broad passageway through the Confederate lines, left, right, and straight ahead, Ferrero's Fourth Division (Colored Troops) would finally be sent in to begin the march all the way to Petersburg.

After giving his divisional commanders their instructions, Burnside advised Ledlie to make a personal reconnaissance of the ground over which they would advance. As he testified to Congress, "General Ferrero, who commanded the colored division, had, with his officers, already examined the ground upon which he was to form, and had made a reconnaissance of the ground over which he was to pass at the time he expected to lead the attack. I sent General Ledlie with his brigade officers to make similar reconnaissances, which they did. At about four o'clock in the afternoon they reported to me that the examination had been made, and they only waited for darkness, and troops to relieve them, in order to get the division in position for the attack." In the meantime, Burnside reported his new plan to Meade, who, in response, "issued his battle order" to the Army of the Potomac.[19]

Meade's orders called for Burnside to "form his troops for assaulting the enemy's works at daylight of the 30th" and to "prepare his parapets and abatis for the passage of the columns, and have the pioneers equipped for work in opening passages for artillery, destroying enemy's abatis, and the intrenching tools distributed for effecting lodgments, &c." The inclusion of "pioneers equipped for work in opening passages for artillery [and] destroying enemy's abatis"[20]—work that should be accomplished by the explosion of the mine—suggests that Meade, even at this late hour, had doubts that the detonation would be effective.

In addition to specifying the actions of Burnside's IX Corps, Meade's orders of the 29th provided for major troop movements (as Burnside explained in his congressional testimony) "to relieve my troops from their position on the line, in order that we might make the concentration for the assault." What Meade's orders failed to contemplate was what Burnside described as "the difficulty of moving large bodies of troops at night."[21] Such difficulty had already afflicted the Army of the Potomac in earlier phases of the Overland Campaign, and Meade should have been wary of the problem, which was likely to be particularly acute among battle-weary troops. Moreover, divisional commanders were not handed their orders until 9 o'clock at night, a circumstance that served to compound the "difficulty."

As the general commanding the Army of the Potomac, Meade—properly—did not concern himself with operations below the corps level. His orders, therefore, did not mention the movements of Burnside's divisions, but merely specified that "At 3.30 in the morning of the 30th Major-General Burnside will spring his mine, and his assaulting columns will immediately move rapidly upon the breach, seize the crest in the rear [Cemetery Hill], and effect a lodgment there." On the corps level, this advance was to

> be followed by Major-General Ord [XVIII Corps], who will support [Burnside] on the right, directing his movement to the crest indicated [Cemetery Hill], and by Major-General Warren [V Corps], who will support him on the left. Upon the explosion of the mine the artillery of all kinds in battery will open upon those points of the enemy's works whose fire covers the ground over which our columns must move, care being take to avoid impeding the progress of our troops. Special instructions respecting the direction of fire will be issued through the chief of artillery.

> . . . Corps commanders will report to the commanding general when their preparations are complete, and will advise him of every step in the progress of the operation, and of everything important that occurs.

> . . . Promptitude, rapidity of execution, and cordial co-operation, are essential to success, and the commanding general is confident that this

indication of his expectations will insure the hearty efforts of the commanders and troops.[22]

The heavy rains that had broken upon the parched Virginia landscape on July 24, threatening the mine with collapse, had long since passed, and the intense heat of that dry and dusty summer had returned with a vengeance. July 29 had been an especially stifling day, hot and breezeless. Night brought remarkably little relief as the benighted soldiers of Ord's corps groped through the dark in an effort to find their positions, so that Burnside's men could take up theirs. As Ord's men dribbled in, the soldiers of Burnside's three white divisions began to form in the trenches and the covered ways in preparation for their advance. Jammed into these miserable, log-walled ditches, the men were hot, thirsty, and sleepless.

In some places, Ord's troops were so thoroughly lost that they failed to relieve IX Corps units. Ord's Third Division, consisting of seven "colored" regiments, did not arrive at Robert Potter's assigned position within the Union works until 3 a.m.—a mere half-hour before the mine was scheduled to be sprung and the assault begun. Accordingly, Potter exercised common sense and declared that he would leave his men where they were and attack from his present positions. He had, however, decided to excuse altogether one of his regiments from the assault. The 48th Pennsylvania, which had built and charged the mine, was to stay out of the fight. The regiment's commanding officer, Henry Pleasants, agreed that his men had earned their rest, but he told Potter that he would accept none of that for himself. Instead, he volunteered to serve on Potter's front-line staff as an aide. He was determined to claim ownership of this battle, which he had made possible. Potter welcomed him.

While the men of Potter's division remained in their assigned positions and the troops of Willcox's division crowded up front to their assault positions, the First Division, under James Ledlie, the unit that was to lead the assault, had yet to reach its assigned staging area. Although the division was to take the lead, it had been posted farthest from the front lines and, therefore, had the longest march to make. The

First Brigade of the First Division, for example, was relieved by Ord's men about 10 p.m. It was then marched to the rear, only to be brought up to the front, in preparation for the assault. Indeed, it was midnight or later before the whole of the First Division was formed up and ready to move toward its staging area—and this for an assault just three and a half hours away.

"The men were cautioned to prevent the rattling of tin cups and bayonets, because we were so near the enemy that they would discover our movements," Major Charles Houghton of the 14th New York Heavy Artillery (one of many heavy artillery units serving as infantry, and a part of the First Division) recalled. "We marched with the stillness of death; not a word was said above a whisper. We knew, of course, that something very important was to be done and that we were to play a prominent part."[23]

Houghton's recollection suggests something of the intensity of anticipation on the eve of battle, in the close, hot stillness of the loneliest hours of night and predawn morning; and it also suggests something more. "We knew," Houghton wrote, "that something very important was to be done." *Something.* In that single word was a wealth of portent. The change in orders putting Ledlie's division in place of Ferrero's had come so late that this regimental major had not been informed of the nature of the division's mission beyond his sense that it was "something very important." Bewildered, groping through the darkness of July 29/30, the men of IX Corps were destined to be even more profoundly lost after daybreak.

The soldiers of the Fourth Division, in contrast to those of Burnside's white divisions, had known for nearly a month what they were preparing for. But about 11 p.m. on July 29, the officers of that division were told that they were not going to lead the attack after all. It fell now to each of them to pass the word to their "men er war." Colonel Henry G. Thomas, commanding the Second Brigade, was not merely disappointed, but fully aware that so late a change in plan hardly boded victory. "I returned to that bivouac dejected and with an instinct of disaster for the

morrow," Thomas wrote. "As I summoned and told my regimental commanders, their faces expressed the same feeling."[24]

For all the last-minute, haphazard activity of that summer night and
early morning, which included the often bumbling movements of some
nine thousand men, the Confederates, just one hundred yards away,
never suspected what was happening. Incredibly, secrecy and surprise
were preserved.

Item number one of Meade's orders of July 29 specified that "General
Burnside will . . . prepare his parapets and abatis for the passage of the
columns." In his testimony to Congress, Burnside alluded to this,
pointing out that "This part of the order was necessarily inoperative,
because of lack of time and the close proximity to the enemy, the latter
of which rendered it impossible to remove the abatis from the front of
our line without attracting, not only a heavy fire of the enemy, but also
his attention to that point, and letting him know exactly what we were
doing." The "failure" to remove the abatis and clear other obstructions
was destined to haunt Ambrose Burnside during the inquiries that followed the Petersburg assault. By allowing these obstacles to stand, it was
alleged that Burnside had fatally retarded the charge of his men over
their own parapet. To Congress, Burnside claimed: "It was afterwards
found that the abatis which had to be removed when our troops did
advance did not delay them more than five minutes."[25] Under the circumstances, even five minutes under fire was not insignificant, yet it is
also true that the labor of clearing the obstacles would almost certainly
have tipped the Union's hand. For there is only one reason why an enemy
would clear his own trenches of obstacles: to make way for an attack.

And so, despite the radical change in plan, despite the confusion,
despite the suffocating heat in which weary men trudged and shuffled,
then finally stood, crammed together for sleepless hours in filthy
trenches—despite all of this, the impending attack maintained surprise
in its favor.

Ambrose Burnside, having managed somehow to absorb the crushing
command to hold his specially trained Fourth Division in reserve and

turn over the assault on Petersburg to an entirely unprepared division, testified to Congress that James Ledlie, after drawing the short straw that put him at the head of that assault, had "left my headquarters in a very cheerful mood." Perhaps that mood had been hysterical rather than cheerful. Or maybe what Burnside saw was a commander already in his cups. On the morning of July 30, while his men were already fighting and dying, James Ledlie—according to Burnside—"was quite sick." Yes, Burnside admitted to the Joint Committee, "I thought afterwards, [that Ledlie] ought to have gone to the crater the moment his men were in. But I understood that he was very sick." Perhaps that "sickness" was already on display the night before battle, as General Ledlie hunched in the trenches with his men, men who had tolerated him well enough when all they had to do was quietly tend coastal artillery in North Carolina but who, ever since Ox Ford and that May afternoon of ill-considered combat and blood spilled in vain, were learning more and more to see their commanding officer as a weak man, incompetent, cowardly, and dangerous.[26]

CHAPTER

- 6 -

Sprung

I received orders from corps headquarters, on the 29th of July, to fire the mine at half past three a.m., July 30," Henry Pleasants told the congressional Joint Committee on the Conduct of the War. There were three parallel fuse lines, each of which ran (according to Pleasants) for ninety-eight feet. This meant that the fuse lines began about four hundred feet into the tunnel, so that whoever lighted the fuses would have to venture four-fifths of the way into the tunnel, apply the match, turn about, and, at a crouching trot, exit via that same four hundred feet. Lieutenant Jacob Douty (also spelled Doughty) and Sergeant Henry Reese, who had served as the foreman-ramrod for the entire project, volunteered to accompany Pleasants into the tunnel to light the fuses. Pleasants estimated that it would take fifteen minutes for the ninety-eight feet of fuse to burn all the way to the powder charge, so, as he told the court, "I lighted the fuze at 3.15 a.m."[1]

Pleasants had profound misgivings, as he detailed to the Joint Committee:

Question. What means did you use to insure the explosion of the powder?

Answer. I used three lines of fuze, called the blasting fuze. I asked for fuze, and they sent me this common blasting fuze. There were troughs running from one magazine to the other, half filled with powder; and then from where the two lateral galleries joined there were two troughs with fuzes in them. The troughs were half filled with fine powder; then from a certain distance out there was nothing but three fuzes, without any powder. The fuze I received was cut in short pieces; some of them are only ten feet long.

Question. Why was that?

Answer. I do not know.

Question. Was not [there] an objection to it?

Answer. A great objection.[2]

Nor was Pleasants the only officer harboring doubts that moonless morning. At "about 3.15 o'clock, when I was about preparing to go forward to General Burnside's headquarters," George Gordon Meade testified before the army's Court of Inquiry, "I found that it was very dark, and suggestions being made by some of my officers that it was too dark to operate successfully and that a postponement of the explosion of the mine might be advantageous, I accordingly addressed a dispatch to General Burnside to the following effect":

HEADQUARTERS ARMY OF THE POTOMAC,
July 30, 1864–3.20 *a.m.*

Major-General BURNSIDE:

As it is still so dark, the commanding general says you can postpone firing the mine if you think proper.

A. A. HUMPHREYS,
Major-General and Chief of Staff[3]

Burnside telegraphed a curt reply. He had no time to explain that match
had already been touched to fuse:

> NINTH ARMY CORPS,
> *July* 30, 1864–3.20 *a.m.*
>
> Major-General HUMPHREYS:
> The mine will be fired at the time designated. My headquarters will be
> at the fourteen-gun battery.
>
> A. E. BURNSIDE,
> *Major-General*[4]

But 3:30 came, and 3:30 passed, bringing no roar of exploding powder
to rend the thick predawn air, no flash of detonation to illuminate the
darkness. In his forward command post, fourteen-gun battery—also
called Fort Morton, after an officer who had fallen in the earlier assault
on Petersburg—Burnside, "like every one else, awaited with great anxiety the explosion of the mine."

> I need not say to this Court that my anxiety on the occasion was extreme,
> particularly as I did not know the reason of the delay. I waited for sev-
> eral minutes, and thinking that there was some miscalculation as to the
> time it would take the fuse to burn up to the charge, when I sent an aide-
> de-camp to find out what was the reason of the delay. Soon after that I
> sent a second aide-de-camp. Soon after that time [Burnside's staff officer]
> Major [James] Van Buren arrived at my headquarters and told me the
> cause of the delay.[5]

In the meantime, "Captain Sanders, I think, or some other one of General
Meade's staff, came to my headquarters to know the reason. I said to him
that I had sent to ascertain the reason; that I could not tell him then."
Moments later, "Another dispatch, either written or verbal, came to know

the reason; and I sent word again that I did not know the reason, but as soon as I could ascertain it I would give the general the reason."[6] Finally:

> I then got another dispatch from General Meade that if the mine had failed I must make a charge independent of the explosion of the mine. Having almost made up my own mind that the mine had failed, or that something had occurred which we could not discover during that morning, and feeling the absolute necessity, as General Meade expressed in his dispatch, of doing something very quickly, I was on the eve of sending an order for the command to be ready to move forward as directed by General Meade, but I said again, "I will delay to ascertain what is the reason of the non-explosion of the mine." I had nothing that I could report up to the time that Major Van Buren came to my head-quarters. I gave to those aides freely the statement that I did not know the reason of the non-explosion of the mine, but that as soon as I learned it I would inform the commanding general.[7]

The first dispatch from Meade, asking "Is there any difficulty in exploding the mine? It is three-quarters of an hour later than that fixed upon for exploding it," had been sent at 4:15. The final dispatch—"The commanding general directs that if your mine has failed that you make an assault at once, opening your batteries"—was sent twenty minutes later, at 4:35, simultaneously with another dispatch, vague and freighted heavily with consternation:

> HEADQUARTERS ARMY OF THE POTOMAC,
> *July* 30, 1864–4.35 *a.m.*
>
> Major-General BURNSIDE:
> If the mine cannot be exploded something else must be done, and at once. The commanding general is awaiting to hear from you before determining.
> **A. A. HUMPHREYS,**
> *Major-General and Chief of Staff*[8]

Burnside could not reply to this series of insistent queries until Major Van Buren returned from the mine. The major returned quickly, but it must have seemed an eternity. He told Burnside "that the fuse had gone out, and that a gallant soldier named Sergeant Reese, of the Forty-eighth Pennsylvania, had volunteered to go into the gallery to ascertain whether the fuse was really burning still and burning slowly, or whether it had failed."[9]

Pleasants told the Court of Inquiry that "having waited till 4.15 a.m.[,] an officer and sergeant of my regiment volunteered to go in and examine into the cause of the delay."[10] In fact, both Reese and Douty had volunteered to go in earlier, but Pleasants insisted on waiting until he was reasonably certain the fuse had failed and the mine would not explode—with the two men inside. At 4:15, he finally allowed Reese, armed with a lantern, to go in alone.

On January 13, 1865, the chairman of the Joint Committee pressed Henry Pleasants on the matter of the fuse his superiors had supplied him, the wrong kind of fuse, whose multiple short lengths had to be spliced in many places.

Question. Was there any danger that it would not communicate at those parts where it was joined?

Answer. It did not, and had to be relighted.

Question. Who had the courage to go down into the mine and relight it?

Answer. I had a lieutenant and a sergeant with me in the mine when I lighted it the first time.

Question. How far in did it go out?

Answer. I had a fuze about ninety feet long, and it burned about forty feet the whole three fuzes.[11]

Pleasants knew the fuse had burned for forty feet, because it was at this point that Sergeant Reese discovered all three lines had sputtered out at a splice. This meant that Reese was fully 440 feet inside of the tunnel, hunched over the fuse, a burning lantern in hand. He must have breathed a sigh of relief to find that all three lines were out—that the fuse was indeed dead. For up to this point, as he ventured deeper and deeper into the cramped shaft, he had had no way of knowing whether the fuse had been extinguished or was just burning very slowly, its progress retarded by dampness and multiple splices, ready to flame into life at any moment and ignite the four tons of powder toward which he was advancing step by step.

But Reese's relief must have dissolved almost instantly into an agony of frustration. As he stared at the burned-out fuse, he saw that he could not resplice the fuses without first slicing out the portions that had put out the fire. The trouble was, in his haste to enter the mine, Henry Reese had neglected to bring along a pocket knife. Without a tool to cut away the bad fuse, there was nothing for it now but to leave the mine, get a knife, return with it, and do the job.

Reese was crouching his way toward the entrance when he was met by Lieutenant Jacob Douty. The Pottsville, Pennsylvania, boilermaker drew out of his pocket a knife, and the pair returned to the fuses, then repaired and relit them. Aware that the burn had only sixty feet more to travel whereas they had 440, Reese and Douty made their way along the shaft as quickly as half-bent men could. Emerging from the shaft entrance, they told Pleasants that the blast should come in a matter of minutes—at 4:45, they said. Pleasants relayed the information to General Potter, who told Major Van Buren, who dashed off to Burnside.

Burnside must have received the information from a breathless Van Buren just moments before the explosion. Most accounts report that the detonation occurred at 4:44.

Before the soldiers of the North and South had scratched, sliced, and gouged parallel scars of trench into it, the land above and around Elliott's Salient had been grazed by the cows of one William Griffith, Virginia farmer. Now that war-battered pasturage received a new insult, far more catastrophic.

At first, it was a "low rumbling," as Benjamin A. Spear, Company K, 57th Massachusetts, put it, followed by "a tremble not unlike an earthquake." Lieutenant J. J. Chase, 32nd Maine, actually thought it *was* an earthquake. He had been sleeping and was "suddenly . . . awakened. Oh horrors! Was I in the midst of an earthquake? Was the ground around me about to part and let me into the bowels of the earth[?] Hardly realizing where I was or what it all meant, this terrible thunder, accompanied by the upheaving and rocking of the ground, springing to my feet I recovered my senses enough to understand that [an] explosion had taken place. Glancing in the direction of Cemetery Hill, I beheld a huge mass of earth being thrown up, followed by a dark lurid cloud of smoke." Unlike Chase, Spear did not have to look as far as Cemetery Hill to behold the explosion: "It seemed for a moment or two as though Co. K would be covered with dirt, fragments of gun-carriages, timbers and distorted fragments of human beings," he recalled. Frederick Cushman, of the 58th Massachusetts, heard "a dull rumbling sound, followed by an immense quantity of earth, parts of caissons, such as wheels, boxes, &c., thrown into the air to a height of 30 feet."[12]

Byron Cutcheon of the 20th Michigan remembered "First . . . a deep shock and tremor of the earth and a jar like an earthquake," succeeded by

a heaving and lifting of the fort and the hill on which it stood; then a monstrous tongue of flame shot fully two hundred feet into the air, followed by a vast column of white smoke, resembling the discharge of an enormous cannon; then a great spout or fountain of red earth rose to a great height, mingled with men and guns, timbers and planks, and every other kind of debris, all ascending, spreading, whirling, scattering and falling with great concussion to the earth once more.[13]

To Major William H. Powell, one of Ledlie's staff officers, "It was a magnificent spectacle," whereas the 14th New York Heavy Artillery's Charles Houghton called it a "terrible and magnificent sight."

The earth around us trembled and heaved—so violently that I was lifted to my feet. Then the earth along the enemy's lines opened, and fire and smoke shot upward seventy-five or one hundred feet. The air was filled with earth, cannon, caissons, sand-bags and living men, and with everything else within the exploded fort. Once large lump of clay as large as a hay-stack or small cottage was thrown out and left on top of the ground toward our own works.[14]

Magnificent.

Terrible and magnificent.

However, the detonation of four tons of powder beneath the men and machines of war was no merely emotional or aesthetic experience. The attackers were, in virtually every sense, unprepared for the event they themselves had caused to take place. Powell explained: "as the mass of earth went up into the air, carrying with it men, guns, carriages, and timbers, and spread out like an immense cloud as it reached its altitude, so close were the Union lines that the mass appeared as if it would descend immediately upon the troops waiting to make the charge. This caused them to break and scatter to the rear, and about ten minutes were consumed re-forming for the attack."[15]

From Burnside's testimony to the Court of Inquiry, we know that there had been much anxiety among the soldiers of IX Corps prior to the explosion. The men were primed to panic. "I witnessed this anxiety among the troops with a good deal of concern," Burnside told the Court of Inquiry.[16] He attributed the mass anxiety to the fact that officers and even some enlisted men had been prompted—presumably by Meade and his chief engineer, Duane—to question the amount of powder Pleasants and Burnside proposed to pack into the mine. These questions had led many to believe that they would be blown up along with the Confederates.

When the mine was detonated, many of the soldiers who had been formed up for the charge—crammed sleepless into the trenches and covered way—were indeed panic stricken.

The sound of the explosion itself was surprisingly unimpressive: "dull sounding, . . . like a heavy gun, far away." But the sight was terrifying. One of Potter's men recalled how the dense black smoke "slowly mounting into the air to a height of some two hundred feet, and then, spreading out like a fan, fell back again into the excavation made by the explosion." A soldier from a Maine regiment said that "Earth, stones, timbers, arms, legs, guns unlimbered and bodies unlimbed . . . ascended in fearful confusion and havoc." It is little wonder, then, that Ledlie's men, at the forefront of the front lines, feared that they would be buried by debris. Instead of immediately commencing their charge out of the entrenchments, they either stood, transfixed by the spectacle, or recoiled. It took the stern and vigorous work of officers to push men back into their formations, where they were showered with dust and small clods of earth, but not buried alive.[17]

The *National Park Service Historical Handbook* for Petersburg National Battlefield reflects the long-held consensus of modern historians that "The awesome spectacle of the mine explosion caused a delay in the Union charge following the explosion."[18] After the failure of the assault, it is true that everyone agreed that the advance of the First Division had been ineffectual—and ultimately disastrous—as were the advances of the other divisions that followed. However, there was much bitter and rancorous dispute about the precise nature and cause of the failure. Some insisted that it began with the front-line panic caused by the explosion itself. Burnside addressed this theory at the Court of Inquiry: "I understand that there was considerable anxiety among the men after and before the explosion as to the effect that it might have upon them, and I have been informed by Colonel Loring, my [assistant] inspector-general . . . who was with the column, that it took probably five minutes to get the men in perfect condition to dash forward. After their ranks were re-established, they went forward, as far as I could see or know or hear, in the most gallant possible style until they arrived within the crater." When the Judge Advocate pressed this issue further with Burnside, his answer remained consistent, although he also admitted the possibility of error:

Question. What time elapsed from the springing of the mine to the forward movement of the assaulting columns, and how long was it before the crater was reached by the storming party?

Answer. At the risk of involving the same difference in time as in similar matters I will state that it was about five minutes until the advance column moved forward, and say ten minutes before the leading column reached the crater. This delay occurred in consequence of the hesitation which has been already alluded to in my evidence, but not personally known to me. And it is not impossible that I may be mistaken as to the time.

Later, testifying to the Joint Committee of Congress, Burnside spoke of a delay "of from five to ten minutes after the explosion of the mine."[19]

As we will see, there were other, far more serious impediments to the initial assault than panic and disorder caused by the spectacle of the explosion itself. True, the white soldiers of IX Corps—especially the lead division, Ledlie's First—were tired, unprepared, and apprehensive, but the fact that these men charged into the site of a massive explosion five, even ten minutes after it occurred was hardly evidence of panic or cowardice or a deficiency of what Meade, at the congressional hearing, called "vim." On the contrary, it was evidence of courage, remarkable and resilient. Frederick Cushman provided a vivid picture: "At the instant of the explosion," he wrote, Union artillery opened fire against the Confederate line. Whereas the sound of the mine detonation itself had been curiously muffled, the cannonade was "perfectly deafening." Captain R. G. Richards of the 45th Pennsylvania wrote of "about 150 pieces of artillery" opening fire so that they "simultaneously crashed their thunders . . . until it seemed as if the vaulted dome above us was bursting asunder." This—not the detonation of the mine, but the unleashing of the artillery barrage almost simultaneously with it—caused the "men [to become] frantic with excitement," according to Cushman. As this eyewitness saw it, they were ready to fight and to win. "Everything looked propitious for a grand success."[20]

"The size of the crater formed by the explosion was at least 200 feet long, 50 feet wide, and 25 feet deep," Henry Pleasants wrote in a letter to the Court of Inquiry. "I stood on top of our breast-works and witnessed the effect of the explosion on the enemy. It so completely paralyzed them that the breach was practically 400 or 500 yards in breadth. The rebels in the forts, both on the right and left of the explosion, left their works, and for over an hour not a shot was fired by their artillery. There was no fire from infantry from the front for at least half an hour; none from the left for twenty minutes, and but few shots from the right."[21]

There is no question that, taken completely by surprise and overwhelmed by the blast, the Confederates could not instantly reply. "The earth seemed to tremble," an Alabama officer recalled, and whereas the sound of the detonation had been muffled and distant to the ears of the Federals, the Alabaman spoke of "a report that seemed to deafen all nature" in the "next instance" after the trembling of the earth. Southwest of the Alabama officer's position, a Virginia soldier described a "deep rumbling sound, that seemed to rend the very earth in twain." It "startled me from my sleep," he wrote, "and in an instant I beheld a mountain of curling smoke ascending towards the heavens." North Carolina lieutenant A. B. Thrash was perhaps two hundred yards from Elliott's Salient, the epicenter of the blast. In the predawn gloom, two sights burned themselves into his memory: the skyward ascent of a gun carriage, detached from the 12-pounder Napoleon it had carried, and the accompanying ascent of a human body. Standing near Thrash's position, an adjutant of an artillery battalion watched the descent of such material: "hurtling down with a roaring sound showers of stones, broken timbers, and blackened human limbs." This was followed by "the gloomy pall of darkening smoke flashing to an angry crimson as it floats away to meet the morning sun."[22]

Such Confederate eyewitness accounts of the moment of the blast are few and sketchy. It is not surprising. Thirty gunners serving in Captain Richard Pegram's four-gun battery were positioned directly above the powder-packed magazines, as were some three hundred South Carolina troops in the closely adjacent trenches. In the first earth-heaving, heaven-rending seconds of the Battle of the Crater, most of these men were killed or wounded. These were the direct casualties of the Petersburg mine explosion.

Almost all the men at Elliott's Salient were buried in earth and debris, some buried dead, some alive—only to be suffocated under a mountain of clay, wood, shrapnel, and blasted human remains. Yet a few, Lazarus-like, emerged from the mass grave of the Confederate fort. Among these was Wilson Moore, Company B, 22nd South Carolina, who had just gotten off guard duty minutes before the detonation. He made his way to a ditch behind the trench, his usual sleeping place, where he was greeted by the sight of his fellow soldiers stretched out in various attitudes of deepest slumber. Finding no room to stretch himself out, Moore propped his back against the side of the ditch and nodded off sitting up. As he began to doze, the earth erupted, and in a twilight consciousness between waking and sleeping, he reflexively thrust his arms and hands above his head. Like his fellow sleepers, he was buried alive, but, unlike them, his hands waved frantically above the surface of the fallen clay. A survivor above grasped his hands, but could not pull him up, so settled for clearing the earth from his face. Moore could now breathe, unlike his supine comrades, but it was not until Union soldiers swept through that he was freed from neck-down entombment.

Two officers of Company B also survived living burial. Captain George Lake and his lieutenant, a W. J. Lake, were completely buried by the explosion, the blast having thrown the lieutenant atop the captain and the earth having covered them over. By some quirk of fate or physics, the pair occupied a small void in the heaped-up debris, which kept them from immediate suffocation. But, fully conscious, both men were acutely aware of the hopelessness of their plight. Lieutenant Lake tried to push the earth up and away with his back, but it was too heavy. Moreover, his leg had been shattered, so he found it almost impossible to move. The men were discussing their impending end when incoming Union troops of the First Division's Second Brigade paused to dig them out. Along with Moore, the pair was sent to the rear as prisoners of war.

Perhaps the most incredible survival story is that of an engineer sergeant and his crew who had been serving under Captain Hugh Douglas, digging one of the countermines intended to intercept and destroy the Union mine. The sergeant and three of his men were below the surface, working in the countermine gallery when the Union mine was sprung. Above, on the surface, were five other engineer troops. The sergeant recalled how the "gallery heaved and waved as from an earthquake,"[23] yet although it was only a few feet from the Pleasants shaft—perhaps as little as five feet above it—the countermine did not cave in. The sergeant and his three-man crew were able to scramble to the surface. The five others who had been working up top were nowhere to be seen. Glancing forward, however, the sergeant saw blue-coated men approaching and, with the other three survivors, high-tailed it to the rear, where they were soon reunited with all but one of the surface workers.

Within five—perhaps ten—minutes of the explosion, as a total of 110 Union cannon and 54 mortars poured fire on some two miles of the Confederate front (24 pieces were directed at the Crater itself), the men of Ledlie's First Division began to mount the Union parapet to start their advance on the Confederate line. Although Burnside, fearful of alerting the enemy to the impending assault, had not leveled the parapet or removed the abatis at the point through which the storming division was to "debouche," Ledlie's men had constructed impromptu stairways over the parapet using stacked sandbags. In some places, bayonets were inserted into the log-reinforced wall of trench and parapet to serve as improvised risers, and sandbags laid across them as equally impromptu treads. In testimony after the battle, Burnside claimed that the parapet, abatis, and other defensive obstacles did not delay the advance more than five minutes—that is, five minutes in addition to the five or ten minutes' delay created by the spectacle of the explosion itself.

James Ledlie personally ordered Colonel Elisha G. Marshall to lead off with his Second Brigade; the First Brigade, under William Francis Bartlett, would follow. Ledlie watched the men of these brigades scramble over the parapet, then, deciding he had seen enough, turned away from the fight.

During the proceedings of the Court of Inquiry, the judge-advocate questioned O. P. Chubb, surgeon of the 20th Michigan Volunteers, IX Corps:

Question. Were you at the assault on the 30th of July?

Answer. I was.

Question. State what you did there.

Answer. I accompanied the Second Brigade of the Third Division of the Ninth Corps across the ravine and up to within ten rods of our breast-works, at the point where the troops passed through immediately after the explosion of the mine. I took position in a bomb-proof which had been used as some regimental headquarters, and remained there for the purpose of dressing wounds. This bomb-proof is located at a point about ten rods [165 feet] in rear of our line. Shortly after I took up that position General Ledlie, of the First Division, and Ferrero, of the Fourth, came up to the front of the bomb-proof, and shortly afterward came in and took seats. This was in the morning about half an hour after the explosion of the mine.

. . . Question. Do you know any reason why [Ledlie] was not with his troops himself?

Answer. No, sir. But during almost the last moments of his stay there he sent an aide to ascertain how things were going on, and remarked that he could not go himself as he had been hurt in the side by a spent ball. I cannot state positively when this occurred; it seemed to be after I first saw him, but I recollect him having mentioned that fact quite late in the forenoon, nearly noon, for the first time. . . .[24]

Later, the judge-advocate questioned another surgeon, H. E. Smith, 27th Michigan Volunteers, IX Corps, who elaborated on Ledlie's stay in the bomb-proof: "General Ledlie asked me for stimulants, and said he had the malaria and was struck by a spent ball. He inquired for General Bartlett, as he wanted to turn the command over to him and go to the rear. It was one of General Bartlett's aides, I believe, who replied that he was in the crater."[25]

. . . Question. You mention stimulants. What were they—hartshorn, *materia medica*, or what?

Answer. It was rum, I think. I had rum and whisky there, and I think I gave them [Generals Ledlie and Ferrero] rum.

Question. How often did you administer stimulants to those two officers during that day?

Answer. I think that once was the only time. I was not in the bomb-proof all the time while they were there. *It was perfectly safe in there*, but it might not have been outside. I had to go out to look after the wounded.[26]

Of Colonel Henry G. Thomas, commanding officer of the Second Brigade, Fourth Division, which was brought into the battle late, the judge-advocate asked a question to which the answer was painfully obvious: "Was the bombproof a good place to see what was going on?"

> Answer. No, sir; there were places near there where something could be seen, but the earth about the crater prevented almost anything being seen immediately to the left of it. The dirt was thrown up very high. There were, I think, however, places near there where a view could be got.[27]

Both Marshall and Bartlett were fine officers; indeed, they were as competent and gallant as Ledlie was not. Elisha Marshall was a West Point man, Class of 1850, who had served in every major Army of the Potomac action until he was grievously wounded at Fredericksburg. After a long bed convalescence, he was given light-duty assignments, briefly left the army, then returned to command the 14th New York Heavy Artillery until he was elevated to brigade command in IX Corps. Wounded very early in the Petersburg campaign, he was on sick leave until shortly before the Battle of the Crater. His heavy artillery brigade consisted of garrison rather than combat soldiers, the 14th New York Heavy, the 179th New York, the 2nd Pennsylvania Provisional Heavy Artillery, and the 3rd Maryland Battalion. Virtually all of the troops were new to infantry action of any kind, and they were certainly not the stuff from which shock troops are made.

Yet they charged out of the Union lines gamely, even courageously, the 2nd Pennsylvania first, the 14th New York next, and the 179th New York and 3rd Maryland last. Captain Stephen M. Weld was part of the advance. He left a detailed picture of the difficulties of climbing over the trench and parapet: "the only chance to get over our line of breastworks was a space not over ten feet wide, where sand-bags had been piled up by the troops who preceded us. I tried to climb the parapet in two or three places, but was unable to do so. Soldiers with muskets and accoutrements could not get over." Yet, somehow, they did, and, as for the abatis on the engaged side of the parapet, it presented "practically no impediment." Despite the struggle to go over the top, Weld reported that "in five minutes from the time of the explosion," men were running toward the crater—albeit not "in a line of battle," but in a "straggling line of men by twos and threes."[28]

Bartlett's men similarly sortied out, and, like Marshall's, had trouble coalescing themselves into an organized advance. Like Marshall, Bartlett was a wounded veteran, but whereas Marshall had recovered from his wounds by the time of the Crater, Bartlett had suffered a wound from which there was no recovery. He had left a leg at the Battle of Yorktown in 1862. (More recently, at the Wilderness, he had been hit by a minie ball, but quickly recovered.) His brigade was more battle hardened than Marshall's, consisting of three veteran regiments—the 21st and 29th Massachusetts and the 100th Pennsylvania—as well as three newer Massachusetts regiments, the 56th, 57th, and 59th. Nevertheless, like Marshall's men, they could not seem to coalesce into a line of battle, but walked toward the Confederate lines no more than two or three abreast.

Capable and courageous, Marshall and Bartlett led men who were, for the most part, unsuited to serve as the advance guard of a major assault. Worse, thanks to the last-minute change of plan imposed by Meade and Grant, they were entirely unprepared for the assault. Most incredibly of all, James Ledlie, drunkenly cowering in the "perfectly safe" bomb-proof, had never bothered to communicate to his brigade commanders the objective of the assault as laid down by General Burnside as well as General Meade. (Perhaps he had already been too drunk to remember to tell them, or perhaps he had been too drunk even to understand the orders Burnside had given him and the other division commanders.) It was to advance on Cemetery Hill, behind the Confederate lines, take that hill, and hold it. Unapprised of this, Marshall and Bartlett led their brigades toward the Crater rather than the high ground behind it.

It must have appeared to those who watched it a most peculiar advance. At first, it hardly resembled an attack at all. For a long while, there was no fire to oppose the assault, which was made, however, not in a great, swift, sweeping wave of blue, but in a mere trickle of men, walking rather than charging across the scarred interval between the Union and Confederate lines. The advancing men stared ahead dumbly at the devastation wrought by the mine, and, individually, they fre-

Alfred Waud sketched this "Scene of the explosion Saturday July 30th." He wrote the following description: "The advance to the 'crater' after the explosion of the mine. In the middle distance are the mounds of earth thrown up by the explosion: beyond upon the high ground cemetery hill the Confederates inner line of works, which if they had carried, would have given the Union Army Petersburg and Richmond. In the foreground troops are seen advancing to and beyond Burnsides [sic] outer intrenched line and moving upon the Confederate defences. These were—on the left Bartletts [sic] Massachusetts brigade, and on the right, the Negro troops—this sketch was made about 8 AM July 30th 1864. A point in the Rebel works known as Elliots [sic] Salient over this part was held by the 18th and 23rd S. Carolina infantry and a battery of artillery blown up in the explosion." Why the artist depicted the figure at the lower left with comically oversized shoes is anyone's guess. This feature was omitted when the drawing was published in *Harper's Weekly* on August 22, 1864. (Library of Congress)

quently stopped, stooping to aid Confederate soldiers buried in the clay. "Little did these men anticipate what they would see upon arriving at [the Crater]," Major William H. Powell wrote. It was

> an enormous hole in the ground . . . filled with dust, great blocks of clay, guns, broken carriages, projecting timbers, and men buried in various ways—some up to their necks, others to their waists, some with only their feet and legs protruding from the earth. One of these near me was pulled out, and proved to be a second lieutenant of the battery which had been blown up. The fresh air revived him, and he was soon able to walk and talk. He was very grateful and said that he was asleep when the explosion took place, and only awoke to find himself wriggling up in the air; then a few seconds afterward he felt himself descending, and soon lost consciousness. The whole scene of the explosion struck every one dumb with astonishment as we arrived at the crest of the debris.[29]

It was a vignette typical of the advance, as Benjamin Spear, 57th Massachusetts, reported: "The earth . . . had opened and great fissures or rents had been made in the center of this fort. . . . In many of the rents lay half buried the bodies of rebel soldiers still alive, which caused us for a while to help them out and give a drink of water to revive them . . ."[30]

Caused us for a while to help them out. It was as if this sight, so novel and nightmarish, compelled or even extorted repeated acts of compassion from soldiers who were supposed to be acting as what the "colored troops" had called themselves: "men er war."

But they were hardly men of war, not under the abrogated leadership of Ledlie—or even of Meade and Burnside—not in the undisciplined manner of their advance, not in their fatal failure to understand their assigned objective, and least of all in their unextinguished humanity. Each pause to gawk or to give aid slowed them more and further disordered their ranks. These men had a golden span of minutes—perhaps a half hour, and by some accounts even more—during which the Confederate side was too stunned to shoot. Had they marched like men of war toward their assigned objective, Cemetery Hill, they might well have taken it before the enemy could shake off the effects of the blast, organize resistance, and mount a counterattack. In his answer to a member of the Joint Committee on the Conduct of the War, George Meade explained what happened instead. He began by addressing the delays in beginning the assault, but made it clear that these were not the principal problem:

Question. Was there any delay in making the assault after the mine was exploded?

Answer. Yes, sir; not so much delay in making the assault as delay in taking advantage of the occupation of the crater of the mine within the enemy's line. There was some delay in making the charge. Arrangements which should have been made preparatory to that charge were not made so far as I can ascertain. There was not a sufficient debouche from our line of works. There was a high parapet in front of our lines, an abatis and other obstacles to keep the enemy from us. Those obstacles should have been removed to enable our troops to move out promptly. There was but a small opening made, by which the 9th corps, 15,000 men, moved out by the flank; whereas there should have been an opening sufficiently large to have allowed the whole corps to move out and to have gone to the crest in not more than thirty minutes.[31]

Meade went on to explain the far more serious tactical source of the failure of the assault:

The explosion of the mine was simply a preliminary operation for the purpose of making an opening in the enemy's line through which we might pour our troops and get in rear and occupy a hill behind their line which commanded all their works. But, after getting into the crater of the mine, the troops never advanced beyond. No effort was made to gain possession of the hill [Cemetery Hill] beyond until the enemy had collected such a force that our troops were repulsed.[32]

Despite this response, the questioner returned to the subject of the commencement of the assault. Meade obliged with an answer designed to ensure that blame was fixed on Burnside:

Question. Could this abatis have been cleared away prior to the springing of the mine?

Answer. Certainly; and it ought to have been done, and it was ordered to [be] done during the night previous.[33]

However, when the questioner asked "about how much delay there was, after the springing of the mine, before the charge was made," Meade returned to the more critical tactical error: the fact that Ledlie's men went after the wrong objective—

Answer. The charge never was properly made. I think that in the course of twenty or twenty-five minutes the troops advanced and occupied the crater of the mine. But the charge was to have been made from the mine [that is, the Crater]. There was no firing upon our troops until they got to the mine—nothing but marching ahead for the first half hour. During that time anybody could walk across and get to the mine. The charge was to have been made from the mine to the hill beyond. That charge never was made. But the troops kept crowding into this crater, which was a large hole some 150 feet in length by 50 feet in width and 25 feet in depth. The troops just crowded into that hole and the adjacent parts of the enemy's lines which had been abandoned for about a hundred yards on each side of the crater. That was immediately filled up by our troops. There they remained, and the more men there were there the worse it was. Their commanders could not keep order among them. The difficulty was to get the men out of this crater and to the hill beyond.[34]

This was certainly one of the most succinct and accurate descriptions of what went wrong in the assault on the Petersburg line. It was a failure both cataclysmic and elementary. Essentially leaderless, the troops headed for the wrong place. With a twist of unconscious irony, Meade added to this explanation:

> I probably ought to add that the condition of the army, from the long campaign in which it had been engaged, the number of battles it had fought, and the frequent attempts it had made to take the enemy's works, which had resulted unsuccessfully, the heat of midsummer—from all these causes the condition of the army was in some measure unfavorable for all operations of this kind. The men did not fight at that time with the vim with which they fought when we first crossed the Rapidan.[35]

The poor "condition of the army" was precisely the reason Burnside had argued for using the "colored troops," who had seen little combat, in the initial assault. In effect, therefore, Meade's added testimony was a condemnation of his own decision to remove the Fourth Division from the first wave. But the main part of what he told the committee was analytically objective and incisive: the Federal troops failed to sweep across the no-man's land between their lines and those of the enemy. Then they failed to skirt the Crater and head for Cemetery Hill. Instead, as the Confederate defenders recovered from their initial shock and as their commanders rallied more and more men to the breach, rebel fire began to bear down on the advancing bluecoats. Out of the relative safety of their trenches, exposed to the increasing volume of fire, many of the men did what Burnside had predicted they would do. They behaved like men weary of battle. Gun shy, they sought whatever shelter they could find. And there was no bigger, deeper shelter than the great Crater itself.

Although some individuals and units operated effectively—the New York artillerists, for instance, found a pair of Confederate cannon, minus their crews, and deftly turned them against the enemy at close range; other men quickly dug in or found natural cover and vigorously returned fire against the defenders—most of Ledlie's division blindly piled into the Crater as one disorganized unit collided with another. Without overall leadership, the unrehearsed, unprepared, battle-weary white troops were transformed from an army into what Captain Weld called a "confused mob," moved by only one imperative: to find cover from fire—

> Here, in the crater [Weld later wrote] was a confused mob of men continually increasing by fresh arrivals. Of course, nothing could be seen from this crater of the situation of affairs around us. Any attempt to move forward from this crater was absolutely hopeless. The men could not be got forward. It was a perfect mob. . . . To ask men to go forward in such a condition was useless. Each one felt as if he were to encounter the whole Confederate force alone and unsupported. The moral backing of an organized body of men, in which each would sustain his companions on either side, was wanting.[36]

"Everything looked propitious for a grand success," Frederick Cushman remarked just after the great blast heaved the earth, tearing open a doorway to Petersburg and victory. Now, less than an hour later, the men of the Army of the Potomac drifted swiftly, numbly, heedlessly into what those who somehow survived could justly call the horrid pit.

- 7 -

A Perfect Mob

E verything looked propitious for a grand success," Frederick Cushman of the 58th Massachusetts pronounced as Ledlie's men began their charge. And even as the dust and lighter debris from the explosion continued to drift and settle, eighteen-year-old Sergeant Edward Parsons, 9th New Hampshire Regiment, carried the Stars and Stripes up the rubble heap that had been Elliott's Salient. As he drove then augured the end of the flagstaff into the loose clods of clay, a Confederate minie ball, a pointed mass of hot, soft, expanding lead, tore into his groin. Comrades scrambled up the rubble heap, got a purchase on a shirt or belt, and pulled Parsons down the heap, then bore him to the rear, where he soon died.

The flag fluttered.

It was probably the first Union banner planted on the Confederate line, and the sight must have cheered any bluecoat who watched from a distance—much as, a year earlier, on the third day of Gettysburg, the sight of the Confederate battle flag flapping briefly atop Cemetery Ridge had cheered the fated men in gray. But, like Pickett's Charge, the advance of Ledlie's men was doomed, and the planted flag—as many as a dozen more national and regimental colors would follow it—signified nothing beyond a fleeting elevation of emotion.

The truth was that as soon as the defenders of the Petersburg line began to shoot back, the great majority of the First Division men took cover, most of them in the Crater. At first and for many minutes, the shooting was sporadic. Stephen Elliott, commanding the brigade that had manned the now-ruined salient named for him, scrambled among the survivors who were clustered just north of the Crater. Individual soldiers were taking potshots at the incoming Union troops, but Elliott knew that the key to a credible response was speedy organization, not catch-as-catch-can fire. He was therefore determined to organize not merely a defense, but a counterattack focused on the Crater, which (he saw to his astonishment) was rapidly filling with Union troops. Elliott gathered the 26th South Carolina and the surviving fragment of the 17th South Carolina, pulling them back from the main trench and deploying them within the cover provided by a ravine behind what had been Elliott's Salient.

Stephen Elliott had a single regiment and a fragment of another, both units dazed by the explosion and the chaos that followed. He could clearly see more and more Federal troops coming his way. His senior colonel, Fitz William McMaster, thought that counterattacking with so small and obviously demoralized a force was suicidal. But within Elliott there burned something of the same spirit that had driven the Spartans to stand at Thermopylae in 480 BC, three hundred against a Persian army of 120,000, perhaps more. Nor was it the first time Elliott had made such a stand. With a garrison of no more than 300 men, he had held Fort Sumter against bombardment by eight Federal monitors and an ironclad under Admiral Samuel Du Pont in April 1863, then resisted a combined naval and infantry assault in August-September. Into Colonel Alexander Smith, commanding the 26th South Carolina, Elliott managed to infuse some of his fire, and the two exhorted their men to assault the Crater.

It is unclear how many actually followed Elliott and Smith over the brow of the ravine behind which Elliott had re-formed them. The number was doubtless small, and in any case the counterattack dissolved completely when Elliott was grievously wounded in the shoulder. The agonizing wound knocked him out of the action, and McMaster, his chief down, wasted not a minute in countermanding the order to charge.

He then withdrew both the 26th and the remnant of the 17th behind a trench at the rear of the Crater and ordered the men to lie down and remain out of sight. They were to open fire only if the Union troops made an attempt to advance beyond the Crater.

Before he was shot, Elliott had essayed a bold, romantically desperate counterattack worthy of the Spartans, but it was McMaster's more prosaic defensive deployment that more closely mirrored the situation at Thermopylae. Initially, McMaster mustered just two hundred men. Before they were reinforced by the 25th North Carolina, these two hundred were all that stood between the Army of the Potomac and the city of Petersburg.

While Elliott rallied a counterattack and McMaster redeployed it into a last-ditch defense, Major James Coit, commander of the artillery battalion of which Pegram's battery—now blasted to bits—had been a part, dashed up Cemetery Hill, where he was able to direct artillery fire from Captain Samuel T. Wright's four-gun battery. At about this time, too, Major Wade Gibbs, seeing an abandoned cannon south of the Crater, cobbled together a gun crew from staff officers and eight surviving privates who had been attached to Pegram's devastated battery. The cannon bore directly on the Crater, and Gibbs directed it in highly effective fire against Ledlie's left until a Union rifleman managed to hit him in the neck. Seeing this, Colonel John T. Goode sent a company of the 34th Virginia, under Captain Samuel Preston, to ensure that the gun remained in play.

The detonation of the Petersburg mine confused and demoralized those it did not kill or wound. The psychological effect was sufficient to silence Confederate fire for at least a half hour, perhaps more. When the defenders began firing again, it was at first sporadic—but, soon, remarkably soon, effective fire was organized from muskets as well as artillery. The organization of this response outpaced the ability of the Union to advance in effective numbers. When the attackers then obliged the defenders by leaping into a hole in the ground, the battle was as good as lost, a magnificent opportunity squandered.

Generations of historians and Civil War enthusiasts have debated the relative merits of "Billy Yank" versus "Johnny Reb." There is no need for that debate here. At Petersburg, both the Union troops and the Confederates were suffering from varying degrees of exhaustion and "nostalgia"—shell shock, combat fatigue, post-traumatic stress, what you will. There is no doubt that the Crater blast traumatized the Confederate soldiers who were near enough to experience it firsthand without getting killed. But even terrorized, the defenders had something the attackers sorely lacked: effective leadership. And that made all the difference.

Wholly unprepared and uninformed or unmindful of their mission—to occupy Cemetery Hill—most of the leaderless men of Ledlie's First Division made for the Crater as if it were their objective. Within this "horrid pit," they degenerated beyond recovery into what Captain Stephen Weld had called them: a mob—and not just a mob, but "a perfect mob." Weld had chosen his words carefully; for, as a *perfect mob*, the men behaved as panic-stricken individuals rather than as an army under competent command: "Each one felt as if he were to encounter the whole Confederate force alone and unsupported. The moral backing of an organized body of men, in which each would sustain his companions on either side, was wanting."

Modern military commanders define a "force multiplier" as anything that serves to amplify the effectiveness of whatever force is at hand. At the Crater, the attackers' status as a "perfect mob" was a force multiplier—for the enemy. In the absence of opposing fire, it squandered opportunity, and when fire finally erupted, haltingly and sporadically at first, the mob mentality amplified and multiplied its effect. The mere crackle of musketry was sufficient to send most of Ledlie's men into the Crater. As the Confederate fire grew in volume and discipline, the mob mentality of the attackers continued to multiply the effect of its devastation far beyond what was being delivered against them in actual powder and lead.

"Any attempt to move forward from this crater," Weld said, "was absolutely impossible." In part, the reason was psychological: to ask a perfect mob "to go forward . . . was useless." But the physical structure of the Crater itself made it far easier to climb into the hole than out of it. On December 20, 1864, Lieutenant Colonel Charles G. Loring, Burnside's assistant inspector general, testified before the Joint Committee on the Conduct of the War that he "went into the crater of the mine" shortly after the initial assault. There he "found the brigade that first started [the Second Brigade] crowded together":

> The crater presented an obstacle of fearful magnitude. I suppose it was a hole of about 200 feet in length, by perhaps 50 or 60 feet in width, and nearly 30 feet in depth. The sides of it were composed of jagged masses of clay projecting from loose sand. The upper surface had been of sand, with a lower stratum of clay. It was an obstacle which it was perfectly impossible for any military organization to pass over intact, even if not exposed to fire. The whole brigade was broken up in confusion, and had utterly lost its organization. The officers were endeavoring to reform their men, but it was an exceedingly difficult operation.[1]

It was nearly impossible to find sufficient toeholds and handholds in the wall of the Crater to climb it. Men turned around, faced inward, and put their backs up against the sheer Crater wall. Then, digging their heels into the wall, they slowly scaled it, so that they emerged at the lip of the Crater facing the wrong way, unable to see who was firing at them. It was like charging into battle backwards. When Elisha G. Marshall, commanding the Second Brigade, sent word back to Ledlie that the situation was chaotic, with advance impossible, the general—who had left the surgeon's bomb-proof and was now in a "protected angle of the works,"[2] offered no reply other than a reminder to Marshall that General Burnside had ordered an immediate advance.

While Ledlie's men languished under intensifying fire in the Crater, Robert Potter's division followed its orders and attacked to the north (right) of Ledlie's First Division and, therefore, to the north (right) of the Crater. In the lead was the Second Brigade, commanded by Brigadier

General Simon G. Griffin, who traced his military heritage to the American Revolution. The 9th New Hampshire was in the brigade's vanguard (its Sergeant Parsons planted the flag at Elliott's Salient), and close behind was the 31st Maine along with a battalion of the 2nd Maryland. Daniel White, colonel of the 31st Maine, led his regiment as well as the Marylanders in an attempt to cover Ledlie's flank, so that the First Division might emerge from the Crater to resume its advance. By this time, however, fire from the 25th North Carolina, which had reinforced the 26th South Carolina, pressed upon White's men, sending many of them into the Crater as well. Those who managed to stay out of the hole dueled viciously with the Carolinians.

White's battle on the flank of the First Division soon became desperate. Those of his men who managed to stay out of the Crater endured a brutal artillery crossfire consisting mostly of canister shot. Canister rounds were essentially tin cans filled with small cast-iron or lead balls (or with oblong slugs of metal) set in sawdust. When fired from a light artillery piece known as a Napoleon, the canister would break apart almost immediately on exiting the muzzle, spraying the balls or slugs for up to four hundred

Waud sketched Union artillerymen firing a Napoleon, the 12-pounder wheeled cannon standard with both sides in the Civil War. It could be loaded with solid shot or with antipersonnel canister shells. (Library of Congress)

yards. Canister was strictly an antipersonnel weapon. It served much the same purpose as the machine gun would in World War I: to sweep the field, killing or disabling as many of the enemy as possible. Men who were hit by canister shot at close range were all but vaporized. Those hit at longer range typically sustained multiple, man-stopping wounds.

By this point in the battle, those who either drifted into the Crater or deliberately plunged into it, seeking refuge from the canister, found themselves the target of a different kind of projectile: the mortar round. Confederate gunners had started to man a battery of mortars, which, having been deployed in an arc behind Elliott's Salient, had been temporarily abandoned in the immediate aftermath of the blast. Now a dozen of the squat artillery pieces were lobbing their high-trajectory shells into the Crater.

As mortar rounds began to rain, Captain Stephen Weld decided he'd had enough of the Crater. He rallied as many men as he could and sent them up the Crater wall and into the Confederate works to the north (right) of the Crater. As he and his men struggled up into this area they discovered a new landscape of nightmare. Assistant Inspector General Loring described it:

> The lines of the enemy were found to be of the most intricate nature. There was one uniform front line; then in the rear there were various lines, traverses between them, and bombproofs. It was more like a honey-comb than anything that can be seen on our lines; so that it was exceedingly difficult for troops to spread themselves either way, either to the right or to the left. It had to be done, not by any movement of a mass of troops, but by hand-to-hand fighting.[3]

Having emerged into this "honey-comb," Weld "tried to re-form" his men. There was a parapet, "some feet higher than the enemy's front line, [which] led from the crater obliquely to the rear." This should have been ideal to cover Weld's advance toward Cemetery Hill, but it ran through a heavily occupied area, which was "cut up in every way by bomb-proofs, traverses, and pits." Weld pushed his regiment "down to the right, and endeavored to clean out the pits still further," but the "fire was too hot to do much, and the ground too broken. The enemy by this time was using artillery, chiefly canister."[4]

Under heavy fire, Weld's men intermingled with the men of Griffin's brigade, including some of White's troops. They all waded through the confusion of the Confederate honeycomb, often as crowded and jammed in the enemy's vacated trenches as they had been in their own when they awaited the springing of the mine. A honeycomb? It was more like fly-paper, and they were the flies.

The men of the combined forces of the 17th South Carolina Regiment and the 25th North Carolina poured fire on them, knowing that, if the Yankees broke loose, they would find themselves overwhelmed. Soon these regiments were joined by men of the 49th North Carolina, under Lieutenant Colonel John Fleming.

The North and South Carolinians understood that these Yankee flies would not stay stuck forever. Their fire, therefore, had to be swift and merciless. In the close quarters of the cut-up ground, neither side could manage a broad front of fire. The Confederates therefore did all they could to keep their front-most line armed. Men in the rear ranks loaded muskets and passed them forward. The front-line troops seized each musket, fired it, then sent it back for reloading as they took hold of a fresh weapon sent up from the rear. Ordinarily, the nine awkward steps required to load and fire a rifle musket of the era limited each man to two or three shots a minute. With others doing the loading, fire became continuous. It was a remarkably deadly close-quarters tactic. Fleming paid with his life—shot through the skull—but his men continued to fire nonstop, as if they were part of some massive killing machine.

Not that Civil War combat was ever exclusively mechanical in nature. Part of the enduring fascination of this conflict is its position on the cusp joining industrialized warfare to the most primitive and atavistic kind of killing. In the honeycomb maze of the Confederate works just behind the

Crater, men not only shot each other with nearly mechanical efficiency, but also tangled hand to hand and at the point of the bayonet. "We made barricades to oppose [the attackers]," McMasters wrote, but "they would run down in front of the line and jump over and were met with bayonet and clubbed with musket. . . . Few battles could show more bayonet wounds than this." In such close combat, the Confederates got as good as they gave, giving the lie to the myth of rebel superiority soldier on soldier. "After a severe hand to hand fight," McMasters wrote, the Confederates lost "Lieutenants Lowry, Pratt, McCorwell and Captain Dunovant, whose arm was shot off, and many brave men . . ."[5]

The combination of unrelenting fire and hand-to-hand ferocity pinned White down after he had advanced some two hundred yards, which was two hundred yards farther than the First Division. He dashed off a message to General Griffin: "General. We have taken the enemy's works and hold them. How are our lines doing on the right and left?" In other words, why isn't the First Division moving forward? "We are much in advance and are getting short of ammunition. Quite a force of rebels on our right." Griffin replied as soon as he received the message: "We hold the fort [Elliott's Salient], and are all right. Hold what you have gained. First division is now advancing. All looks well as far as we have gone."[6]

Was the oddly buoyant optimism of this reply the product of the fog of war, of hopeful thinking, or of nothing more than a desire to maintain the morale of a subordinate? We do not know. We do know, however, that Daniel White folded the reply—which had been scrawled on the back of his own message—put it in his pocket, and carried it throughout the rest of the war, which he spent as a POW after he was captured in the Confederate counterattack at the Crater.

A few units of the First Division did advance beyond the Crater. The 179th New York, the 3rd Maryland, and the 2nd Pennsylvania Provisional Heavy Artillery all made it to the periphery of the Confederate "honey-comb" just beyond the lip of the Crater. But they were held there by fierce Confederate resistance on their flanks—the very positions Burnside had been so anxious to neutralize with a swift advance that included wheeling movements to right and left made simultaneously with the main thrust straight ahead. It was a remarkable example, on the Confederate side, of tactical jiu-jitsu, the use of an opponent's own strength to defeat him. The Union had blasted a hole in the Confederate line, putting Petersburg and, with it, the entire Southern cause in mortal jeopardy. Yet because Confederate commanders at every level organized effective resistance, developing the flanks on either side of the Crater, that hole was transformed from the attackers' gateway to their tomb. The first fatal error had been to march into the Crater, but even when the portions of the divisions that followed Ledlie's attempted to surge right and left, they were driven by intense musket and artillery fire back into the Crater or the area immediately adjacent to it. It was ground on which an army became a "perfect mob," incapable of combat and ripe for slaughter.

Major William H. Powell, one of James Ledlie's disgruntled staff officers, declared it "as utterly impracticable to re-form a brigade in that crater as it would be to marshal bees into line after upsetting the hive; and equally as impracticable to re-form outside of the crater, under the severe fire in front and rear, as it would be to hold a dress parade in front of a charging enemy."[7]

As Ledlie's First Division wallowed in and around the Crater and Potter's Second Division struggled to protect the First Division's flank on the northern rim of the Crater, Orlando Willcox's Third Division advanced to the Crater's southern side. As Burnside had originally conceived the assault, a single division, Ferrero's Fourth, was to advance against the Confederate lines. As the main body of the assault skirted the Crater and made for Cemetery Hill, two units would simultaneously peel off, left and right, to suppress Confederate flanking fire. Only after this initial assault—center, left, right—had succeeded would the rest of IX Corps be thrown into the attack. Meade's last-minute change of plan, however, sent an entire division—Ledlie's First—straight ahead, followed *in sequence* by the Second Division's advance to the right (north) and the Third's advance to the left (south). The problem was that the First Division stalled in or near the Crater. Elements of Potter's Second Division continued their advance to the north and found themselves well forward of the stymied First Division—whose flank they were supposed to protect—even though "well forward" was no more than about two hundred yards ahead.

Advancing toward the southern rim of the Crater, the Third Division, did not get nearly so far. The lead unit of the division's assault was the First Brigade, commanded by John F. Hartranft, who had just earned his brigadier's star on May 12, on the strength of his gallant leadership at Spotsylvania. This promotion was the culmination of a career in the war that can best be characterized as steadfast. Born near Pottstown, Pennsylvania, he earned a college degree in civil engineering, worked for eastern Pennsylvania railroads, then entered the family business in Norristown. He rose to prominence in his hometown as deputy sheriff of Montgomery County and as a member of the local fire company. In 1860, he was admitted to the bar and also appointed colonel of the Pennsylvania Militia. With the outbreak of war, he raised a Montgomery County regiment of ninety-day volunteers in Norristown and was named colonel of the 4th Pennsylvania Volunteer Infantry. On the very eve of the First Battle of Bull Run, even as the opening shots were being fired, the regiment dissolved from under him, the members' terms of enlistment having expired. Hartranft pleaded and cajoled with his men, but they left just the same, and when they left, Hartranft insisted on remaining with the army. This act earned him a Medal of Honor (conferred on August 21, 1886) for voluntarily acting as an aide to Brigadier General William B. Franklin and brilliant participation in combat "after expiration of his term of service, distinguishing himself in rallying several regiments which had been thrown into confusion."[8] That is the kind of leader John F. Hartranft was. It was he who marched at the head of the 51st Pennsylvania Infantry in the charge across "Burnside Bridge" at Antietam, the regiment suffering 120 casualties. It was the most celebrated charge of the battle.

Hartranft's failure now to advance his brigade at the Crater resulted from a combination of physics and military orders. The physics was simple: two bodies cannot occupy the same space at the same time, and Hartranft could not get his men through or around the stalled First Division. The matter of orders was rather more complex. Whereas Potter's brigade commanders had received orders from Burnside to continue pressing forward, Hartranft adhered to the original order he had been given, which was to keep pace with the advance of the First Division, moving when it moved, pausing when it paused. Since the First had stopped, Hartranft also called a halt, even though that left his brigade strung out, entirely in the open, between the Union and Confederate lines, a field swept by fire. His halt in turn jammed up the rest of Willcox's Third Brigade units, some of which had yet to exit the covered way in the Union's works.

At the army's Court of Inquiry, the judge-advocate questioned Hartranft:

Question. Were you at the assault on the 30th of July, and what was your command?

Answer. I was there. My command was the First Brigade of the Third Division (General Willcox's) of the Ninth Corps.

Question. Did you regard the attack as a failure?

Answer. I did.

Question. What, in your opinion, were some of the causes of that failure?

Answer. The massing of the troops in the crater where they could not be used with any effect. I think that the troops, instead of being sent to the crater, should have been sent to the right and left, so as to have moved in line of battle, then they could have advanced in some kind of shape; but after they came into the crater in the confusion they were in, other troops being brought up only increased the confusion, and by that time the enfilading [flanking] fire of the enemy's artillery and infantry had become very annoying, which also made it very difficult to rally and form the troops.[9]

Even among officers of higher rank and greater fame, John Frederick Hartranft must have been a most impressive presence on the witness stand. He was a handsome man, in his mid thirties, adorned with a florid but neatly trimmed martial moustache. His courage—his steadfastness—was beyond reproach. But what happened at the Crater reduced even General Hartranft to confusion. "Do you know any reasons why the troops did not go to the right and left of the crater? Were there any physical obstacles to prevent them?" the judge advocate asked.

> Answer. No; I think troops could have been sent there. The Second Brigade of my division was sent to the left of the crater; they took a portion of the pits. If a vigorous attack had been made on the right and left of the crater I think the enemy's pits could have been taken without any difficulty and the line occupied.[10]

It was a perfectly cogent response—except that the Second Brigade was sent to the *right* of the Crater. It was Hartranft's own brigade, the First, that was sent to the left. Although no one corrected his slip, Hartranft went on to explain correctly that he was assigned to protect the *left* flank of the First Division. His further testimony also laid bare the fatal flaw in his orders:

> Question. What was the formation of your command in moving forward?
> Answer. I formed my command, which was immediately in rear of the First Division (which was the assaulting division), in one or two regiments front—I put two small regiments together—and my instructions were, *after I passed through the crater with my advance*, to form to the left of the First Division, protecting its left flank while they were advancing,

and form my line as the regiments would come up, so as to form a line of battle on the left of the First Division.[11]

Burnside intended—and believed he had so ordered—his forces to skirt the Crater, not to descend into it. It is not difficult to believe that the First Division's James Ledlie had failed to understand such an order, but Orlando Bolivar Willcox, commanding the Third Division, to which Hartranft's brigade belonged, was no dipsomaniac "political general." He was a West Point graduate (Class of 1847) and had seen service in the U.S.-Mexican War, the Indian wars in the West, and the Third Seminole War before leading a brigade in Heintzelman's Division at First Bull Run. Captured in that battle and exchanged a year later, he was awarded (in 1895)

Brigadier General Orlando Willcox (seated) with the staff of his Third Division, IX Corps. (Library of Congress)

a Medal of Honor in recognition of his "most distinguished gallantry" at Bull Run.[12]

By the time of the Overland Campaign and operations at Petersburg, Willcox was a major general of volunteers. Yet could this highly trained, highly respected, and thoroughly seasoned officer have misunderstood Burnside's orders as badly as Ledlie had? Or, in the rush to prepare for the assault, did he fail to convey them to his brigade commanders? Or did the fault, after all, lie with Ambrose Burnside? Perhaps he had failed to make his orders clear.

We cannot know. All we do know is that Hartranft understood that he was to *pass through*—not skirt—the Crater, and *then* "form to the left of the First Division" to protect its flank. Apparently, he did not question this highly questionable tactic, nor did he (or any other commander, for that matter) think through the implications of the prescribed route. Ordered to march his men into a steep-walled hole, shouldn't Hartranft have thought to equip his troops with siege ladders in order to scale the wall? Every unit that descended into the Crater found it a Herculean labor to climb out and judged that it would have been difficult, even if the ascent did not have to be made under the most withering fire. Yes, it is dumbfounding to contemplate that the lead commander in a major assault—an assault that might well have shortened the war—was a drunken, incompetent, and cowardly military non-entity. Yet here was a fine brigade commander, a gallant professional, who also failed to exercise the commonest of common sense.

Of course, no one in the Court of Inquiry so much as mentioned "common sense." Indeed, the judge advocate apparently assumed that the order to advance into the Crater had been perfectly sound:

Question. If the troops that first went into the crater had not delayed there, could they not, considering the consternation that the explosion of the mine made in the enemy's camp, have got forward to the crest of Cemetery Hill?[13]

The judge advocate did not question the wisdom of marching into the Crater in the first place, but instead addressed his query exclusively to the issue of the delay in leaving the Crater. Hartranft answered him: "I think [the First Division troops] could have moved up to that crest immediately, if they had made no halt at all, under the consternation of the enemy. . . ."[14] Like the judge advocate, Hartranft did not question the descent into the Crater, even though common sense should have dictated that climbing a mass of men into and out of a deep hole would necessarily impose a "halt," even if opposing fire had not been an issue. The only way to have avoided a halt would have been to avoid stepping into the Crater in the first place. At this battle, a great many men died because of multiple failures of leadership coupled with multiple failures of common sense.

By 5:45 on the morning of July 30, Hartranft's brigade was stalled behind the stalled First Division. By lot—the drawing of three straws from a hat—an unprepared garrison-quality division nominally led by a drunken coward had been chosen to spearhead a high-stakes assault. Of course, this was only the culmination of a plan that had been wrecked at the last minute for reasons of perceived sociopolitical propriety and public relations. Leaving the choice of assaulting force and commander to random chance was symbolic of the entire operation, in which orders were poorly formulated and inadequately communicated, and on which the lives of thousands depended—the lives not just of IX Corps men, but also of those Northerners and Southerners who would be forced to fight the battles that success at the Crater might have made unnecessary.

- 8 -

The Ground Blue with Union Dead

S o far as my recollection goes," George Gordon Meade testified to the army's Court of Inquiry, "the mine was exploded about 4.40 or 4.45. At 5.45 a.m., one hour after the explosion of the mine, the following dispatch was sent to General Burnside":

> HEADQUARTERS ARMY OF THE POTOMAC,
> *July* 30, 1864—5.40 *a.m.*
>
> Major-General BURNSIDE:
> What news from your assaulting column? Please report frequently.
>
> > **GEO. G. MEADE,**
> > *Major-General*[1]

"The following dispatch was received from him apparently as an answer to mine, although through a difference in time it is dated before it":

BATTERY MORTON,
July 30, 1864—5.40 *a.m.*

General MEADE:

We have the enemy's first line and occupy the breach. I shall endeavor to push forward to the crest [Cemetery Hill] as rapidly as possible.

A. E. BURNSIDE,
Major-General[2]

"About this time, 5.45 or 5.50—I see by reference to the dispatch that it is 5.45—an orderly came up to me and delivered me a dispatch which, upon opening, I found to be a dispatch from Colonel Loring, [assistant] inspector-general of the Ninth Corps, written at the crater and addressed to General Burnside, which dispatch the orderly, not knowing where to find General Burnside, had brought to his old headquarters, where it found me. That dispatch, so far as I recollect the purport of it, was to the effect that General Ledlie's troops occupied the crater, but in his (Colonel Loring's) opinion he feared the men could not be induced to advance beyond. That dispatch was telegraphed to General Burnside, and sent to him by an officer, so that I have no copy of it. That was the substance of it, however. It was shown to General Grant and General [A. A.] Humphreys [Meade's chief of staff], both of whom can give their recollection of it in confirmation of mine. It is an important matter to be taken into consideration here, that as early as 5.45 a.m. a dispatch was placed in my hand, stating that General Ledlie's troops could not be induced to advance. In addition to that the following dispatch was sent to him":[3]

HEADQUARTERS ARMY OF THE POTOMAC,
July 30, 1864—5.40 *a.m.*

Major-General BURNSIDE,
Commanding Ninth Corps:

The commanding general learns that your troops are halting at the works where the mine exploded. He directs that all your troops be pushed forward to the crest at once. Call on General Ord to move forward his troops at once.

A. A. HUMPHREYS,
Major-General and Chief of Staff[4]

"Fearing that there might be some difficulty on the part of General Burnside's troops, I thought it possible that by another corps [X Corps, attached to Edward O. C. Ord's XVIII Corps] going in on his right encouragement might be given to his men and a prompt assault might be made. The next dispatch I received was from an aide-de-camp, whom I had sent to General Burnside's headquarters, to advise me of what was going on. It is dated 5.50, and is from Captain Sanders":[5]

HEADQUARTERS,
Fourteen-Gun Battery, July 30, 1864—5.50 a.m.

General MEADE:

The Eighteenth Corps have just been ordered to push forward to the crest. The loss does not appear to be heavy. Some prisoners coming in.

W. W. SANDERS,
Captain and Commissary of Musters[6]

"The next dispatch that I will read is one addressed to General Burnside at 6 a.m.":

HEADQUARTERS ARMY OF THE POTOMAC,
July 30, 1864—6 a.m.

Major-General BURNSIDE:

Prisoners taken say there is no line in their rear, and that their men were falling back when ours advanced; that none of their troops have returned from the James. Our chance is now; push your men forward at all hazards (white and black), and don't lose time in making formations, but rush for the crest.

GEO. G. MEADE,
Major-General[7]

". . . The next dispatch was received from Captain Sanders at 6.10 a.m. as follows":

HEADQUARTERS,
Fourteen-Gun Battery, July 30, 1864—6.10 *a.m.*

General MEADE:

General Burnside says that he has given orders to all his division commanders to push everything in at once.

W. W. SANDERS,
Captain and Commissary of Musters[8]

Before the members of the Court of Inquiry, General Meade was anxious to demonstrate that he had aggressively attempted to push the advance against Petersburg. The series of dispatches he presented, however, reveal that the Army of the Potomac commander was out of touch with his forces and the circumstances of the assault. His heedless blanket order to push, push, push, together with his unilateral decision to add an entire new corps (actually, only the Second Division of X Corps) into the advance, failed to take into account the reality of the terrain and the rapidly growing enemy resistance. To put the situation in terms both prosaic and anachronistic, Meade responded to a hopeless traffic jam by sending in more cars. Even worse, Ambrose Burnside, although he was closer to the action and should have known better, instantly caved in to his commanding officer's pressure by simply giving "orders to all his division commanders to push everything in at once." The result was merely to increase the size and, therefore, the disorder of the "perfect mob."

"Before Petersburg at sunrise. July 30th 1864," by Alfred Waud. (Library of Congress)

John Hartranft, who had been holding in place both because the stalled First Division was in his way and also because his orders had been to await the advance of that division, received Burnside's new orders and immediately ordered in turn the resumption of his brigade's advance. He sent the 27th Michigan Regiment to penetrate the Confederate trenches then push southward, thereby clearing the way for the rest of his brigade to come up into the Confederate lines. By this time, however, troops of the 22nd and 23rd South Carolina Regiments, reinforced by the 26th and 59th Virginia had been deployed to the area adjacent to the southern perimeter of the Crater. They set up a fierce fire, which killed the 27th Michigan's colonel and pinned the unit in place. The rest of Hartranft's brigade moved up nevertheless, but because the Michigan men had been unable to push through the Confederate resistance, the brigade collided with and waded into the mass of Ledlie's forces, both inside and outside of the Crater.

While the situation south of the Crater was rapidly deteriorating, Robert Potter, whose Second Division units north of the Crater, though bogged down, were already farther advanced than any others, responded to Burnside's latest order by throwing in his only uncommitted brigade, the First, under Colonel Zenas R. Bliss.

Bliss sent his 4th Rhode Island Infantry through the covered way first, followed by the 45th Pennsylvania and a portion of the 58th Massachusetts that had been separated from the elements of this regiment that had gone out with the First Division. Had the assault proceeded as planned, the First Division would have taken all the risk in advancing across the interval of ground separating the Union and Confederate lines. Once these "shock troops" had cleared the way, subsequent units could have expected to encounter far less resistance. But, of course, the assault, barely planned to begin with, had not gone as expected, and whereas many of the men of the First Division had walked across no-man's land largely unopposed, Bliss's brigade was exposed to a murderous fire. As the 45th Pennsylvania's Captain Theodore Gregg later wrote, "severe fire from the enemy's works on the right and left. The whole space was swept with canister, grape and musketry."[9] Men did not simply fall dead or wounded, but were mutilated and mauled by a horizontal hail of antipersonnel projectiles. Arms, legs, noses, jaws, whole faces, or entire heads were torn away and carried off by high velocity clusters of canister. Most men thus wounded died, either on the field or in a field hospital, but some carried their cruel deformities for the rest of their lives.

Frederick Cushman, of the 58th Massachusetts, made it across the field and entered the Crater area, where "we were obliged to pass other troops"—Ledlie's men—"lying in utter disregard of order, behind debris and the now vacated works running from the fort so recently in the possession of the enemy." The effect of this passage was all too typical. It multiplied the prevailing disorder as "the right and left wings of the [58th Massachusetts] regiment became separated."[10]

As more of Bliss's brigade came into the vicinity of the Crater, they were able to inflict significant casualties on the defenders. But the combination of broken ground, debris, the Crater itself, the crowded disorder of the Federal troops, and fierce Confederate resistance prevented the effective use of massed firepower. The experience of the 51st New York and the 2nd New York was typical. They pressed ahead, taking their toll on the defenders, only to bog down under intense musket and artillery fire. Once their advance was slowed or stopped, the bluecoats ceased to be soldiers and became so many targets. When the colonel of the 51st fell, the regiment's major took command. He was George Washington Whitman, brother of the poet Walt and of another Civil War officer, Andrew Jackson Whitman. Whitman's tenure was brief, however, as he was soon wounded.

Mired as they were, elements of both Griffin's and Bliss's commands nevertheless continued to claw their way forward by dint of main strength. Suddenly, they burst through the line of Confederate defenders and found themselves on open ground, not far from Cemetery Hill.

The openness here soon proved illusory—and deadly. Although they had gotten beyond the riflemen, they were now in a field swept by the crossfire of no fewer than three artillery batteries, two positioned to the northwest and a third due west. From this battery came an especially intense barrage of canister. The desperate Federals decided to make for a barnlike house the Confederates knew as the residence of a farmer named Gee. It stood just west of the Jerusalem Plank Road and was actually beyond Cemetery Hill. If the men of Griffin and Bliss could reach the Gee House before they were whittled away to nothing, they would be behind the Confederate artillery and relatively safe. They would also be in a position to attack Cemetery Hill from behind, if they chose to do so, or to serve as the anchor for the formation of a Union line, which could then advance to Petersburg.

What Griffin's and Bliss's men did not know is that the Gee House was an objective of even greater value. It served as Confederate headquarters for this part of the Petersburg line. To take it would, at the very least, greatly disrupt the defense. It might even result in the capture of high-ranking Confederate officers. The gunners of Henry Flanner's battery, facing the Federal advance from the west, and those of Samuel T. Wright to the north were not about to allow Gee House to fall.

"We were ordered to charge upon a battery which was in position a quarter of a mile in rear of the fort we had mined," Cushman later wrote. The open field across which the men would have to charge was "Fully in range of the enemy's fire, both musketry and artillery." Cushman remarked that the "task assigned us to perform was replete with difficulty and danger. It even savored of impossibility; yet the order to charge was obeyed promptly and without a murmur."

But even at this critical juncture orders were garbled or misinterpreted. Some of the 58th sheared off to the right, "in the direction of another battery. . . . There was evidently a misunderstanding as to which battery it was intended to capture." The result was "hesitation and confusion." The "line of battle wavered and finally broke, the men filing off into the fort [that is, the Crater], and into the saps and trenches that led from it." Once again, the "order came to charge upon the battery across the field." The charge was made, "but fruitlessly, the men returning to the fort and filling every portion of it to overflowing."[11]

Elements of the 45th Pennsylvania Regiment, perhaps ninety men under Captain Theodore Gregg, also charged Flanner's battery and the Gee House nearby. They were swatted down by flanking fire, artillery as well as muskets. They, too, fell back upon the remnant of the Confederate works adjacent to the Crater, but instead of securing shelter there they were surprised to find themselves face to face with the enemy.

Quite literally face to face.

A Confederate major leveled his revolver at the chest of a Federal captain named Richardson, whereupon Gregg snatched the major's gun from out of his hand and sent him, along with a pair of Confederate privates, to the rear as prisoners. Saved from a bullet in the chest, Richardson was given the unenviable task of holding his position in the Confederate works with a small detachment while Gregg and most of the other surviving members of the 45th Pennsylvania continued their withdrawal toward the Crater. Richardson and his tiny command were a miniature Alamo, no more than fifty feet from a large contingent of Confederates and entirely cut off from the rest of IX Corps, the Army of the Potomac, and, for that matter, the United States of America.

Finally—also in obedience to Burnside's order for an unconditional advance—Orlando Willcox, commanding officer of Third Division, sent his last brigade, the 2nd, toward the Confederate line. The brigade was already out of the Union's works when its colonel, William Humphrey, formed up its seven regiments, which included Company K of the 1st Michigan Sharpshooters, made up exclusively of Chippewa Indians. Willcox assigned Humphrey the immediate objective of silencing the single surviving gun of what had been "Davidson's battery," on the Confederate right (the position south of the Crater). It was, in fact, a reasonable assignment—one of the few feasible missions of the entire assault, because Humphrey, on the Union's far left, which was not jammed with soldiers, had the freedom of maneuver denied to the units that had directly assaulted the Crater itself. Humphrey hoped to move quickly enough to flank the Confederates—Henry Wise's Virginia brigade under the command of Colonel John T. Goode—but they, along with adjacent South Carolina regiments, pivoted deftly to meet the advance both straight-on and also at a raking angle. The result was a deadly crossfire that sent the 46th New York running, along with the 50th Pennsylvania, the 24th New York, and the 60th Ohio—all of Humphrey's left. Despite the collapse of this flank, the rightmost regiments, all from Michigan—the 1st Michigan Sharpshooters, and the 2nd and 20th Michigan—stormed the Confederate works, not only taking them, but sending a bag of prisoners to the rear, before turning a pair of captured guns back upon the enemy line. It was the one ray of hope in an otherwise uniformly bleak assault.

O. P. Chubb, surgeon with the 20th Michigan, testified to the Court of Inquiry that "General Ledlie, of the First Division, and Ferrero, of the Fourth, came up to the front of the bomb-proof, and shortly afterward came in and took seats."[12] That is where they spent most of the assault.

At 6:00 a.m., Meade sent Burnside a nearly frantic message: "Our chance is now; push your men forward at all hazards (white and black), and don't lose time in making formations, but rush for the crest." *White and black.* Burnside sent an order to Edward Ferrero to send in—at long last—his Fourth Division, the "colored troops" who had been groomed for the initial assault.

Surgeon H. E. Smith, 27th Michigan Volunteers, was in the same bomb-proof as Chubb. "I was there when the colored troops were ordered to advance," Smith told the judge advocate presiding over the Court of Inquiry, "and heard General Burnside's aide give repeated orders to General Ferrero to take his troops up and charge toward Petersburg. I think he gave the order three times. The third order General Burnside sent to General Ferrero was an imperative order to advance. To the previous orders General Ferrero would make the answer that the other troops were in his way and he could not possibly advance while they were there, and if they would be taken out of the way he would go ahead."[13]

Question. General Ferrero was present?

Answer. Yes, sir.

Question. Any other generals?

Answer. General Ledlie was present. Those were the only generals I saw.

Question. Did General Ledlie make any reply that you heard when this order was given to General Ferrero?

Answer. I did not hear him make any reply or any statement on the subject of that order from General Burnside.

Question. What troops did you understand General Ferrero to allude to as being in the way?

Answer. I did not understand. I supposed they were those troops that had made the charge. The general was in front of a bomb-proof, which had been used as a regimental headquarters, and was situated about ten or twelve yards, as near as I could judge, in rear of the work. This bomb-proof was fronting to the rear.

Question. Did General Ferrero leave that place and accompany his troops to the front when they left?

Answer. He did. General Ledlie, I think, left the bomb-proof for a very short time. That was about the time of the stampede of the darkeys. Then, I think, both General Ledlie and General Ferrero returned about that time. I am not positive, however, for I was busy seeing that the wounded were being attended to. General Ledlie asked me for stimulants.[14]

Such testimony makes it easy and obvious to lump Edward Ferrero with James Ledlie and conclude that they were made of the same sorry stuff. Both cowered in a bombproof and—together—consumed the "stimulants" (that is, rum) proffered by the regimental surgeon. By his conduct and by all accounts, Ledlie was an incompetent, a scoundrel, a drunk, and a coward. Although it is tempting to dismiss Ferrero—the dancing

These surgeons of Fourth Division, IX Corps, posed at Broadway Landing, Virginia, in July 1864. (Library of Congress)

master—similarly, his combat record did not warrant so doing. As mentioned in Chapter 4, he had shown himself to be a solid if not exceptional commander under fire.

Did Edward Ferrero simply lose his nerve at Petersburg?

Perhaps. To Burnside's repeated orders that he advance his Fourth Division, Ferrero replied that "the other troops were in his way and he could not possibly advance while they were there, and if they would be taken out of the way he would go ahead." The few historians who have commented on this judge the reply an evasive excuse or a "cryptic comment."[15] They point to the desperate situation at the Crater and the fact that the "colored troops" of the Fourth Division had been waiting, eager, and ready since the detonation to move forward.

Shortly after 5:30, Colonel Henry G. Thomas, Second Brigade, Fourth Division, heard a "quiet voice" behind him as, with his brigade, he awaited orders. "Who commands this brigade?" the voice asked.

> "I do," I replied. Rising, and turning toward the voice, I saw General Grant. He was in his usual dress: a broad-brimmed felt had and the ordinary coat of a private. He wore no sword. Colonel Horace Porter, his aide-de-camp, and a single orderly accompanied him. "Well," said the general, slowly and thoughtfully, as if communing with himself rather than addressing a subordinate, "why are you not in?" Pointing to the First Brigade just in my front, I replied, "My orders are to follow that brigade." Feeling that golden opportunities might be slipping away from us, I added, "Will you give me the order to go in now?"[16]

Ulysses S. Grant was doing something George Gordon Meade disdained to do. He was making a personal reconnaissance of the situation. Nevertheless, he was apparently unwilling to break the chain of command. "After a moment's hesitation," Grant answered Thomas "in the same slow and ruminating manner, 'No, you may keep the orders you have.' Then, turning his horse's head, he rode away at a walk."[17]

Although Ferrero responded with an "excuse" to Burnside's repeated order to advance, he did move his division closer to the front at 5:45. Fifteen minutes later, however, the division halted in the covered way. Here the men of the division became unwilling spectators to a procession of the wounded. Some, Colonel Thomas remarked, were lighthearted, clearly relieved to have been put out of the action: "I'm all right, boys! This is good for thirty days' sick-leave."

> Others were plucky and silent, their pinched faces telling the effort they were making to suppress their groans; others, with the ashy hue of death already gathering on their faces, were largely past pain. Many, out of their senses through agony, were moaning or bellowing like wild beasts.[18]

Thomas and his men "stood there for over an hour with this endless procession. . . . There could be no greater strain on the nerves. Every moment changed the condition from that of a forlorn hope to one of forlorn hopelessness. Unable to strike a blow, we were sickened with the contemplation of revolting forms of death and mutilation."[19] Awaiting the word to charge, the Fourth Division's "men er war" were being thoroughly, almost systematically, demoralized.

But were they really being forced to wait because Ferrero busied himself drinking with Ledlie in a bombproof?

William W. Loring, Burnside's assistant inspector general, had spent just ten minutes in the Crater, but it was long enough for him to judge that the situation was one of hopeless confusion. He did not, of course, personally venture beyond the Crater, into what he called the "honey-comb" of the Confederate trenches and traverses. "All that I know of what took place beyond those lines I know from hearsay only," he admitted to the Joint Committee on the Conduct of the War, "as the lines were so high as to cut off the view." But, concluding that the situation there was even more desperate than in the Crater itself and that the Union advance was stalled at and around the Crater, as well as just beyond it, Loring returned to the Union's front lines.

Nothing especial occurred, so far as I saw, until about half past seven o'clock, when the colored division was ordered in. At that time I was standing in our front line. General Ferrero, who commanded the colored division, was standing near me when the order [apparently Burnside's third] was brought to him, by one of General Burnside's staff, to lead his division also into the crater, and to push for the top of the hill. The order struck me as being so unfortunate that I took the liberty to countermand it on the spot.[20]

Now that Ferrero was out of the bombproof and apparently at last prepared to commit his division, it was Loring, Burnside's own aide, who stopped him. "General Ferrero hesitated," Loring testified, "as he said here was a positive order from General Burnside." To this, Loring responded by telling "him that I was the senior staff-officer present, and that, in General Burnside's name, I would countermand the order until I could go up and inform General Burnside of the state of affairs."[21] What was the state of affairs?

I went up and represented to General Burnside that this colored division *could not be expected to pass the lines of the old troops*; that it was impossible to expect green troops to succeed where old troops had failed before them; and furthermore that, *instead of accomplishing any good result, they would only throw into confusion the white troops that were already in that line and holding it.*[22]

Loring countermanded Burnside's orders for the very reason that Ferrero had repeatedly given for not ordering his men to advance. Loring reported that the Fourth Division "could not be expected to pass the lines of the old troops" and an attempt to do so would only create more "confusion." Ferrero had put it more simply: "the other troops were in his way."

But by this time Ambrose Burnside was clearly not interested in the reality of the battlefield. Loring testified: "General Burnside did not reply to me, as he usually does to his staff officers, by stating his reasons for disagreeing with them, but simply repeated his previous order." The motivation for this uncharacteristic behavior was made clear to Loring "that evening, after the affair was all over" when "General Burnside showed me a written order from General Meade, directing him to throw in all his troops and push for the top of Cemetery hill; and he added that under those instructions he felt that he could not have done otherwise than he did."[23] It was yet another disastrous abrogation of command responsibility. Instead of holding back the Fourth Division, acknowledging that throwing more troops into the swirling chaos of the failing assault would only intensify the disorder, Burnside blindly obeyed the orders of a commander who had not even bothered to inspect the battlefield for himself.

Loring trudged back to Ferrero to tell him that the advance had to be made after all. Surgeon H. E. Smith testified that Ferrero left the area of the bomb-proof "about the time of the stampede of the darkeys." Although, in his testimony to the Joint Committee, Colonel Loring stated that "The colored division went in very gallantly indeed,"[24] all that most of the white officers back at the Union lines noted was the rout—a "stampede"—that followed it.

"You say that during the stampede Generals Ferrero and Ledlie returned to the bomb-proof," the judge-advocate asked Surgeon Smith. "How long did they remain there?"

> Answer. General Ferrero remained a very short time. He was exhausted. I think he came in for the purpose of getting some stimulants, too, and I think he went out immediately after I gave him the stimulants. . . .[25]

Modern commentators have pointed to this as further evidence of Ferrero's command malfeasance. Reluctantly and after much delay, he finally sent his troops into battle, remaining behind, then turning to drink as they stampeded in disordered retreat.

There is no question that Edward Ferrero, like every other IX Corps division commander, chose not to lead his troops into battle at the Crater, but whereas James Ledlie drank on this occasion because he was both a habitual drunk and a physical coward, Edward Ferrero drank quite possibly to dull the pain of witnessing the consequences of having followed an order to send his soldiers to a purposeless doom. He appeared before the army's Court of Inquiry on August 31, 1864:

Question. Were you at the assault on the 30th of July, and what was your command?

Answer. I was commanding the Fourth Division of the Ninth Army Corps (colored troops).

Question. What was their formation for the attack?

Answer. There was no formation further than moving down in rear of the Third Division, as directed in the orders, by the flank, in the covered way.

Question. Was this the most judicious?

Answer. It was the only formation that could be adopted under the circumstances.

Question. Please to state the circumstances?

Answer. There being no position to mass the troops.

Question. Why was there no position?

Answer. On account of there being three other divisions in advance of mine, which would occupy all the available ground where my troops could have been formed.[26]

When the judge advocate asked Ferrero to further characterize the advance of his division, he replied:

I would state that the troops went in in the most gallant manner; that they went in without hesitation, moved right straight forward, passed through the crater that was filled with troops, and all but one regiment of my division passed beyond the crater. The leading brigade engaged the enemy at a short distance in rear of the crater, where they captured some 200-odd prisoners and a stand of colors, and recaptured a stand of colors belonging to a white regiment of our corps. Here, after they had taken those prisoners, the troops became somewhat disorganized, and it was some little time before they could get them organized again to make a second attempt to charge the crest of the hill. About half an hour after that they made the attempt and were repulsed by a very severe and galling fire, and, I must say, they retreated in great disorder and confusion back to our first line of troops, where they were rallied, and there they remained during the rest of the day and behaved very well. . . .

Question. If your division had been the leading one in the assault would they have succeeded in taking Cemetery Hill?

Answer. I have not the slightest doubt from the manner in which they went in, under very heavy fire, that had they gone in in the first instance, when the fire was comparatively light, but that they would have carried the crest of Cemetery Hill beyond a doubt.[27]

Ferrero was understandably more circumspect—not to say slippery— where his own role in the advance was concerned:

Question. Did you go forward with your division?

Answer. I went to our first line of works and there remained to see my command go through. I would state that I deemed it more necessary that I should see that they all went in than that I should go in myself, as there was no hesitation in their going forward whatever. I was at no time at a farther distance than eighty or ninety yards from my division.

Question. Where were you after they had all passed the crater, and were, as you say, at one time half an hour in reorganizing?

Answer. I was immediately in front of the crater on our front line of works. I would also state that one regiment was checked between the crater and our front line unable to get through, and I was at that time making every effort to get that regiment through with the intention of passing through myself as soon as they got past, but it was impossible for me to do so from the crowded state of the troops that were there.[28]

It is doubtful that many members of the Court swallowed whole Ferrero's self-justification, but no one—in the courtroom or in the field—could in good conscience doubt at least the initial gallantry of his "colored troops." The First Brigade, under Joshua K. Sigfried, went first, with Thomas's Second close behind. Immediately upon emerging from the covered way, these brigades came under intense fire. As Lieutenant James H. Clark of the 115th New York (part of X Corps) narrated—

We watch them eagerly; it is their first fight and we wonder if they will stand the shock. Noble fellows! Grandly they cross the field; they are under a withering fire, but still rush on regardless of fallen comrades, and the storm of pitiless lead and relentless grape that pours upon them [from] three sides, and gain the works with a ringing cheer."[29]

The flanking fire was such that the men of Sigfried's brigade suffered the same fate as those of the first three divisions. Many of the troops were unable to get around the Crater and were instead forced into it. The result was precisely what Loring—and Ferrero himself—had predicted: an exacerbation of the prevailing chaos. The influx of fresh troops destroyed whatever vestige of order may have clung to the First Division's formations, even as the collision with First Division broke up what little order existed in the Fourth Division's charge.

As Sigfried saw it, there was nothing to do but try to bull his way through. At least three of his four regiments soon emerged from the Crater and into the warren of Confederate works. The 30th, 43rd, and 27th U.S. Colored Troops turned sharply north (right) and reinforced Griffin's Second Brigade, Second Division against the Confederate units under Fitz William McMaster. In the process, these two regiments sent some one hundred Confederate prisoners to the rear. The 115th New York's Lieutenant Clark marveled at how the colored troops "sweep everything before them."[30]

Henry Thomas had been ordered to lead his Second Brigade in support of Sigfried on Sigfried's left. That, however, would have pushed the Second Brigade into the already jammed Crater along with Sigfried and the bulk of the First Division. To avoid this, Thomas decided to veer farther north. But even this maneuver gained him little or no freedom of movement. The Second Brigade ended up wallowing in what had been the Confederate trenches, where, as Frederick Cushman wrote, an "indescribable scene of confusion immediately followed" as "Colors which had been planted by our troops, sanguine of success, on the parapet in the early part of the day, were thrown down and trampled under foot in the mud. White men and negroes lay indiscriminately together, piled up three and four deep." Any attempt to rise and extricate oneself from the roiling mass in these trenches and rifle pits invited instant death from what Colonel Thomas described as "a deadly enfilade from eight guns on our right and a murderous cross-fire of musketry." Thomas saw officer after officer fall dead—"Major Rockwood of the 10th . . . mounted the crest [of a trench] and fell back dead, with a cheer on his lips"—and with the white officers, "hundreds of heroes 'carved in ebony' fell" as well.[31]

It was, as Thomas described it, both a grotesque charnel house and a poetic ecstasy of violent death. "Two of my four orderlies were wounded: one, flag in hand; the remaining two sought shelter when Lieutenant Pennell, rescuing the guidon, hastened down the line outside the pits." Thomas's narration conjures a vignette of mythic intensity:

With his sword uplifted in his right hand and the banner in his left, he sought to call out the men along the whole line of the parapet. In a moment, a musketry fire was focused upon him, whirling him round and round several times before he fell. Of commanding figure, his bravery was so conspicuous that, according to Colonel Weld's testimony, a number of his [Weld's] men were shot because spellbound, they forgot their own shelter in watching this superb boy, who was an only child of an old Massachusetts clergyman; and to me as Jonathan was to David.[32]

For all its terrible beauty, Thomas's appreciation of Pennell's moment of supreme heroism did not prevent his seeing the bigger picture: "The men of the 31st making the charge were being mowed down like grass, with no hope of any one reaching the crest [of Cemetery Hill], so I ordered them to scatter and run back." So intense was the fire "that Captain Dempcy and myself were the only officers [of the Second Brigade] who returned, unharmed" from the charge.[33]

Where the 31st U.S. Colored Troops had failed, the 28th, also of the Second Brigade, hoped to succeed. They found passage toward Cemetery Hill via an abandoned Confederate covered way and punched through—until they hit a wall consisting of some two hundred (some reports double this number) firmly entrenched Confederates. Unable to emerge from the covered way into a line of battle—and therefore unable to bring effective fire to bear against the Confederates—the men of the 28th recoiled then fell back entirely.

The Crater was a rare occurrence in military history: a battlefield so overcrowded that the chances for the attackers' victory were, for all intents and purposes, *inversely* proportional to the strength of forces fielded. The more men the Union commanders jammed into the blasted Confederate lines, the less effective each individual soldier could be. Those in and around the Crater were rapidly coming to understand this bizarre situation. Those in command, however, were far from the Crater, saw none of the battle for themselves, and apparently discounted the reports of those who were actually there. A heedless Meade ordered Burnside to send in everything he had, which, thanks to General Meade, now included Edward Ord's XVIII Corps—or, more precisely, Second Division, X Corps, which was attached to it.

The division was commanded by Brigadier General John W. Turner, who had until recently served exclusively as a staff officer, but who took to field command with gusto. Of all the division commanders on that July morning—Ledlie, Potter, Willcox, Ferrero—only Turner actually visited the Crater. It was not that he sought glory, but that, of all the division commanders, he was the only one who seemed to grasp the consequences of failing to understand just what was going on in this cauldron. Before committing his men to the crowded confusion, he wanted to see for himself just where he could best send them in.

He saw—for himself—that "the crater was full of men; they were lying all around, and every point that would give cover to a man was occupied." Returning to the Union lines, he reported to his commanding officer, General Ord, that "unless a movement is made out of the crater towards Cemetery hill, it is murder to send more men there." He observed that the "colored division should never have been sent in there"; but no subordinate relishes telling his commander that what he has been ordered to do is impossible. After essentially declaring precisely this, Turner paused, then allowed that the zealous blacks had created "a furor," so that they might be able to "move off sufficiently for me to pass my division out." In contrast to both Meade and Burnside, Ord responded quite reasonably, instructing Turner that he should make an advance *if* the troops ahead of him managed to advance.

John Turner kept his eyes glued to the Crater. Suddenly, he perceived movement, and it seemed to him that men in blue were indeed and at last moving toward Cemetery Hill. Perhaps the situation was not hopeless after all.

Taking up a position at the head of his division, which he had decided to lead to the northern lip of the Crater, Turner drew his sword and called out: "Come on my brave boys!"[34]

Thus it began, a glorious storybook charge. The Third Brigade, commanded by Colonel Louis Bell, led off, with the Second (William B. Coan) and First (N. Martin Curtis) behind. All aimed themselves north of the Crater, the lead-off brigade in the center of the advance, the Second to the right (north) of the Third, and the First to the left (south) of the Third. Lieutenant James H. Clark's 115th New York was part of Bell's brigade. Clark recalled vividly how the regimental color bearer unfurled the flag, pointed to the Confederate works, and stepped forward amid shouts of "Forward, hundred and fifteenth!" Clark remembered how each man "dreamed that he would stem the tide of battle, and that some other poor fellow would fall." And he remembered even more vividly the reality: how "We left the ground covered with killed and wounded."[35]

Yet they push onward: "The colored troops hold the two first lines, and we hold the third." That put the "rebels . . . on the same line with us, on our right and left." On both flanks, they engage us . . . with infantry, at the same time sweeping our lines with a cross of grape."[36]

But still they persevere, advancing to "the mined fort," where, "amid gun carriages and timbers, lay the naked corpses of the South Carolinians blown up by powder." They gaze at this, then look round the Crater and behold "a large body of Union soldiers, lying as though in line of battle waiting for the command to move forward." Clark supposes "they are some regiment or brigade." And he pushes farther forward still with his ever-dwindling brigade until, reaching "the spot [where the soldiers lie in line of battle], what is our horror to find that they are all Union dead! There they lay both white and black, not singly or scattering, but in long rows; in whole companies." Clark is unable to avert his eyes: "The ground is blue with Union dead."[37]

- 9 -

Counterattack

H ow did your particular command retire from the front?" the army's judge-advocate asked Colonel Henry G. Thomas.

Answer. In confusion.

Question. Driven?

Answer. Driven back by a charge of the enemy.

Question. And not by any orders?

Answer. No, sir; they received no orders. They were ordered to stop by myself and all my staff officers who were in the pits. When I got into this position on the right of the crater the fire was very severe; there was also a very severe enfilading fire from the right. I attempted one charge without success the moment I reached there. I could not get more than fifty men out. I sent word to General Burnside by Major Van Buren, of his staff—as he was the only staff officer I saw in the pits except my own—that unless a movement was made to the right to stop the enfilading fire not a man could live to reach the crest; but that I should try another charge in ten minutes, and hoped I would be supported.[1]

The survivors of Thomas's first charge fell back just in time to receive a new order from Edward Ferrero "in pretty near these words, 'Colonels Sigfried and Thomas, commanding First and Second Brigades: If you have not already done so, you will immediately proceed to take the crest in your front.'"[2]

Question. Where was the division commander [Ferrero] all this time?

Answer. I do not know. When I went up with my brigade he was in the bomb-proof on the left, with the commanding officer of the First Division. Generals Willcox, Ledlie, and Ferrero were in the bomb-proof on the left.

Question. Was the bomb-proof a good place to see what was going on?

Answer. No, sir. . . .[3]

The only evidence Ferrero had of what was going on at the Crater were the hundred or more prisoners Sigfried's brigade had sent back, together with a Confederate battle flag. From this, he must have assumed that that there was at least the beginning of a breakthrough, and so he sent— blindly—the new order to Thomas. Although already beaten back with severe casualties, Thomas gamely tried to obey the order. He began by attempting to re-form as much of his brigade as possible, sending officers and non-coms to unknot the disorganized soldiers of the 23rd, 28th, and 29th U.S. Colored Troops from the equally disorganized body of white troops in and around the Crater. "Colonel Sigfried had, I think, already received [Ferrero's new order] as he was in the crater," Thomas told the judge-advocate. "I sent word to Colonel Sigfried's brigade, on my right, where I supposed the colonel to be, that I was about to charge, that we should go over with a yell, and that I hoped to be supported."[4]

Thomas knew he had surely seen hell. But he did not then know it was about to get a whole lot uglier. While Thomas was being driven back the first time, two of Sigfried's regiments, the 30th and 43rd U.S. Colored Troops, had (as noted in Chapter 8) succeeded in overrunning the Confederate entrenchments just to the north of the Crater. They had charged the trench with a cry that both terrified and enraged the Carolinians defending this portion of the Petersburg line.

It was "Remember Fort Pillow!"[5]

No one on either side could have mistaken the import of these three words.[6] Fort Pillow stood on a high bluff above the Mississippi River, at Henning, Tennessee, about forty miles north of Memphis. Built by Confederate brigadier general Gideon Johnson Pillow early in 1862, it was occupied by Union forces on June 6, 1862, and used to defend the river approach to Memphis. When some fifteen hundred Confederate troops arrived to retake Fort Pillow on April 12, 1864, the fort was garrisoned by 262 black soldiers and 295 whites. Nathan Bedford Forrest assumed personal command of the Confederate assault and sent a surrender ultimatum to Major William F. Bradford, who had assumed command of the Fort Pillow garrison after Major Lionel F. Booth, its original commanding officer, had fallen to a sniper's bullet. Bradford asked for an hour to decide. Forrest granted the hour, but, observing what he took to be truce violations, he suddenly demanded an answer before the time was up. To this, Bradford responded "I will not surrender," whereupon the Confederates quickly overran the fort.

Union losses were approximately 231 killed and 100 wounded; 168 whites and 58 blacks were taken prisoner. (Forrest lost 14 killed and 86 wounded.) Partisans of Forrest maintained that the Union casualties were incurred while the garrison fought its way back to the river bank before finally surrendering, but Union sources claimed that surrender came as soon as the fort was overrun, and that Forrest's men—shouting "No quarter! No quarter! Kill the damned niggers; shoot them down!"—murdered much of the garrison. Indeed, the Committee on the Conduct of the War, in House Report 65, 38th Congress, 1864, catalogued a litany of atrocities at Fort Pillow, ranging from cold-blooded murder, to setting ablaze the tents that sheltered the Federal wounded, to burying some black prisoners alive.

Historians have long disputed both Southern and Northern versions of what happened at Fort Pillow, but Confederate refusal to accept the surrender of black troops, the murder of black wounded on the battlefield, and the execution of those taken prisoner—and their white officers—was widespread both in the eastern and western theaters in the last two years of the war, as was retaliatory killing by blacks. In any case, on July 30 at the Crater, no one in blue doubted that the rebels had been guilty of a massacre. As "Remember Fort Pillow!" attested, the men of 30th and 43rd thirsted for revenge. In response to the battle cry, at least one Confederate captain was heard to holler, "Kill 'em! Shoot 'em! Kill the damned niggers!"[7]

That particular captain was silenced by the thrust of a bayonet, but the presence of the black troops took the combat to a place remote from military motives, necessity, or any vestige of rationality. Officially, on May 1, 1863, the Confederate Congress had authorized President Jefferson Davis to "put to death or . . . otherwise [punish]" any black soldiers taken as prisoners of war. Soon, the authorization was extended to the white officers who led them. But the defenders of Petersburg needed no presidential authority to tell them they should be merciless with the black men in blue. Racism was a motive for murder, true enough, but the Petersburg Confederates also believed—and it was a belief actively nurtured by their commanders—that the fury of the black soldiers knew no bounds. "Ah, boys," one Confederate officer rallied some nervous Virginia troops, "you have hot work ahead; they are negroes and show no quarter."[8]

The phrase *no quarter* was repeated frequently in and around the Crater. In strictly military terms, it meant that defeated troops would be killed rather than allowed to surrender, and that was bad enough; but the defenders of Petersburg also believed that "no quarter" would be the fate of the citizens—male and especially female—of Petersburg, should that city fall to black soldiers.

Colonel Henry Thomas did not receive the support he hoped for. Nor did he wait for it to materialize. After re-forming his regiments as best he could, he ordered their renewed advance. Lieutenant Colonel John Bross, 29th U.S. Colored Troops, seized his regiment's colors, mounted the lip of the Crater, and rallied his men toward Sigfried's 30th and 43rd U.S. Colored Troops, who, still exulting in their conquest of the Confederate entrenchment, nevertheless were pinned down, enduring a hail of canister. Although Thomas's men were on the move, the white troops of Simon Griffin's and Zenas Bliss's brigades were all but paralyzed. They had been exposed to withering fire for so long that most of their officers were dead. To make this situation even worse, just as some of these shattered, leaderless units were struggling to re-form, Sigfried's 30th and 43rd had come storming through, bringing renewed chaos. But seeing Thomas's men starting to advance toward those of Sigfried, elements of the white regiments began to move ahead as well.

Among those who watched these fitful advances was Brigadier General William Mahone. He had assumed command of Richard H. Anderson's Division of the Confederate III Corps after Anderson himself was promoted to replace James Longstreet, wounded at the Wilderness. Mahone and his division of about three thousand men had been posted at Lieutenant Creek, two miles south of the Crater when the explosion took place. As soon as he had been informed of the springing of a mine and the Union advance that followed it, Robert E. Lee had sent one of his staff officers, Charles Venable, straight to Mahone. Lee admired that brigadier, a graduate of Virginia Military Institute who had demonstrated conspicuous gallantry at Second Bull Run and Chancellorsville. Short yet gaunt—his uniforms seemed to hang off of him—Mahone was dubbed "Little Billy" by his men. It was a term of affection rather than a slur on his command presence. For Mahone had a way with troops, and Lee was aware that, in his hands, Anderson's Division had become a crack outfit, the perfect unit to repel what Lee assumed would be an all-out Union offensive.

Venable told Mahone that Lee wanted him to send two of his brigades to support Major General Bushrod Johnson, who was in command of the

Two views of William Mahone. (Library of Congress)

South Carolina troops at the Petersburg line. For reasons he did not explain—perhaps he did not fully trust Johnson, perhaps he simply could not bring himself to relinquish to another command the troops he loved well—Mahone replied to Venable, "I can't send my brigades to General Johnson. I will go with them myself."[9] After he spoke these words, he ordered his men to strip down to combat trim, discarding heavy knapsacks and, in fact, to throw down everything except rifles, cartridge boxes, and canteens. He listened carefully to Venable's situation report, then instructed the commanders of his Georgia and Virginia regiments to march the men to the front cross-country rather than by road. This, he explained, would screen their advance from the Union's signal towers. With that, Mahone rode off to reconnoiter the developing battle.

Enroute to a point from which he could observe, Mahone called at Bushrod Johnson's headquarters. There he met briefly with General P. G. T. Beauregard and Johnson. Beauregard suggested to Johnson that he give Mahone his "outlying troops" to assist in the counterattack. In contrast to Mahone, Johnson had no qualms about relinquishing a portion of his command. Not only did he agree, but he showed far more interest in finishing his interrupted breakfast than in participating personally in the defense of Petersburg. When Mahone asked that he lead him to a good spot for reconnoitering, Johnson called to one of his staff lieutenants and resumed eating. Mahone must have silently congratulated himself on having declined to give Johnson the loan of his men.

The nominated lieutenant pointed out to Mahone a slope from which, he said, "you can see the Yankees." He did not, however, offer to lead the general up the slope himself, and Mahone did not press him to do so. Instead, he mounted the rise alone and, reaching the summit, must have stared openmouthed at the spectacle of thousands of blue-coated troops moving in and around the Crater as well as passing through the trenches and traverses just beyond it. In one particular spot, he counted no fewer than eleven flags of Union regiments.

Mahone instantly realized that two brigades—about fifteen hundred men—were no match for the Union swarm he was gazing on. After sprinting down the slope, he sent for a third brigade. Combined with the two brigades he had already pulled from the Confederate right, this had the effect of drastically weakening the Confederate position south of the Crater.

Mahone went about organizing the counterattack, and as his units moved north, they passed the fleeing defenders of the entrenchments that had been taken by the two regiments of Sigfried's black troops. The men were clearly frightened, some gasping out that they had been overrun by "niggers" who "gave no quarter." Mahone personally arrested the flight of one man, asking him to say precisely what had happened. The reply was unmilitary but quite cogent: "Hell is busted back thar," he said, then resumed his exodus.[10]

The retreat and the colorful comments accompanying it did not dispirit Mahone or his command. On the contrary, it served to fire them. They, too, would give no quarter.

David Weisiger was in the lead of Mahone's men, with a Virginia brigade of eight hundred. In the words of Major William H. Etheredge,

Artist Alfred Waud titled this "Capture of Petersburg." (Library of Congress)

commanding the 41st Virginia Regiment, they "headed towards the cemetery, and when arrived at the mouth of the covered way, used to protect our men when relieving the picket, we marched up that covered way until we reached an angle, we then left the ditch, flanked to the right and marched a short distance down a ravine until nearly opposite the point where the mine was sprung, and we were ordered to lie down." Moving into a position north of the Virginia brigade was Wright's Brigade, a Georgia unit commanded (in the absence of its namesake) by Matthew R. Hall. The Virginians lay in the ravine behind the ruined Confederate front-line trenches. Quietly, the word was passed to fix bayonets and to fire only when they saw the whites of the enemy's eyes. In his 1866 *The Lost Cause*, Edward A. Pollard, who edited the *Daily Richmond Examiner* during 1861-1867, wrote more specifically that Mahone's soldiers "were ordered not to fire until they could see the whites of the negroes' eyes."[11]

The Georgians had yet to get down into the ravine and their position when some of the Virginians saw an officer rise up from the Federal line. It was almost certainly John Bross, with the flag of the 29th U.S. Colored Troops in his hand. The Confederates had no choice but to assume that the

Union troops were rising to the charge. Major Etheredge, commanding the 41st Virginia, was even certain he heard Federal officers calling for bayonets to be fixed and "no quarter" to be given. At this, Weisiger was not content to wait for the onslaught, let alone the whites of the enemy's eyes—nor even for the positioning of the Georgians. He told Captain Victor Girardey, one of Mahone's staff officers who had just delivered a message to him, to return to Mahone, advise him of the movement in the Federal line, and get his permission to commence a counterattack.

Girardey ran back to "Little Billy," gasping out: "General, they are coming!"[12]

Mahone needed no persuasion to order an immediate counterattack. "Tell Weisiger to forward," he barked.[13]

Girardey burned with a fire. Instead of conveying the message with which he had just been charged, he effectively usurped Weisiger's role, drawing his own sword, waving his hat, and shouting to the Virginians, "Forward! Charge!"[14]

In this way, the Confederate counterattack began.

It did not start out as a picturebook charge. The Virginians slowly rose from their prone positions in the ravine and walked ahead at an almost leisurely trail arms. Their imperfectly dressed ranks bowed inward, so that the flanks led while the center formed a concavity. One of the residents of Petersburg who watched the battle said later that the advancing line resembled a great scythe.

It was not until the Virginians reached the crest of the rise overlooking the jammed Union positions that they broke into the Rebel Yell—a battle cry at once celebrated and mysterious, with no two authorities agreeing on exactly what it sounded like. Some heard in it the call of the Southern fox hunter, others an Indian war whoop or perhaps an ancient Celtic battle cry, while still others thought it more animal than human. Whatever it was, the Rebel Yell could be produced only by the blended voices of men together, and its effect was invariably inspiriting to the attackers and unnerving to those who were attacked.

By this time, too, the Virginians' scythe-like line of battle had been augmented by the arrival of other soldiers, including those of the 17th and 26th South Carolina and the 25th North Carolina on the line's left wing and the 61st North Carolina behind the line. The counterattacking troops had been warned that they would be facing black Yankees, but the reality of it seemed to hit them only when they actually laid eyes on the "colored troops" for themselves. The clash that resulted was one of utmost brutality. It could be characterized as bestial, were it not for the fact that animals lack the human faculty of hatred.

Among the first to fall in the counterattack was John Bross, cut down by musket fire, the regimental flag torn from his grasp. Other rebels shot pointblank into the black faces that loomed before them. Few of the Virginians had time or space to reload as they recklessly closed with the Federals. Instead, they plied their bayonets or clubbed their muskets, swinging the heavy stocks into faces and skulls.

No quarter. The Virginians believed that the black Yankees proposed none, and they, in turn, were determined to offer none. Students of the Civil War have often pointed out the inefficiency of the typical soldier, how disproportionate quantities of powder and lead were required to kill a single man, and how, for example, 27,574 muskets were recovered from the battlefield at Gettysburg, of which a total of 24,000 were loaded, 12,000 loaded more than once, and 6,000 loaded three to ten times (one musket was stuffed with 23 charges and rounds). Yet when the keening Virginians descended on the Union's "colored troops" at the Crater, men killed with prodigious efficiency. William C. Smith of the 12th Virginia recounted how Emmet Richardson, an orderly sergeant of the regiment, "a tall, strong, athletic fellow . . . after discharging his gun, did terrible work with the bayonet and the butt of his gun. No less than five of the enemy fell beneath the terrible strokes of this powerful man."[15]

Some witnesseses reported that he went on to kill a total of seven. One soldier of the 41st Virginia reportedly dispatched fourteen Federal troops in the opening phase of the Confederate counterattack.

Unblooded before the Petersburg battle, the soldiers of the Fourth

Division (Colored Troops) nevertheless performed as Ambrose Burnside had predicted they would, attacking with a boldness and enthusiasm that continuous combat had bled and beaten out of the white troops of IX Corps. But now, mired in the human morass of the Crater and feeling the full fury of the Virginians, whose wrath was a combination of atavistic racial hatred and a righteous passion for defense of self and homeland, the inexperienced black troops panicked. Many threw down their muskets, bayonets and all, and ran, the rebels picking them up and hurling them like spears into the roiling masses struggling in the "honey-comb" of works surrounding the Crater.

As the incoming black troops had collided with the whites, so now they again crashed and tangled in their disordered exodus. Union soldiers, white and black, bayoneted one another, accidentally or on purpose, as each strove to move past the other in the packed traverses adjacent to the Crater.

Just south of the Crater, many Fourth Division men managed to break free, as did many white troops, and, together, they swarmed back to the Union lines. This was the view from the bomb-proof in and around which Ledlie and Ferrero had passed the battle. As Surgeon Chubb testified to the Court of Inquiry, what must have seemed an eternity to those in or near the Crater was in reality "a very short time."

> I stepped out [Chubb testified] and saw them [the two Fourth Division brigades] go over our works just in front of where General Ledlie's division passed over. Then they passed out of sight of where I was standing, but in a very short time I heard they were coming back, and, sure enough, they poured down all along in that vicinity with a good many white troops mixed with them. About that time General Ferrero returned [to the bombproof]. I am not positive if General Ledlie returned or not, and in answer to somebody who asked him how the battle was going, General Ferrero said we had lost everything, or something to that effect; that we were repulsed. He said it was nonsense to send a single body of troops (colored or white) forward at one single place, in front of lines held

by us, to throw them in the face of a re-enforced enemy, or an enemy who had opportunities to bring other forces to bear. General Ferrero said he thought his division was needlessly slaughtered.[16]

In the traverses adjacent to the Crater, the view was quite different. Corporal Newell Dutton, color bearer of the 9th New Hampshire, said it was "a mass of worms crawling over each other."[17] The Virginians viewed this mass down the barrels of their muskets, pouring fire into it, then jumping down into the moiling men mainly to wrest from them as many stands of regimental and national colors as possible.

As chaotic as was the situation of Thomas's troops, the disorder was even more intense to the north of the Crater, as Sigfried's black regiments broke and flooded back through the right wing of Bartlett's brigade. South of the Crater, men crawled over each other in the traverses like worms. Here, the traverses were so crowded that they did not permit even this degree of movement. Man was pinned to man. No one could move. And whereas many black as well as white troops were able to break out of the "honey-comb" south of the Crater and dash back to the Union lines, here they were stuck. Stephen Weld, with Bartlett's brigade, could not so much as raise his hands from his sides—either to loft a weapon, to defend himself, or even to surrender.

The Virginians leveled their muskets into this solid mass of humanity. Some opened fire. Others acceded to pleading offers of surrender.

But even surrender accepted was no guarantee of safety. As the POWs began to move out of the traverses (Weld reported) he heard someone call: "Shoot the nigger, but don't kill the white man."[18] Was this an officer's command or merely the urging of one soldier to another? Whatever it was—according to Weld—a pair of rebels turned their muskets on the black soldier standing beside him and fired pointblank. Others poked about the ruined works, eagerly finishing off each wounded black man they encountered.

North of Weld's position, more of Sigfried's routed troops collided with the X Corps brigade commanded by Louis Bell. In their panic, the black troops lashed out at Bell's men, overrunning them and even stabbing them with bayonets. Bell reported that he and his officers used their "sabers freely on the cowards but could not stop them and were all driven back—pell mell,"[19] carried, as it were, by a resistless tide of retreat.

That tide continued its rush, even as the routed men reached the Union's own covered way. The defeated "men er war" pushed aside and back the X Corps brigade of Martin Curtis, which was just coming up through the covered way headed for the front.

The flight of Sigfried's regiments and the forced retreat of Bell's brigade, carried on the tide of the routed black regiments, laid open the northern flank of the Crater, exposing the Union troops who remained there to severe enfilading fire from North Carolinians under Lee McAfee. This had the effect of pushing those Federals who occupied the trenches and traverses north of the Crater into the Crater itself.

The most industrious military historian would be hard pressed to find an instance in which the very space of the battlefield was as disastrously mismanaged as it was at the Crater. Nevertheless, despite the horror, atrocity, and panic, the battle was, at this point—about nine in the morning—not as one-sided as it seemed to virtually everyone except Ambrose Burnside.

While the other Union commanders focused on what was indeed the hopeless chaos in and immediately around the Crater, Burnside seized upon a series of messages coming to him (as he recounted to the Court of Inquiry) "from my signal officer, Captain Paine." He consistently reported from "a signal station in front of my line . . . that the enemy's right was very much weakened."[20] It was clear to Burnside that Robert E. Lee was prodigally pulling troops out of the line well south of the Crater.

Signal towers such as these were used by both sides to observe action developing behind the enemy's lines. (*Harper's Pictorial History of the Civil War,* 1866)

Burnside testified that he was at Robert Potter's headquarters when Paine's information first reached him. Accordingly, he made his way back to his own headquarters, from which he telegraphed General Meade to send in Gouverneur K. Warren's V Corps, which occupied the Union line immediately opposite the weakened Confederate right. This was not only a good idea, it was *the* imperative move at this critical juncture—probably the only positive, productive move the Union could make, and one that might just have saved the day. To his credit Burnside realized this, yet he somehow failed to communicate the importance of making the move *right now.*

Hours earlier, Meade had been quite anxious to send in Warren's V Corps:

HEADQUARTERS ARMY OF THE POTOMAC,
July 30, 1864—6.05 *a.m.*

Major-General BURNSIDE,
Commanding Ninth Corps:
The commanding general wishes to know what is going on on your left, and whether it would be an advantage for Warren's supporting force to go in at once.

A. A. HUMPHREYS,
Major-General and Chief of Staff [21]

188

Aware that the front was jammed, Burnside replied:

HEADQUARTERS NINTH CORPS,
July 30, 1864–6.20 *a.m.*, (*Received* 6.20 *a.m.*)

Major-General MEADE:

If General Warren's supporting force can be concentrated just now, ready to go in at the proper time, it would be well. I will designate to you when it ought to move. There is scarcely room for it now, in our immediate front.

A. E. BURNSIDE,
Major-General[22]

Burnside's tone irked Meade—always testy, and especially contemptuous of Burnside—who seems to have regarded the answer as so much evidence of his subordinate's lack of aggressiveness and all-round efficiency rather than as a straightforward (and accurate) assessment of the condition of the battlefield:

HEADQUARTERS ARMY OF THE POTOMAC,
July 30, 1864–6.50 *a.m.*

Major-General BURNSIDE:

Warren's force has been concentrated and ready to move since 3.30 a.m. My object in inquiring was to ascertain if you could judge of the practicability of his advancing without waiting for your column. What is the delay in your column moving? Every minute is most precious, as the enemy undoubtedly are concentrating to meet you on the crest, and if you gave them time enough you cannot expect to succeed. There is no object to be gained in occupying the enemy's line; it cannot be held under their artillery fire without much labor in turning it. The great point is to secure the crest at once, and at all hazards.

GEO. G. MEADE,
Major-General[23]

In fact, it was about this time that Mahone had begun moving first two brigades, then a third, from their positions some two miles south of the Crater, thereby greatly weakening the Confederate front here. Like Burnside, Meade began hearing reports that the Confederate right was weak, and, through his chief of staff, queried Warren as to whether he could make an immediate attack:

HEADQUARTERS ARMY OF THE POTOMAC,
July 30, 1864–7 *a.m.*

Major-General WARREN,
Commanding Fifth Corps:
What about attacking the enemy's right flank near the lead-works with that part of your force nearest to it?

A. A. HUMPHREYS,
Major-General and Chief of Staff[24]

It was not that Meade thought that Warren could actually break through the Confederate lines, but he did hope that such an attack would create a diversion from the growing Confederate concentration at the Crater, perhaps allowing a breakthrough there. Warren replied that one of his divisional commanders, General Crawford, was making a reconnaissance and that it would be "some time" before he would be heard from. After an hour, at 8:00 a.m. Warren passed on to Meade's chief of staff Crawford's report: "He says 'the lead-works are over a mile from the angle of my picket-line. I do not think an attack upon the enemy's works at or near that point at all practicable with the force I can spare. . . .'"[25] With this, a magnificent opportunity was squandered; for the fact was that Warren could have sent at least twenty-six regiments against the mere fifteen considerably understrength regiments that now defended the far southern flank of the Crater. Warren did not question his subordinate's report, however, and Meade, in turn, did not question Warren when he reported that an attack was not in the cards.

An hour later, at 9:00 a.m., acting on his signal officer's report of even greater weakness on the Confederate right—by this time, there were only eight understrength regiments there—Burnside sent Meade a note that completely failed to convey the key message:

> HEADQUARTERS NINTH CORPS,
> *July* 30, 1864—9 *a.m.*
>
> General MEADE:
> Many of the Ninth and Eighteenth Corps are retiring before the enemy. I think now is the time to put in the Fifth Corps promptly.
>
> **A. E. BURNSIDE,**
> *Major-General*[26]

Instead of explaining that the front before V Corps was now observed to be very weak and vulnerable, Burnside noted only that his IX Corps and Ord's XVIII (actually elements of the X Corps attached to it) were falling back. His message, therefore, was not *Strike while we have a golden opportunity,* but *I have failed; give me more troops*—a message Meade would mentally complete: *so that I may uselessly spill their blood as well.*

With Burnside's grossly inadequate dispatch in hand, Meade's chief of staff received a new message from Warren, dated just fifteen minutes later. Giving up on the idea of Warren's making an independent assault on the Confed-erate right, Meade had ordered him to do no more than assault a one-gun battery to the left of the Crater. Even to this modest proposal Warren responded:

> HEADQUARTERS FIFTH ARMY CORPS,
> *July* 30, 1864—9.15 *a.m.*
>
> Major-General HUMPHREYS:
> Just before receiving your dispatch to assault the battery on the left of the crater occupied by General Burnside, the enemy drove his troops out of the place and I think now hold it. I can find no one who knows for

certainty or seems willing to admit, but I think I saw a rebel battle-flag in it just now, and shots coming from it this way. I am, therefore, if this [be] true, no more able to take the battery now than I was this time yesterday. *All our advantages are lost.* I await further instructions, and am trying to get at the condition of affairs for certainty.

> G. K. WARREN,
> *Major-General* [27]

All our advantages are lost. At 9:30 a.m., just as Ambrose Burnside was pinning his hopes on Warren's striking the manifestly vulnerable Confederate right, Meade's chief of staff sent him this message:

> HEADQUARTERS ARMY OF THE POTOMAC,
> *July* 30, 1864–9.30 *a.m.*

Major-General BURNSIDE,
Commanding Ninth Corps:
The major-general commanding has heard that the result of your attack has been a repulse, and directs that, if in your judgment nothing further can be effected, you withdraw to your own line, taking every precaution to get the men back safely.

> A. A. HUMPHREYS,
> *Major-General and Chief of Staff*

General Ord will do the same.

> A. A. HUMPHREYS,
> *Major-General and Chief of Staff* [28]

It was based not only on Warren's pessimism, but on a personal reconnaissance by no less than U. S. Grant, who had witnessed the flight of

Ferrero's division, including how they ran through the white units. From this, the commanding general could draw no other conclusion than that the Petersburg assault had completely broken down.

It was, nevertheless, a premature conclusion. The enemy was still highly vulnerable, and its weak right was not its only vulnerability. As one-sided as the Crater struggle seemed, the Virginia brigade, which was meting out so much punishment, was getting brutally battered in return. After all, the Confederates were to a large degree constrained by the very conditions that had bogged down the Union assault: a massively overcrowded battlefield. Of one hundred men in the 6th Virginia Infantry who participated in the "scythe" counterattack on Union forces adjacent to the Crater, eighty fell in the course of the operation. Nor were these casualties exceptional. Losses of 50 percent and more prevailed among all counterattacking units. In some cases, whole companies were simply wiped out. Mahone concluded that he could not capture the Crater using the Virginians alone, and it would take time to get the Georgians into a position where they could help. Mahone used that time to lob mortar shells into the Crater, each salvo sending a certain number of Federals clambering out of the pit and into the clutches of the Confederates, who took them prisoner. But Mahone, quite aware of the weakness he had created on the Confederate right, did not deceive himself into believing that time was on his side. He could not wait for attrition to do its work, but wanted desperately to bring the Battle of the Crater to a decision.

As for Burnside, persuaded by his signal officer's assessment, he was determined to convince Meade that now was not the time to quit, that something further could indeed "be effected." However, at 9:45, Meade ordered Hancock, Warren, and Ord to break off all offensive operations. To Burnside, Meade's chief of staff sent a one-line order, which allowed no latitude for the exercise of the IX Corps commander's "judgment":

HEADQUARTERS ARMY OF THE POTOMAC,
July 30, 1864–9.45 a.m.

Major-General BURNSIDE,
Commanding Ninth Corps:
The major-general [commanding] directs that you withdraw to your own intrenchments.

A. A. HUMPHREYS,
Major-General and Chief of Staff[29]

Throughout the entire Petersburg operation, Ambrose Burnside had yielded to George Gordon Meade, even when doing so meant abandoning his own judgment and abrogating his own command responsibility. Easygoing and compliant to a fault, even Burnside had finally reached his limit. In company with General Ord, he rode to Meade's tent and, by all reports, exploded. In language and tone Meade's staff characterized as "extremely insubordinate," Burnside asserted that the enemy's line *could* be broken, especially south of the Crater.

Meade—and, for that matter, everyone else in the United States Army—was familiar with what happened the last time Ambrose Burnside had insisted that repeated assaults would break the enemy's line. The slaughter of Fredericksburg had happened.

Moreover, Ord sharply disagreed with Burnside. He believed the battle had indeed been lost. And that ended the matter—or so Burnside, Ord, and Meade thought. But at the very moment that Ord delivered his opinion, a telegram arrived from Brigadier General Julius White, who was acting as Burnside's chief of staff. He suggested that, even if breakthrough to Petersburg was no longer possible, the Crater itself could be held and made part of the Union's siege lines. Burnside brightened at this, but Meade rejected the proposal out of hand, insisting on withdrawal from the Crater, moving back to the present Union lines, and resuming the siege. When Burnside objected that the severe Confederate crossfire *behind* the Crater made immediate withdrawal suicidal, Meade conceded this, and put modified withdrawal orders in writing:

HEADQUARTERS ARMY OF THE POTOMAC,

July 30, 1864–10 *a.m.*

Major-Generals BURNSIDE and ORD:

You can exercise your discretion in withdrawing your troops now or at a later period, say to night. It is not intended to hold the enemy's line which you now occupy any longer than is required to withdraw safely your men.

GEO. G. MEADE,

Major-General [30]

Orders in hand, Burnside and Ord left their commanding general's tent. Burnside paused to look his colleague in the eye. Remarking that some fifteen thousand Union soldiers were at that very moment massed in the vicinity of the Crater, he said, as if thinking aloud: "It is strange if you cannot do something with them." Perhaps the musing was intended as merely rhetorical, but Ord took it as an accusation. Raising his arms in a gesture of helplessness, he asked: "If you are held by the throat, how can you do anything?" [31]

Burnside's response, if any, is not recorded. We can only wonder if he asked himself just whose hands were at *his* throat. Those of Robert E. Lee, his officers, and men? Or those of Major General George Gordon Meade?

- 10 -

Put in the Dead Men

By the time Generals Burnside and Ord met with General Meade, the survivors of IX Corps occupied very little of the Confederate trenches. Most of the men had been pushed into the Crater, except for a portion of First Brigade, Third Division, under the command Brigadier General John Hartranft. These soldiers clung, Alamo-like, to the traverses of the demolished Confederate fort immediately adjacent to the Crater.

Despite the carnage they were meting out, Mahone's Virginians were also absorbing terrific punishment, in large part because, even with the trenches cleared of Yankees, they could barely move for all the bodies now heaped in them. The commanding officers of the 41st and 61st Virginia Regiments reluctantly pulled men out of the firing line to make some maneuvering room by dragging and heaving some of the corpses over the parapets. It was ghastly work, the men toiling in pools of blood that oozed over the tops of their brogans. Colonel David Weisiger, commanding the Virginia brigade, did not witness this gruesome labor. He had sustained a severe wound in his side and, assuming his wound mortal (it proved not to be), he turned over command of the brigade to 6th Virginia CO Colonel George Rogers. After suffering momentary capture followed by a lightning rescue, Weisiger retired to the Gee house to get his wound dressed. There General P. G. T. Beauregard, the very commander who had presided over the opening shots of the Civil War against Fort Sumter, greeted him. "Colonel," he intoned in an orotund drawl that was outdated even in 1864, "you have covered yourself with glory."[1]

Regiments from North and South Carolina moved up to augment the Virginia brigade in its ongoing effort to clear the Crater, the central feature of a front that was now no more than a hundred yards across yet occupied by several thousand men. To bring maximum pressure to bear against the Federals occupying the Crater, two Coehorn mortars were ordered forward from their battery at the Jerusalem Plank Road so that they could be positioned in the recaptured trenches just a few yards from the Crater. Coehorns—they were named after their late-seventeenth century Dutch inventor, Baron Menno van Coehoorn—were compact and portable smoothbores designed to lob heavy shells at high trajectory into enemy works. They were short-range artillery requiring little powder, and because they weighed less than three hundred pounds each (when mounted on a block or platform), they could be readily manhandled into position. Yet it was still no easy task to drag nearly three hundred pounds through an area in which some traverses were still held by a shooting enemy. John Haskell, the Confederate artilleryman in charge of moving the Coehorns, encountered a white Union officer with two black soldiers. Haskell and the Federal regarded one another with momentary astonishment before the Union officer ordered his men to open fire. Haskell, however, had the drop on him, shooting him dead with a pistol he had borrowed from a fellow officer. He then called to Confederate infantrymen to climb into the trenches. Flushing out a dozen or more black soldiers, they took them prisoner. With these Yankee diehards out of the way, Haskell and his men placed the Coehorns where they could fire 24-pound shells directly into the Crater using no more than an ounce and a half of powder.

As the Federals endured a ceaseless crescendo of shelling in the Crater, Mahone decided it was time to add Lieutenant Colonel M. R. Hall's Georgia brigade to the Virginians and Carolinians. He wanted the Georgians to clear Hartranft's Michigan men out of the trenches, so that the final assault on the Crater could get under way. What Mahone did not realize was that, by this time, most of Hartranft's men were long gone from the trenches. The only regiments remaining there were elements of the 20th Michigan, the 2nd Michigan, and the 1st Michigan Sharpshooters. The largest contingent, 20th Michigan men, had actually withdrawn earlier only to be recalled by Hartranft not to renew the assault on the Confederates, but to try to stem the rout of Ferrero's broken Fourth Division. Now the men of the Fourth were either back in the Union lines or stuck in the Crater, and the three Michigan regiments found themselves the unwilling defenders of an impromptu Alamo.

John Hartranft set about trying to bring some semblance of order to his brigade as well the survivors of William Humphrey's brigade. He therefore took on the responsibility of divisional command outside of the Crater. Simon Griffin, commander of the Second Brigade of Robert Potter's division, assumed command of the forces in the Crater itself. Brigadier General William Bartlett, who had led the First Brigade of Ledlie's division in the initial assault, was still alive, but he was out of action. Bartlett had gone into the battle with a prosthetic leg made of highly compacted cork. The leg was light and gave him considerable mobility, but it was not sturdy, and when an exploding shell kicked up heavy clods of clay, one or more struck his cork limb, shattering it. When that happened, Bartlett was sent sprawling. Officers rushed to help.

"Put me any place where I can sit down," Bartlett instructed them.

"But you are wounded, General, aren't you?"

"My leg is shattered all to pieces."

"Then you can't sit up," the incredulous officer exclaimed. "You will have to lie down."

"Oh, no. It's my cork leg that is shattered. I have only one leg to go on now."[2]

Thanks largely to Hartranft, Hall's Georgians did not encounter a defenseless mob when they descended on the Michigan men and the Crater. Hartranft rallied his riflemen, and his ad hoc artilleryman, Sergeant Wesley Stanley, of the 14th New York, turned a pair of captured Napoleons against the Georgia brigade. The pieces were loaded with the Confederate canister shot that had already taken a grim toll on the Union troops.

Hartranft's soldiers fought with last stand desperation, Stanley directing a merciless fire from his two-gun battery. The Georgia brigade fell back, first into trenches and traverses, and then all the way behind the Virginians. Some few were even captured by Hartranft's men.

Mahone realized that he could not take the Crater with his Virginia brigade alone. He had hoped that the addition of the Carolinians would make the capture possible, but when that proved insufficient, he threw in the Georgians. Incredibly, they, too, were beaten back. He turned now to Bushrod Johnson, who, apparently having finished his breakfast, deigned to visit the battlefield. Mahone could see that his brigades were badly hampered by a crowded battlefield thoroughly cut up by traverses and trenches. He knew that the Yankees could not hold out here, of course, but he was also keenly aware that each passing minute brought danger

This half of a stereograph shows a dead Confederate soldier in a forward trench beyond the cheval-de-frise—the defensive obstacle (at the lower right) made of sharpened wooden cross-members. (Library of Congress)

south of the Crater, where the Confederate line was delicate as gossamer.[3] He therefore proposed that Johnson send those of his troops who were now south of the Crater against the Union left, while also ordering Alfred Colquitt's brigade to provide a heavy crossfire from behind. While these operations were under way, Mahone would commit the Alabama brigade under John C. C. Saunders to an attack from the southwest—a direction across a much more open landscape relatively free of trenches and traverses. Coordinated with these fresh assaults, the already involved Virginia troops of John T. Goode and Weisiger would continue to apply pressure, moving additional mortars closer and closer to the Crater and increasing the frequency of fire. Even with all three brigades and more committed to the counterattack, the Confederates were still greatly outnumbered. It was therefore a singularly bold plan for envelopment, intended not only to retake all of the original Confederate line, but to bag or kill every IX Corps soldier remaining in and around the Crater.

There would have been a kind of mercy in Mahone's projected endgame, had he been able to play it immediately to its conclusion. But it would take time to get Saunders's Alabamans in place, and the enveloping attack was not set to commence until 1 p.m. Mahone was not interested in merely driving the Yankees from the Confederate lines. He wanted to kill or capture them. Therefore, it became imperative to hold them in place until the arrival of Saunders. That meant maintaining a deadly thick enfilading fire in front of the Crater and across the no-man's land separating the Union and Confederate lines even as more and more mortar fire was concentrated on the Crater itself. The fighting in this corner of the Civil War had begun as a great explosion followed by an inept attack met by a fierce defense. The defense rapidly evolved into a brutal counterattack. And now that counterattack had mutated into a kind of torture, a large-scale version of what boys might do to captive insects before, at length, weariness of the game prompted finishing them off.

Mortar and canister fire rained into the Crater from three sides. This produced two effects. It sent some men cowering, desperately seeking shelter the confines of the Crater did not afford. The fire drove others to attempt escape from the Crater. The Confederates had thought of this, however; they posted sharpshooters all around the Crater, and any man whose head rose above the rim became a target. Not content with the accelerating tempo of the Coehorn rounds the artillerymen lobbed into the Crater, Confederate infantry troops occupied themselves gathering abandoned muskets or prying bayonet-bearing muskets from the dead grasp of casualties, then hurling these, harpoon-like, over the Crater rim and into the mass of men within.

Some Federals stationed themselves at the lip of the Crater, digging their toes and the balls of their feet into whatever concavity they could find or make. The danger in this position was chiefly from sharpshooters, but it was the only position from which it was possible to fight back. The besieged Union riflemen took a significant toll, but each shot also drew the enemy's fire. Connecticut sergeant John Lathe was a marksman who notched five Confederate hits that day before an enemy round took off two of his fingers and tore into the flesh, muscle, and bones of his hand, cleaving the appendage as far as the wrist. The excruciating wound sent Lathe sliding down the Crater wall. A lieutenant from his regiment recognized him and shepherded him to the rear of the Crater, where, using his handkerchief, he bound the hand as tightly as he could. Lathe later managed to escape to the Union lines.

Among those still just outside of the Crater were the 1st Michigan Sharpshooters, including Company K, made up of Chippewa Indians. Their fire was especially deadly, but they, too, were doomed, both by the attrition of their numbers and the dwindling of their ammunition.

As was to be expected in such a stand, the shortage of ammunition soon grew general. Hartranft sent a runner, who managed to get to General Willcox at the Union lines. The general organized members of the 51st Pennsylvania into teams of four. A shelter half was laid out in front of each team, and cartridge tins were dumped onto it. Then each man in the team picked up a corner of the shelter half and made a mad dash across the bullet-swept reaches of no-man's land. Astoundingly, ten thousand rounds reached Hartranft by this means.

Even as Hartranft found new ways to keep his men in the fight, the Confederates devised new ways to kill them. Mortar fire was the ideal artillery weapon against the Crater, but Napoleons loaded with canister were more effective over topography that allowed for a shallower trajectory. For the most part, the cut-up ground around the Crater provided shelter from canister—until the Confederate artillerists located the trenches that ran straight out from the Crater on its north side. These provided ample avenues for enfilading artillery fire. By shooting through—along the length of—these alleyways, the artillerymen could gouge deeply into the masses of tightly packed Union troops. Now low-trajectory canister poured into the Crater through the slots created by the trench ends.

Exhausted, beaten, shattered as they were, it did not seem possible that the soldiers in the Crater could be menaced by any novel means of horror. The introduction of the canister shot, however, created an entirely new level of panic. Bartlett, unable to move, watched his agitated men mill aimlessly under the new barrage. Something had to be done.

He ordered the black troops to build a breastworks to close up the trench ends. They started piling earth, each man struggling to the Crater rim with as many clods as he could carry. But even the labor of this collective Sisyphus would never succeed in closing the gaps.

Then someone realized that the defenders of the Crater possessed an asset yet to be exploited.

"Put in the dead men," that someone shouted.[4]

With that, black men and white began dragging bodies up the wall of the Crater. Seeing what was going on, some of the Chippewas at the edge of the Crater rolled bodies from outside the Crater into the gaps. Sharpshooters who hugged the rim tore out fistfuls of clay beneath the bodies, thereby hollowing out apertures through which to continue firing.

* * *

As morning crawled toward noon that 30th of July, and the naked sun rose higher, a want of water eclipsed the want of ammunition. The wounds, especially those made by artillery fired at short range, were ghastly. Limbs were blown off, and devastating head wounds abounded. Mortar shells shattered skulls, not so much decapitating a man as blowing his head into pieces, often leaving nothing discernable from the neck up. But fragments—of metal and of earth—caused far more injuries than the direct hits did, and victims of these missiles did not always die instantly, but lived for a time to suffer and to moan. Yet by late in the morning, it was the cries of the desperately thirsty that cut more piteously than those of the wounded. One of the most striking images from the battle were the eyewitness reports of mist—some called it a fog—that arose from the Crater to mingle with the pall of smoke produced by battle. The dewy mist of morning had long since burned off, but this eerie fog lingered, a condensation of breath and the evaporation of sweat from thousands of toiling, desperate, fearful, fighting men.

Some went crazy for want of water. Others were spurred to uncommon valor. A nameless private approached General Griffin, offering to collect empty canteens from the men, venture out of the Crater and into the no-man's land, fetch water, and return. Griffin told the soldier he could try if he wanted to. In truth, the general didn't think the private had a prayer across that killing field, and if he did somehow make it to the rear, he certainly didn't expect him to return. But that would be all right. If he managed to reach the Union lines, he deserved to live.

No sooner did Griffin give this private permission than others sought to do the same. Griffin let them all go. And then he was stunned and profoundly moved when, one by one, those who had lived through the crossfire—likely as not wounded, often in more than one place—valiantly trundled back into the Crater with filled canteens, which, as promised, they quickly shared out.

*   *   *

"How long did your troops remain in the crater before the order was given to retire?" the judge-advocate asked Ambrose Burnside.

> Answer. The order was given to retire, I think, about 9.30. When the order was given to retire I went to General Meade's headquarters, consulted with him, ascertained that it was final, and decided that our best method of retiring was to hold the crater until dark and then retire by trenches.[5]

Apparently dissatisfied with this response, the judge-advocate repeated the question, and "the witness [was] requested to give a more specific answer."

> Question. How long did your troops remain in the crater before the order was given to retire?

> Answer. They remained there until about 2 o'clock. I think the order [that is, Burnside's order to IX Corps] reached them about 11.40.[6]

Even after he had lost the battle with Meade to send Warren's V Corps against the Confederate right, Burnside resisted immediately evacuating IX Corps because he believed that the crossfire sweeping no-man's land was too hazardous. He wanted to retreat under cover of darkness and testified to the Court of Inquiry that he felt confident in "the reports I had received that our people would be able to hold the position which they then occupied until night."[7]

On the surface, it was a judgment call—defensible, although it exhibited dubious judgment. (How could the fire at the Crater be less deadly than the fire between the Crater and the Union lines?) Yet, continuing his testimony, Burnside went on to explain that although he was confident "that our people would be able to hold [their] position . . . until night," he felt that even "if they were not [able to hold], one time for evacuation was about as good as another."[8]

The hallmark of this entire doomed operation was always the triumph of irrationality over rationality. Here was yet another instance. Given the intensity of fire at the Crater, immediate evacuation was clearly the most viable alternative; however, Burnside's proposal to evacuate under cover of darkness was at least rational, but his further remark that "one time for evacuation was about as good as another" smacked of his earlier abrogation of command and decision making. It was an abandonment of rational thought.

And there was worse to come. Burnside testified that he "thought it best to have a perfect understanding as to the method of withdrawal." He therefore met with his divisional commanders, and "it was decided that we should dig a trench or trenches from our main line to the crater, and thereby enable them to withdraw without serious loss. It will be remembered that this distance is but a little over 100 yards, and taking into consideration the radius of the crater it is probably less than that distance. General Willcox had already given instructions, as he informed me and as I know, to dig a trench connecting our advance line with the crater, and I am not sure that the other division commanders had not commenced like operations."[9]

The task proposed was to dig a three hundred-foot trench, eight feet deep and somewhat more than four feet wide, under murderous enemy fire, and to do it not in a matter of days, but hours. Ambrose Burnside and his subordinates—the commanders collectively responsible for the lives of the men in and around the Crater—were proposing to save them not by physically, let alone militarily, feasible means, but by sheer magic.

By late midmorning, a man who risked peering above the lip of the Crater to look back toward the Union lines would have seen scores of soldiers frantically plying picks and shovels. If that same man looked in the other direction, he might have glimpsed the approach of a fresh force come to kill him and his comrades. It was the Alabama brigade.

On Wednesday evening, April 18, 1906, John C. Featherston, "Late

Captain in Alabama Brigade of Gen. Mahone's Division, C.S.A," spoke at the Old Methodist Church of Pottsville, Pennsylvania. His subject was "The Battle of the Crater."

After delivering a competent secondhand summary of the battle, Featherston reached the point in his narrative at which the "Alabama brigade . . . appeared on the scene. (I had the honor to command a company in that brigade.)"[10]

"As soon as we emerged from the covered way into a ravine or swale running parallel with the works held by the enemy, we there met General Mahone himself on foot." Mahone "called the officers to him" and explained that the "Virginians and Georgians had by a gallant charge captured the breastworks on the left, that is north, of the Crater, but the enemy still held the fort and a short space of the works to the right of it." Mahone ordered the Alabamans to "move up the ravine as far as we could walk unseen and then crawl still farther until we reached a point as near opposite the fort as possible." At that point, the brigade was to lie down "until the artillery posted in our rear could draw the enemy's fire. . . . When this was accomplished we should rise up and move at a 'trail arms,' with guns loaded and bayonets fixed but not fire a gun nor yell until we drew the fire from the fort." Once the enemy opened fire, the Alabamans were to "yell and make a dash for the fort" before the Federals could bring to bear what Mahone quite mistakenly believed were some fifty pieces of artillery.[11]

> As we were withdrawing from the presence of the General he said: "General Lee is watching the result of your charge."[12]

Captain Featherston and his fellow officers returned to their men "and ordered them to 'load' and 'fix bayonets.' Then 'right face.'" As Featherston started his company moving—

> a soldier, worse disfigured by dirt, powder and smoke than any I had before seen, came up to my side and said: "Captain, can I go in this

charge with you?" I replied, "Yes, who are you?" He said: "I am ____ (I have forgotten his name), and I belong to ____ South Carolina Regiment. I was blown up in that fort, and I want to even up with them. Take my name and regiment and if I get killed, inform my officer of it." I said: "I have no time for writing. How high up did they blow you?" He said: "I don't know, but as I was going up I met the company cook coming down, and he said he would try to have breakfast ready by the time I got back."[13]

Featherston informed his Pottsville audience that the Alabama brigade "carried into battle 628 men [some sources reported 632], practically the same that the Light brigade carried into the charge at Balacklava [Balaklava in the Crimean War] that Tennyson immortalized."[14]

The men of the Alabama brigade advanced to a point two hundred yards from the Crater before they lay down. To them it did not appear that they were facing a beaten enemy who was under orders to withdraw. Instead, "we could see the fort and the many flags of the enemy which indicated their numbers. We knew the odds were greatly against us, but 'it was not ours to ask the reason why, only ours to do and die.'" The men knew, Featherston explained in an oddly mixed metaphor, "that we were Gen. Lee's last card that he was playing on the checkerboard of war as we were the last of the reserves." Thus, when Mahone "gave the command 'forward,'" the Alabamans went without hesitation.[15]

Soon we saw the flash of the sunlight on the enemy's guns and bayonets as they leveled them over the walls of the fort. Then a sheet of flame flashed out as they fired. Then followed the awful roar of battle. This volley seemed to awaken the demons of hell. There were in gunshot of that fort, I think I can say, fully 20,000 men, including both sides. It seemed to be the signal for everybody within range to commence firing.[16]

The brigade "raised a yell and made a dash to get under the walls of the fort, before their artillery could open on us, but in this we failed." The Federals had but few captured Confederate Napoleons to fire against the Alabamans, but Featherston recalled that "the air seemed literally filled with missiles." Nevertheless, "on the 600 Alabamians went, as it seemed to us, literally into 'the jaws of death, into the mouth of hell.'"[17]

As Featherston's company "reached the walls of the wrecked fort we dropped on the ground to get the men in order and let them get breath. While lying here we could hear the enemy endeavoring to encourage their men by telling them to 'Remember Fort Pillow.'" Featherston's company and others of the brigade "pushed up hats on bayonets and as expected they riddled them with bullets." This ploy was routinely used to induce defenders to fire. Because it took time to reload, there followed an interval of reduced fire. The Alabamans sought to exploit this by "immediately [springing] over the walls and [into] the fort."[18]

> Then commenced that awful hand to hand struggle of which history tells you. Each side were throwing guns, bayonet foremost, at each other over the walls of the fort, also cannon balls, etc.
>
> Whites and negroes were indiscriminately mixed up and it was the first time that our troops had encountered the negroes and they could only with difficulty be restrained.[19]

As Featherston tells it, the Federals put up a gallant fight. Perhaps that was genuinely his impression, or perhaps he crafted his narrative to please his Pennsylvania audience. For Union accounts of the fight within the Crater speak mainly of panic. Although the defenders at the rim of the Crater saw the approach of the Alabamans and defended against it, the bulk of the troops within the blasted fort were totally surprised by the appearance of the Confederates charging over the rim. Most broke and ran—or tried to, stepping upon what some described as a solid layer of the dead and dying. ("In one part of the fort," Featherston himself said, "I counted eight bodies deep.")[20]

Featherston spoke of black and white troops "indiscriminately mixed up." In fact, some white troops began shooting, clubbing, and bayoneting their black comrades for fear that the onrushing rebels would summarily shoot any white man seen fighting alongside a black. As one white officer later wrote to his family, "the men was bound not to be taken prisoner among them niggers."[21]

With more and more Alabamans and others, including members of the Virginia brigade, topping the rim and pouring in, Griffin and Hartranft moved among the thousands within the Crater, desperately trying to bring order and rally resistance. But only a rearguard—one hundred, perhaps two hundred men—offered anything like orderly defensive fire. By this time, pursuant to Meade's order to discontinue all offensive activity, Warren and Ord had completely withdrawn their corps, so that, with each passing minute, the Confederates met less and less resistance from outside the Crater and could therefore turn their full attention on the Crater itself.

As if to symbolize the culmination of total defeat, the few survivors of Company K, 1st Michigan Sharpshooters—Chippewas all—withdrew from the rim and down into a southern corner of the Crater. Here they pulled shirts over bowed heads, and began chanting their death songs to ensure their translation into the afterlife.

"The fort was blown into two compartments," Featherston observed. This was the result of the powder in the mine having been divided between the two galleries that branched off the end of the main shaft. Separated by a wall of clayish earth, the two cavities were of unequal size, the larger to the north. Within this one, Lieutenant Freeman Bowley, an officer of the 30th U.S. Colored Troops, sat with a survivor of his company, a black sergeant, among a tattered collection of other troops. From beyond the wall, Bowley heard a voice: "Every man get his gun loaded, give one spring and go right over." Then: "Forward 41st!"[22] With that, Major William Etheridge of the 41st Virginia, materialized at the top of the wall. Bowley discharged his pistol, but missed the major. A sergeant of the 41st in turn leveled his musket at Bowley, but held fire in response to shouts of surrender coming from all around him.

Etheredge later told his own story of his entrance into the Crater:

I was among the first to jump into the ditch where the Yanks were as thick as they could stand. The first sergeant of Co. D jumped in about the same time I did, and was killed instantly. Where I was there was a small bomb-proof, and two Yanks squatting down near its mouth to keep out of danger (they were white men with muskets in their hands with fixed bayonets). My feet had not more than touched the ground when they rose up and stood before me. Just then the man that killed the sergeant stepped down and picked up a musket evidently with the intention of killing me. I . . . took hold of the two men in front of me and kept them so close together it was impossible for . . . the man that picked up the musket to kill me. . . . Just at that moment our men were jumping into the ditch like frogs. One of them jumped in just behind me, and I sang out to him at the top of my voice to kill the man in front of me. The man . . . stepped one pace to the right of me and killed the Federal soldier as quick as you could wink your eye.[23]

And Bowley's perspective on the Union defeat at the hands of the Virginians was charged with an element of glory: "Here it was that our gallant Capt. Seagrave, with a knee shattered by a bullet, unable to retreat, refusing to surrender, fought with revolver and sword, killing six rebels, until he was shot and bayoneted in seven places."[24]

Federals, white and black, threw down their weapons and raised their hands. Suddenly, however, the Confederates began shooting and bayoneting the unarmed blacks. Those "colored troops" who had not yet shed their arms opened fire, and the hand-to-hand combat resumed.

While this grisly scene was being played out in the northern "compartment" of the Crater, Alabamans were pouring into the smaller cavity to the south. There was firing at very close quarters, as well as fighting with bayonets, knives, and rifle butts. Officers who attempted to wield their swords against the enemy found the space too confined to do much with that weapon.

Even as more and more Confederates poured in, they remained outnumbered better than two to one. But the bluecoats were terrified, shell shocked, exhausted, thirsty to the point of madness, utterly demoralized, and impossible to organize. They were, for the most part, useless as soldiers now. "After we captured the larger compartment," Featherston told his Pottsville audience, "those in the smaller one cried out that they would surrender."[25]

> We told them to come over the embankment. Two of them started over with their guns in their hands, and were shot and fell back. We heard those remaining cry: "They are showing us no quarter; let us sell our lives as dearly as possible." We then told them to come over without their guns, which they did, and all the remainder, about thirty in number, surrendered and were ordered to the rear. In the confusion and their eagerness to get from that point, they went across the open field, along the same route over which we had charged them. Their artillery, seeing them going to the rear, as we were told, under the flag of truce, thought that it was our men repulsed and retreating, and they at once opened fire on them, killing and wounding quite a number of their own men. One poor fellow had his arm shot off just as he started to the rear, and returning, said: "I could bear it better if my own men had not done it."[26]

"Did you remain till the troops retired?" the judge-advocate asked Brigadier General John F. Hartranft.

Answer. Yes, sir.

Question. Did they retire in confusion?

Answer. Yes, sir.

Question. Driven out?

Answer. They were driven out at the same time that I had passed the word to retire. It was a simultaneous thing. When they saw the assaulting column within probably 100 feet of the works, I passed the word as well as it could be passed, for everybody to retire, and I left myself at that time. General Griffin and myself were together at that time. The order to retire we had indorsed to the effect that we thought we could not withdraw the troops that were there on account of the enfilading fire over the ground between our rifle-pits and the crater without losing a great portion of them, that ground being enfiladed with artillery and infantry fire. They had at that time brought their infantry down along their pits on both sides of the crater, so that their sharpshooters had good range, and were in good position. Accordingly we requested that our lines should open with artillery and infantry, bearing on the right and left of the crater, under which fire we would be able to withdraw a greater portion of the troops, and, in fact, every one that could get away.[27]

Thus it was about two p.m. that Generals Hartranft and Griffin, deciding that it was suicide to hold out until nightfall, sent their staff officers through the terrified mob in the Crater with orders to withdraw when the signal was given. That signal was to be the opening of Union artillery—firing from the Union lines—against the area north and south of the Crater. Hartranft gave a staff officer his and Griffin's endorsements of Burnside's withdrawal order—the endorsements now specifying immediate withdrawal—together with a request for the Union batteries to provide a covering barrage against the north and south ends of the Crater. Bearing these documents, the officer dashed back to the Union lines.

"While we were waiting for the approval of that indorsement and the opening of the fire," Hartranft told the Court of Inquiry, "this assaulting column of the enemy came up, and we concluded—General Griffin and myself—that there was no use in holding it any longer, and so we retired."[28]

"At the last assault of the enemy General Hartranft gave the order to his command to withdraw," Ambrose Burnside testified to the Court of Inquiry. "General Hartranft was not, in fact, authorized to make such a movement, but I have not the slightest doubt in my own mind but he thought he was carrying out the spirit of the order." Burnside continued, with the well-meaning magnanimity he customarily showed subordinates: "It was one of those misunderstandings which are so likely to happen at so critical a time. He had before reported that they would be able to hold their position. . . ."[29]

One of those misunderstandings? From behind Union lines, it was one thing to speak of holding until nightfall or even to opine that one time to withdraw was about as good as any other, but in the Crater, under merciless artillery fire, dodging bayonet-tipped muskets hurled like javelins, and locked in combat hand-to-hand, such leisurely options were hardly available.

Hartranft and Griffin got their men moving out of the Crater and across the killing field that was the space between lines of gray and blue. Many fell. To be sure, it was a rout rather than a retreat, a mob of men desperate enough to shove and run their way through a storm of musketry and artillery fire. Many fell, and those who fell wounded were not aided by their comrades, but were supremely fortunate if they somehow escaped being trampled to death by them. The twinned instincts of fear and survival propelled many men to continue their flight despite wounds that should have disabled them. One New Hampshire private took a minie ball in the knee but nevertheless continued his run to the Union's covered way, not even stumbling. Uppermost in his mind was the image of his brother, starving in a Confederate POW camp.

Most of the survivors of the bombardment and assault on the Crater made the flight, but several hundred remained behind. In the first few minutes of the withdrawal, when a great mass of men were in retreat, the law of averages was an ally. Confederate muskets and guns could kill only so many, after all. But as the flow of men petered out, marksmen could choose their targets more deliberately. Those who still occupied the

Crater saw more and more of their comrades fall in flight and some—approximately five hundred—decided to chance the mercy of the rebels.

But the Confederate brigades who continued to swarm into the Crater had embarked on their counterattack armed with stern warnings that black men in Union blue would show them no quarter. For this reason, Union offers of surrender were, more often than not, met with a thrust of the bayonet or a blow of the rifle butt.

What could possibly end this blood frenzy? As it turned out, just a few blunt words of human language.

"Why in hell don't you fellows surrender?" Adjutant Morgan Cleveland, 8th Alabama Regiment, called out above the din.

He was answered instantly by a Union colonel: "Why in the hell don't you let us?"[30]

After this homely exchange, a 4th Rhode Island lieutenant named Kirby withdrew from his sleeve a dirty white silk handkerchief. He tied it to the handle of his sword, grasped the weapon by the blade, and held it aloft, handle topmost. At this, the roar of musketry subsided into a crackle and then silence, a silence made more profound by its sudden contrast with cacophony that had preceded it. The universal quiet was roughly punctuated by the thud and rattle of several hundred Union muskets cast down to clatter into the Crater's bloody clay.

CHAPTER

- 11 -

A Stupendous Failure

T here were but few wounded compared with the killed," Captain John C. Featherston told his Pottsville audience in 1906. Among the wounded was Brigadier General William Bartlett, who "was lying down and could not rise. Assistance was offered him, but he informed those who were assisting him that his leg was broken . . . . One of our officers ordered a couple of negroes to move him, but he protested, and I believe he was given white assistance. . . . One of our soldiers seeing the cork leg and springs knocked to pieces waggishly said, 'General, you are a fraud; I thought that was a good leg when I shot it.'"[1]

Gallows humor, no matter how dark, is humor nonetheless. There would be little enough of it. The Federal prisoners of war began filing out of the Crater between a double row of Confederates. Artillerymen at the Union lines must at first have seen only the men in gray, for they opened fire on the prisoner line. Confederate casualties resulting from this brief barrage—the mistake was quickly discovered—are unknown, but a Union private lost an arm to a Federal cannon ball. As for the black prisoners, the slaughter continued. Confederate artillerist Brigadier General Edward P. Alexander reported that, "Some of the Negro prisoners, who were originally allowed to surrender by some soldiers, were afterward shot by others." Colonel "Willie" Pegram told his sister, "I think over two hundred negroes got into our lines [i.e., as prisoners]. . . . I don't

Waud titled this sketch "Pitkins Station U.S.M.R.R. [United States Military Railroad] Petersburg, Va." Inscribed below this title are two indicators: "New road to City Point" and "Old route to City Point." Petersburg was a key southern road and rail hub, through which both Richmond and Lee's Army of Northern Virginia were supplied. The first Union troops to see this view saw it as prisoners of war, about to be marched through the streets of the city. (Library of Congress)

believe that much over half of these ever reached the rear. You could see them lying dead all along the route to the rear."[2]

Confederate troops were quickly positioned within the Crater. Among the dead bodies and the flies that already swarmed about them in the afternoon sun, the soldiers took up firing positions against the Union lines. They dug a firing shelf into the wall of the Crater facing the Yankees and opened up, determined to prove that the breach blown into their line had been strictly temporary.

"As the dust and smoke cleared away," Captain Featherston recalled forty-two years later, "the firing seemed to lull, but there was no entire cessation of firing that evening. Indeed it was continued for months by the sharpshooters."[3]

Throughout the afternoon, Ambrose Burnside received grim reports from the Crater. General Potter reported at 2:30 that his Second Division had been reduced to a mere shell. More than half the division's regiments had been captured. Ledlie and Ferrero withheld reporting on the condition of their divisions, partly because their units were too disordered for subordinates to make cogent reports to them and partly because the two generals were simply too stunned to report. When General Ord requested Burnside to relieve his battered XVIII Corps (actually a division of X Corps, attached to it), Burnside could do nothing but lamely reply: "We are so situated as to render it almost impossible to relieve your divisions to-night. Hope to be able to make a better report to-morrow night."[4] As it turned out, there was enough left of Willcox's division to fill the Union trenches left empty by the withdrawal of Ord, so Burnside did not have to make a humiliating appeal to Meade to order the relief of the entire IX Corps.

That was small enough comfort. But even as the magnitude of the defeat was brought home to Ambrose Burnside, General Meade remained remarkably ignorant. At 5:00 p.m. he prudently ordered precautions to be taken against a general Confederate counteroffensive:

Major-General WARREN:
Signal officers report the enemy returning rapidly from the north side of the James. Every preparation should be made to restrengthen the line of works where any obstacles have to-day been removed. The lines should be held strongly with infantry and artillery, posted wherever practicable; available reserves held in hand ready for movement in case it becomes necessary. I anticipate offensive movement on the part of the enemy, and expect it will be by a movable column turning our left and threatening our rear. Major-General Hancock will, to-night, resume his former position, and General Ord his also.[5]

Yet little less than three hours later, he sent this message to Burnside:

HEADQUARTERS ARMY OF THE POTOMAC,
July 30, 1864—7.40 p.m.

Major-General BURNSIDE,
Commanding Ninth Corps:

The major-general commanding desires to know whether you still hold the crater, and, if so, whether you will be able to withdraw your troops from it safely to-night, and also to bring off the wounded. The commanding general wishes to know how many wounded are probably lying there. It will be recollected that on a former occasion General Beauregard declined to enter into any arrangement for the succor of the wounded and the burial of the dead lying under both fires, hence the necessity of immediate and active efforts for their removal in the present case.

A. A. HUMPHREYS,
Major-General and Chief of Staff[6]

Did he still hold the Crater? Burnside fumed at the message, flung it down, and refused to answer it. Everyone, he believed, knew very well what had happened. Everyone had seen the rout earlier that afternoon and had by now heard the stories of horror. Could Meade be so ignorant or so heedless? Or—and this was far more likely, Burnside must have concluded—did George Meade know damn well that the Crater had been lost, and was he now deliberately taunting him?

The fact was that Meade did not know. Nor did he make any further effort to find out that night, except to send another dispatch to Burnside—which Burnside also ignored:

HEADQUARTERS ARMY OF THE POTOMAC,
July 30, 1864—10.35 p.m.

Major-General BURNSIDE,
Commanding Ninth Corps:

The major-general commanding desires to know whether you have any wounded left on the field, and directs me to say that he is awaiting your reply to the dispatch of 7.40 p.m.

A. A. HUMPHREYS,
Major-General and Chief of Staff[7]

Apparently, Meade's ignorance of the fate of IX Corps and the Crater did not prevent his going to sleep sometime after midnight, without having had a reply to his questions, including those concerning the welfare of the wounded.

To his Pennsylvania audience, Featherston explained that, "After dark[,] tools were brought, with which we reconstructed the wrecked fort. In doing this we buried the dead down in the fort by covering them with earth. The fire of the enemy was entirely too severe to carry them out. We were therefore forced to stand on them and defend our position, while we remained in the fort, which was until the following Monday night." One Confederate casualty was given special treatment, however. "As we went over the embankment into the fort," Captain Featherston recalled, "one of my sergeants, Andrew McWilliams, a brave fellow, was shot in the mouth, the ball did not cut his lips. It came out of the top of his head. He was evidently yelling with his mouth wide open. He fell on top of the embankment with his head hanging in the fort. We pulled him down in the fort and that night carried him out and buried him."[8]

The ongoing firefight not only kept the Confederates from hauling the dead out of the Crater, it prevented the Union from collecting its wounded. Burnside did not answer Meade's messages to him, but General Ord did reply to those Meade sent him:

HEADQUARTERS ARMY OF THE POTOMAC,
July 30, 1864–7.30 *p.m.*

General ORD:
Can you not get your wounded off after dark to-night? The last time we

had wounded left on the field Beauregard, on my application, refused to have a flag of truce to take off the wounded. It would, therefore, be useless to try it again.

GEO. G. MEADE,
Major-general

*   *   *

HEADQUARTERS EIGHTEENTH CORPS,
July 30, 1864

General MEADE:

The enemy have a terrible cross-fire at short range on the ground. It would be impossible. They have many wounded and dead there, and our trenches rake the place so that an offer might be mutually acceptable.

E. O. C. ORD,
Major-general

*   *   *

HEADQUARTERS ARMY OF THE POTOMAC,
July 30, 1864–8 *p.m.*

Major-general ORD:

Can you not give me an estimate through your medical director of the number of wounded; also the killed to-day in your corps? I want to make a consolidated estimate for General Grant.

GEO. G. MEADE,
Major-General

*   *   *

HEADQUARTERS EIGHTEENTH ARMY CORPS,

July 30, 1864

General MEADE:

The medical director reports 157 wounded sent to hospital. As many more were wounded or fell into hands of enemy, when cross-fire made them jump into enemy's trench to avoid it. This in Turner's division, which agrees with approximate estimate of Generals Turner, 350, and Ames 20 killed, wounded, and missing. Carr's loss will not exceed 30 I hope.

E. O. C. ORD,

Major-General[9]

Thus, except for those taken prisoner, most of the non-ambulatory Union wounded remained on the field through the day and night of July 30 and would do so through all of July 31.

The night of July 30/31, the Confederates made repairs to the ruins of Elliott's Salient. Featherston's men "unearthed numbers of confederate soldiers who were killed and buried by the explosion. I remember in one place there were eight poor fellows lying side by side with their coats under their head. They seemed never to have moved after the explosion."[10]

That night we slept in the fort, over those who slept "the sleep that knows no waking," and with the living that slept that sleep caused by exhaustion. We could hear them crying for relief, but the firing was so severe that none dared go to them either by day or night.[11]

Gouverneur K. Warren also sent Meade's chief of staff an urgent message about the wounded:

HEADQUARTERS FIFTH ARMY CORPS,

July 31, 1864

Major-General HUMPHREYS:

Our helpless wounded are still lying close to the enemy's line and they give them no help. There is no firing going on. Our men and the enemy are standing up on the parapets. They could help them if they would. The wounded seem to be mostly colored men who are writhing with their wounds in this almost insufferable sun, and I think the neglect of them must be intentional. I think we should open fire upon the enemy if he refuses to let us go and take care of these men.[12]

Warren took pains to note that the wounded were "mostly colored men," pointing out that it appeared to him "the neglect of them must be intentional." Was Warren aware that Meade had, at the last minute, barred the use of the "colored troops" of the Fourth Division in the initial assault against the Confederate line, lest their sacrifice in battle suggest that black lives were valued less than white? If so, was his observation concerning the black wounded intended to shame Meade into urgent action? Whatever motivated Warren's remarks, his message elicited the following from Humphreys:

HEADQUARTERS ARMY OF THE POTOMAC,

July 31, 1864—3.45 *p.m.*

Major-General WARREN,

Commanding Fifth Corps:

Your dispatch relative to the wounded lying close to the enemy's line is received. A communication to General Lee upon the subject of the wounded has been made by the major-general commanding, and an informal request concerning them authorized to be made of the immediate commander of the troops by the officer carrying the communication. As yet no reply has been received.[13]

On July 31, Lieutenant Colonel C. B. Comstock, General Grant's aide-de-camp, became sufficiently concerned about the wounded to send a dispatch to General Meade:

> I have been on Burnside's front to-day, and am told that among the large number of our men now lying around the crater some are still alive. As General Grant is now absent at Fort Monroe I am unable to report the fact to him without delay.[14]

Meade replied:

> HEADQUARTERS ARMY OF THE POTOMAC,
> *July* 31, 1864–5.30 *p.m.*
>
> Lieutenant-Colonel COMSTOCK:
>
> General Grant, to whom the fact of wounded being left between our lines was communicated last night, authorized my asking to remove them under flag of truce. General Burnside was authorized this morning to endeavor to make an informal arrangement for the withdrawal of the wounded, which, if unsuccessful, he was furnished with a letter from myself to General Lee asking the privilege. No report has been received from General Burnside.[15]

Read closely and in context, Meade's reply is nothing short of appalling. During the night of July 30, Meade had reported to Grant on the situation of the wounded. The commanding general authorized him to solicit Robert E. Lee for a truce in order to remove the wounded. On July 31—we don't know at what time exactly—Burnside sent the following message to Meade:

> GENERAL: I have the honor to request that a flag of truce be sent out for the purpose of making arrangements for assisting the wounded and burying the dead left on the field of battle. The number of the wounded left between the lines and beyond the first lines of the enemy has been exaggerated by rumor. They are not believed to amount to over 100 in all. Of these there are but few between the lines, the greater part being beyond the first line of the enemy's works.

I have the honor to be, general, very respectfully, your obedient servant,

> A. E. BURNSIDE,
> *Major-General, Commanding*[16]

Meade's assistant adjutant-general replied:

> Your communication of this date, respecting the wounded and dead left on the field in the engagement of yesterday, has been received and laid before the commanding general, and I have the honor herewith to transmit a letter addressed to General R. E. Lee, commanding Army of Northern Virginia, asking for a cessation of hostilities sufficiently long to enable us to bring off our wounded and dead, which you are desired to send to the enemy's lines, and you are authorized to instruct the officer who takes the flag to say to the officer who receives it that the object of the letter is simply to effect the removal of the dead and wounded, and that if an informal arrangement for this purpose can be entered into it will not be necessary to forward the communication to General Lee.[17]

Instead of immediately acting on Grant's authorization to seek a truce from Lee, Meade (through his assistant adjutant) told Burnside to try to make an informal arrangement for the removal of the dead and wounded. Apparently puzzled by this instruction, Burnside sought clarification:

> HEADQUARTERS NINTH ARMY CORPS,
> *July* 31, 1864
>
> Major-General HUMPHREYS:
> The commanding general desires to know if he is to understand the letter to General Lee is to be forwarded sealed.
>
> A. E. BURNSIDE,
> *Major-General*[18]

The assistant adjutant-general replied:

> I am instructed by the commanding general to say that the letter to General Lee is to be forwarded sealed if it is found necessary to send it. In the letter transmitting it to you you were informed of the purport of the letter, and it was stated that it would not be necessary for it to go to General Lee if the officer taking it to the enemy's lines could make an informal arrangement with the officer receiving it for the recovery of our wounded and dead.[19]

Why did Meade consume precious time with this extra step? The only possible reason was his understanding that to request from the enemy commanding general an overall truce would be to admit abject defeat—nothing less than the defeat of the Army of the Potomac by the Army of Northern Virginia. Meade vastly preferred to allow Burnside to admit the defeat of no more than his IX Corps, and he was willing to delay giving aid and succor to the wounded in order to bring this about.

Pursuant to Meade's instructions, Burnside sent one of his staff, under a white flag, to arrange a local truce. "About noon or a little after," Captain Featherston narrated to his Pennsylvania audience, "there went up a flag of truce immediately in our front."

> The flag was a white piece of cloth about a yard square on a new staff. General Saunders ordered the sharpshooters to cease firing. Then a Federal soldier with a clean, white shirt and blue pants, jumped on top of their works holding the flag and was promptly followed by two elegantly uniformed officers. General Saunders asked those of us near him iof we had a white handkerchief. All replied, "No." A private soldier nearby said to the men around him, "Boys, some of you take off your shirt and hand it to the General," to which another replied: "Never do that; they will think we have hoisted the black flag" [traditional signal of "no quarter"].[20]

General Saunders "finally got a handkerchief, which, though not altogether suitable for a drawing room," he "tied to the ramrod of a musket"
and gave to his assistant adjutant general, Captain George Clark, who,
with another man, "went forward to meet the Federal flag."[21] The
meeting took place halfway between the lines, and Clark received Burnside's informal request for a truce. Burnside reported the result to
Meade's chief of staff at 6:00 p.m., July 31:

> I sent one of my staff to endeavor to make the informal arrangement in
> regard to relieving the wounded, and if not made to forward the commu-
> nication to General Lee. He was unable to effect any arrangement beyond
> supplying water and whisky to the wounded between the lines, and
> passing whisky into our wounded in their lines. They declined to receive
> the communication [the letter to Lee] until their general officer could be
> consulted. Pending the answer a cessation of hostilities on our front took
> place for about three hours, when the enemy insisted on resuming firing
> and the flag ceased. There are not more than twenty wounded between
> the lines. The enemy are to inform us when they have permission to renew
> the flag and receive the communication.
>
> A. E. BURNSIDE,
> *Major-General*[22]

At 6:38, Burnside sent another communication to Meade's chief of
staff:

> The enemy informed us of their willingness to receive the communica-
> tion, which was accordingly delivered to one of their company officers,
> the highest officer seen by Major Lydig, who had charge of the [truce]
> flag. They said it would be impossible to say when an answer would be
> given us. The flag still continues.[23]

Meade's "communication" to Lee was as follows:

HEADQUARTERS ARMY OF THE POTOMAC,

July 31, 1864

General R. E. LEE,

Commanding Army of Northern Virginia:

I have the honor to request a cessation of hostilities at such time as you may indicate, sufficiently long to enable me to recover our wounded and dead in the engagement of yesterday, now lying between the lines of the two armies. I make this application that the sufferings of our wounded may be relieved and that the dead may be buried.

Very respectfully,

GEO. G. MEADE,

Major-General, Commanding[24]

Pending Lee's reply, Meade instructed Burnside to suspend the de facto truce immediately:

HEADQUARTERS ARMY OF THE POTOMAC,

July 31, 1864–7 *p.m.*

General BURNSIDE:

The commanding general directs that you at once withdraw the flag of truce. When the answer to the communication addressed to General Lee is ready it can then be received under a flag. The commanding general did not anticipate that the flag would be kept out longer than might be necessary to effect an arrangement for the recovery of the wounded or to deliver the letter for General Lee to the officer sent to receive it.

S. WILLIAMS,

Assistant Adjutant-General[25]

Lee received the letter, but was more concerned with preserving his chain of command than he was with providing immediate relief for the wounded. P. G. T. Beauregard was the commander in charge of the sector that included the Crater; Lee therefore forwarded Meade's letter to him.

The forwarded document did not reach Beauregard until late in the afternoon of July 31, so late that he decided there was not enough time for a truce long enough to allow for the recovery of the wounded and the burial of the dead before dark, and he was unwilling to split the truce across two days. The truce, therefore, would have to wait until August 1. In a letter dated 10:00 a.m. on that day, Meade reported to General Grant: "In reply to my letter to General Lee, I received this morning about 6 o'clock a letter from General Beauregard, consenting to a truce from 5 [a.m.] to 9 [a.m.], for the purpose of burying the dead and removing the wounded."[26]

At 11:30 in the morning, Burnside reported to Meade's assistant adjutant-general that "About 220 dead were found between the lines and are now buried. About twenty wounded were found and brought in. These men were mostly colored troops."[27]

In truth, two days' exposure to the midsummer sun had turned all the dead a livid black, so that the only visible difference between white soldier and "colored soldier" was the texture of the hair. The uniformly black bodies were bloated with the gases of death. Maggots already crawled about them. Most of the corpses were so badly shot up that it would have required detailed autopsies to distinguish ante-mortem from post-mortem wounds. But, of course, there would be no autopsies, and the burials were in mass graves between the lines. "I understand," Burnside wrote to Meade's assistant adjutant, "that as the trenches for burial of the dead were not finished at 9 o'clock, the truce was informally continued till [all] the dead could be buried."[28]

Union and Confederate soldiers worked side by side to dig the burial trenches, into which, Featherston recalled, the "dead were thrown . . . indiscriminately three bodies deep." During the extended truce, soldiers in blue and soldiers in gray traded with one another such small luxuries as coffee and tobacco. Featherston called it "one of the grandest and most impressive sights [he] ever saw. Where not a man could be seen a few minutes before, the two armies arose up out of the ground, and the face of the earth seemed to be peopled with men. It seemed an illustration of Cadmus sowing the dragon's teeth. Both sides came over their works, and meeting in the

Union officers pose outside of an Army of the Potomac headquarters building at City Point, Virginia. (Library of Congress)

center, mingled, chatted and exchanged courtesies, as though they had not sought in desperate effort to take each other's lives but an hour before."[29]

It was reported that, in the midst of the truce, one of the Confederates impulsively leaped up on the parapet and shouted "Let's all go home!"[30] By 11 that morning, however, the dead were all buried, and, even before Burnside had sent off his latest dispatch to Meade's headquarters, the firing resumed on both sides. Nurses in a Petersburg hospital reported that wounded Confederates refused to be parted from their muskets, the locks of which were snarled with the blood- and gore-matted hair of Yankees they had brained at the Crater. The wounded men proudly exhibited the weapons to any and all who cared to examine them.

For the dead—and for the severely wounded returned to Union lines— the war was over. For those taken prisoner, the shooting had ended, but the war dragged on.

The fate of a POW during the closing years of the Civil War was grim for Confederates as well as Union men. The black prisoners who had not been murdered were mostly put to work on various fatigue duties. Both black and white prisoners went a full day after capture with neither food nor water. They were held in an open field, without shelter or even blankets. On the Sunday following the battle, the prisoners were marched through the streets of Petersburg, arranged in a formation their captors had intended as a humiliation before the city's jeering citizens. Four Union officers, marching abreast, led the way. Behind them were four black soldiers, who were followed by four whites, then four more blacks, and so on. This was the shame of racial equality.

After plodding through Petersburg, the prisoners were bivouacked on an island in the Appomattox River. Although, once again, they were afforded neither shelter nor blankets, they were at last issued a slim ration of bacon, raw, and were allowed to drink their fill of river water. On Monday, officers were loaded into cattle cars bound for a prison camp at Columbia, South Carolina. Enlisted men were sent, also by rail, to a Danville, Virginia, camp. Those men too badly wounded to be transported were hospitalized in Petersburg. The Confederate surgeon in charge, Dr. John Claiborne, enlisted the aid of five Union surgeons (captured in various earlier battles) to attend to the wounded. He noted that the surgeons attended immediately and dutifully to the white wounded, but refused to treat the black troops. The day after the Crater wounded were brought in, Dr. Claiborne was summoned to an estate adjacent to the hospital. Its owner complained that some 150 wounded black soldiers had been unceremoniously dumped on his grounds. Many had been stripped of their uniforms. Claiborne called on the Federal surgeons to treat the men, and when they again refused, he threatened to pack them off to a POW camp. That at last induced them to minister to the "colored troops."

To army Chief of Staff Henry Wager Halleck, Ulysses S. Grant wrote that the failed assault on the Petersburg line "was the saddest affair I have witnessed in this war."[31] For more public consumption, in his *Personal Memoirs*, Grant pronounced "the effort . . . a stupendous failure." In the immediate aftermath of the assault, on the evenings of July 31, August 1, and August 2, commanders submitted their routine daily reports to General Meade. Typical of these was General Warren's from 9:15 p.m., August 2: "I have the honor to report that nothing of importance has occurred in my front to-day."[32]

But just fifteen minutes earlier, Brigadier General Edward O. C. Ord had sent a dispatch to Brigadier General Hiram Burnham, commanding a division of his XVIII Corps:

> GENERAL: [Confederate] deserters in to-day and this p.m. state rumors of a mine existing among their men, and they give some details of the point mined, supposed to be the work [redoubt] near the Hare house on General Turner's late front. The last deserter said it would be fired to-morrow a.m., though he said similar reports were circulated yesterday. The last deserter also states that two brigades arrived this evening and are posted in or near the railroad (in front of the left of your line) and under the cliffs this side of Petersburg. It may be well to have your men ready for emergencies. . . .[33]

At 11:40, Ord reported to Meade: "Deserters still report a mine in my front soon to be fired."[34] The Confederates defending Petersburg had been busy tunneling under the Union lines and were about to blast a hole in them.

Butcher's Bill

Rumors of a Confederate mine reached Union commanders along the Petersburg line on August 2. Unlike many wartime rumors, these were quite true.

Captain Hugh Douglas, the Confederate officer who had been in charge of the countermining operations that missed intercepting the Pleasants mine by perhaps no more than five feet, had just finished digging a mine some six hundred yards from the Crater. Its explosive-packed gallery was in front of Gracie's Salient, a short distance to the right of Burnside's position, in the territory covered by Ord's XVIII Corps. Douglas intended to spring his mine immediately after the August 1 truce. No assault was planned to follow the detonation, but the Confederate commanders figured that the explosion itself would not only be destructive, but demoralizing, especially right after the burial of the dead. It would also deliver a satisfying measure of retribution.

At the moment the truce was concluded, 11:30 a.m., Douglas put the match to four individual runs of safety fuse. Twenty minutes, thirty— then forty-five minutes elapsed.

No explosion.

An enlisted man named Black volunteered to enter the Confederate shaft and discovered that three of the four fuses were dead, the fourth sputtering toward extinction.

Instead of trying again that afternoon, Douglas decided to extend his mine. He was now worried that he had stopped short of the Union line. When this new digging was completed, his men moved eight large barrels of powder into two magazines at the end of the extended shaft. At 6:30 p.m. on August 5, Major General A. A. Humphreys, George Meade's chief of staff, telegraphed Ambrose Burnside: "Is that firing of artillery and musketry on your front? What is it?" Burnside returned an immediate reply: "Part of it is. I have sent out to see. We heard no musketry here."[1] An hour and fifteen minutes later, Burnside sent this to Humphreys:

> The enemy exploded a mine in front of General Ames' division. The understanding is the mine exploded short and did not reach our works or do any damage. Firing started at once and extended to our First Division front, but amounted to very little.[2]

There was the sound of a muffled explosion, accompanied by a dirt spout about forty yards in front of Ord's left. Although unimpressive, it had been sufficient to prompt from Ord a fusillade of artillery fire, which was answered by the Confederates. As Burnside reported, the mine had done little or no damage, but Ord reported to Humphreys (in a message Meade's headquarters received at 8:10 p.m.) that "Colonel [Griffin] Stedman [had been] dangerously wounded by canister-shot."[3] When he later succumbed to his wounds, his fellow officers christened one of the line's forts after him.

Either just before or after the Confederates detonated their anticlimactic mine, Burnside sent a message to Seth Williams, Meade's assistant adjutant general. Whether he transmitted it on his own initiative or in response to a query from Meade is not known:

> GENERAL: I have the honor to submit, for the information of the general commanding, the following statement in regard to the [Pleasants] mine: The main gallery is uninjured clear up to the tamping, which extends back thirty-five feet from the end of the gallery. Side galleries

Fort Stedman, one of many strong points in the Union's siege line, was named after Colonel Griffin Stedman, a Union officer mortally wounded by a canister round in an artillery attack that followed the fizzled detonation of a Confederate mine before the Union line at Petersburg. On March 25, 1865, the Confederates would storm and briefly hold Fort Stedman in their last attempt to break the Petersburg siege. (Library of Congress)

could be started from a point twenty-five feet this side of the tamping, running off diagonally to the enemy's works on either side of the old crater. If the commanding general desires to make use of mining in connection with the operations of the army against Petersburg, this work could be done in a few days.[4]

If it seems rather more than incredible that Ambrose Burnside—or anyone else—was seriously contemplating reusing the mine or detonating another, the Confederates were, in fact, expecting just that. General Beauregard or one of his subordinates had assigned Lieutenant Colonel William Blackford to oversee the digging of numerous countermines to locate the original Pleasants shaft and any new Union excavations. After weeks of tunneling, Blackford's men finally discovered the main Union shaft.

The cost of these arduous explorations had been twofold. The men stationed near the Crater so feared a new tunnel that they panicked every time they heard the subterranean sound of picks and shovels. Each time the alarm was sounded, however, the source of the noise turned out to be Blackford's own counterminers.

The second cost was more grim. As Captain Featherston had remarked to his Pottsville audience in 1906, sustained Union fire made it impossible to haul out the dead from the Crater. Instead, they were buried where they lay, in places eight bodies deep. The counterminers soon discovered that the gases of decomposition from these bodies permeated the ground all around the Crater. Every shaft they dug was quickly overwhelmed by the terrible stench of decay, mixed with the trapped sulfurous vapors that had resulted from the imperfect combustion of tons of black powder. The counterminers did their best to improvise ventilation ducts, but the work must have been singularly hellish nevertheless.

It was the kind of labor that magnified the horror of the Battle of the Crater far beyond what the casualty figures alone implied. Of some fifteen thousand Union troops either directly engaged in the assaults on the Crater or deployed along the Union lines near the area of the assault, 504 had been killed or fatally wounded; 1,881 were non-fatally wounded; 1,413 captured. Total Union casualties, therefore, were 3,798, of whom 3,475 were from Burnside's IX Corps and 323 from X Corps (attached to Ord's XVIII Corps). Fourth Division of IX Corps, the "colored troops" who had prepared to make the initial assault only to be thrown into the fray after the battle had turned hopeless, sustained the greatest losses: 1,327 men. Of these, 209 were listed as killed in combat, and 697 as wounded. The remaining 421 were listed as "missing." Some were probably killed in the Crater, their bodies never identified, and the Confederates admitted to holding 150 of them prisoner. The remainder, perhaps from 150 to 200, were murdered after they had been taken prisoner. In some units, losses were especially devastating. Colonel Henry Thomas's Second Brigade, Fourth Division, suffered 40 percent casualties.

Although officers at the highest levels—down to the division commanders—stayed out of the Crater, brigade, regiment, and company commanders were in the thick of the fighting and paid a heavy price. The 28th U.S. Colored Troops, for example, lost seven of its eleven officers, the 23rd lost eleven of eighteen. Of the 58th Massachusetts, just three officers and twenty-five enlisted soldiers returned to Union lines. The others were killed, wounded, or captured.[5]

Confederate losses, in total, were about half those of the Union. Approximately three hundred men were killed in the explosion of the mine. Elliott's Brigade, which had been stationed directly over the site of the explosion, suffered most of these initial losses, and by the end of the battle counted 677 killed or wounded. The Virginia brigade of David Weisiger lost 258 men, killed or wounded, including Weisiger himself, who incurred a wound he believed would kill him. (It did not.) Some Confederate regiments were decimated: seventy-six of 184 men in the 61st Virginia were killed or wounded, as were eighty-six out of ninety-six men in the 6th Virginia. The commanding officers of the 6th Virginia, the 14th Alabama, and the 64th Georgia were killed.[6]

The U.S. Army Court of Inquiry instigated by George Gordon Meade and authorized by Abraham Lincoln, which convened for the first time on August 6, 1864, inflicted its own casualties among the officer ranks, finding five officers "'answerable for the want of success' which should have resulted" from the assault on the Crater:

I. Maj. Gen. A. E. Burnside, U.S. Volunteers, he having failed to obey the orders of the commanding general.

1. In not giving such formation to his assaulting column as to insure a reasonable prospect of success.

2. In not preparing his parapets and abatis for the passage of the columns of assault.

3. In not employing engineer officers, who reported to him, to lead the assaulting columns with working parties, and not causing to be

provided proper materials necessary for crowning the crest [Cemetery Hill] when the assaulting columns should arrive there.

4. In neglecting to execute Major-General Meade's orders respecting the prompt advance of General Ledlie's troops from the crater to the crest; or, in default of accomplishing that, not causing those troops to fall back and give place to other troops more willing and equal to the task, instead of delaying until the opportunity passed away, thus affording time for the enemy to recover from his surprise, concentrate his fire, and bring his troops to operate against the Union troops assembled uselessly in the crater.[7]

The Court of Inquiry was careful to avoid accusing Burnside of outright insubordination or willful dereliction of duty: "Notwithstanding the failure to comply with orders and to apply proper military principles ascribed to General Burnside, the Court is satisfied he believed that the measures taken by him would insure success."[8] Yet, in thus limiting its judgment against him, so that he did not appear deliberately insubordinate, the Court in effect labeled Ambrose Burnside incompetent.

Second named was Brigadier General James H. Ledlie—

he having failed to push forward his division promptly according to orders and thereby blocking up the avenue which was designed for the passage of troops ordered to follow and support his in the assault. It is in evidence that no commander reported to General Burnside that his troops could not be got forward, which the Court regards as a neglect of duty on the part of General Ledlie, inasmuch as a timely report of the misbehavior might have enabled General Burnside, commanding the assault, to have made other arrangements for prosecuting it before it became too late. Instead of being with his division during this difficulty in the crater, and by his personal efforts endeavoring to lead his troops forward, he was most of the time in a bomb-proof ten rods in rear of the main line of the Ninth Corps works, where it was impossible for him to see anything of the movement of troops that was going on.[9]

This was the most stinging rebuke, inasmuch as it labeled Ledlie a coward without calling him one. Although he did not avoid censure, General Ledlie did avoid testifying. Pleading illness, he obtained an extended leave of absence that kept him out of the proceedings.

The Court judged Edward Ferrero culpable on three counts:

1. For not having all his troops formed ready for the attack at the prescribed time.

2. Not going forward with them to the attack.

3. Being in a bomb-proof habitually, where he could not see the operation of his troops, showing by his own order issued while there that he did not know the position of two brigades of his division or whether they had taken Cemetery Hill or not.[10]

Colonel Zenas R. Bliss, 7th Rhode Island Volunteers, "commanding First Brigade, Second Division, Ninth Corps," was censured for having "remained behind with the only regiment of his brigade which did not go forward according to the orders and occupied a position where he could not properly command a brigade which formed a portion of an assaulting column, and where he could not see what was going on."[11]

Finally, Brigadier General Orlando B. Willcox was condemned because "the Court [was] not satisfied that [his] division made efforts commensurate with the occasion to carry out General Burnside's order to advance to Cemetery Hill, and they think that more energy might have been exercised by Brigadier-General Willcox to cause his troops to go forward to that point."[12]

The Court of Inquiry demurred to the extent that it did not intend "to convey the impression that there was any disinclination on the part of the commanders of the supports to heartily co-operate in the attack on the 30th of July," but it concluded with the opinion "that explicit orders should have been given assigning one officer to the command of all the troops intended to engage in the assault when the commanding general was not present in person to witness the operations."[13] This was, in effect, another dig at Burnside, as the responsible officer.

The Court of Inquiry delivered its findings on September 9, 1864. Ambrose Burnside was not present to hear them. He had begun a twenty-day furlough the day after his testimony was concluded on August 12. Shortly before his leave was due to expire, Burnside contacted Grant, asking him where he should await his orders. Grant responded that he should not return to IX Corps at present, because the Court of Inquiry had found him chiefly responsible for the Crater catastrophe. Weeks passed before, at the end of September, Grant ordered Burnside to dissolve his staff, returning the staff officers to duty with the corps.

The intent of this message was unmistakable. Grant was taking Burnside out of the war. Yet, characteristically, Burnside refused to give up. In November, he wrote to Grant seeking permission to visit the army. The commanding general replied with frigid formality: "You are authorized to visit headquarters."[14] When Burnside arrived at City Point, where Grant was still directing the siege of Petersburg, then in its sixth month, the commanding general was absent, having left to visit his wife in New Jersey. Burnside continued on to Washington, where he called on Abraham Lincoln to complain to him that the Court of Inquiry's verdict, combined with his enforced inactivity, made him uneasy about continuing to draw an army salary. He asked the president to accept his immediate resignation. Lincoln gently refused, so that Ambrose Burnside was still an army officer when, on December 15, 1864, Henry Anthony, senator from Rhode Island and a personal friend of Burnside's, succeeded in his motion that the long-established Joint Committee on the Conduct of the War formally investigate the Battle of the Crater.

During the Christmas recess, committee members traveled to the Petersburg front to take testimony from Meade, Grant, James Duane, and others. Later, after Congress reconvened, they heard testimony from Pleasants and from Brigadier General John W. Turner. Turner had commanded the Second Division of X Corps and had the distinction of being

This stereograph from June 1864 shows a captured Confederate encampment near the Petersburg siege line. (Library of Congress)

the only divisional commander who was actually present at the Crater. Despite their being principals in the Crater operations, the army's Court of Inquiry had heard testimony from neither of these officers.

Early in February 1865, the Joint Committee published its findings. They differed dramatically from those of the Court of Inquiry. The committee concluded that the assault on the Crater had failed because General George Gordon Meade had wrecked Burnside's plan. Had Meade allowed Ferrero's division to lead the assault—as Burnside had planned, with a principal thrust against Cemetery Hill and simultaneous flanking movements to suppress enemy flanking fire—the assault most likely would have been successful. Thus the Joint Committee entirely shifted blame for the failure of the Crater from Burnside to Meade—although it did censure Burnside for leaving to chance the choice of the division that finally led the assault.

Just before the Joint Committee published its findings, Burnside again appealed to Grant for his next assignment. To Burnside, Grant replied bluntly that he had no assignment to offer. To Meade, Grant proposed bringing Burnside before a court-martial as the most efficient way of clearing Meade's name.

Grant's eagerness to side with the commander of the Army of the Potomac seems to have distorted his own perception of the battle. To Meade, he remarked that the Joint Committee must have been guided by "General Burnside's evidence," and Burnside (Grant continued) "to draw it mildly, . . . has forgotten some of the facts." Yet, to the Joint Committee, Grant himself had plainly testified that "General Burnside wanted to put his colored division in front, and if he had done so I believe it would have been a success." Be this as it may, Meade demurred at the prospect of a court-martial and managed to talk Grant out of convening one. Meade asked only that the Court of Inquiry do what the Joint Committee had done: publish its findings. He believed that this would vindicate him.[15]

In the end, neither Burnside nor Meade was truly vindicated—or deserved to be. Yet Burnside's military career was over, whereas Meade continued to command the Army of the Potomac and enjoyed the honor of accompanying Grant when Lee surrendered at Appomattox. After the war, as commander of the Third Military District, encompassing Alabama, Georgia, and Florida, Meade, whose prickly personality was infamous, nevertheless earned southern respect and even a degree of gratitude for his firm fairness as a military governor. As for Burnside, although his military career was at an end, he went on to work successfully as a railroad executive and then served as governor of Rhode Island from 1866 to 1869 and as a United States senator from 1874 until his death in 1881.

Zenas R. Bliss, who had earned a Medal of Honor for valor at Fredericksburg, served through the rest of the war after the Crater as a colonel whereas most of his colleagues were liberally accorded brevet promotion to brigadier general. He reverted after the war to the regular army rank of major and remained in the army until 1897, when he retired as a major general.

Orlando Bolivar Willcox continued in divisional command, ending the war in North Carolina and receiving a brevet to major general in the regular army. He served as commander of the Department of Arizona after the war and retired in 1887 at his permanent rank of brigadier general.

Edward Ferrero retained divisional command until he mustered out of the army on August 24, 1865. Returning to New York City, he opened a new dance academy in a ballroom called Apollo Hall, the ancestor of Harlem's celebrated Apollo Theater. In 1872, Ferrero moved from Apollo Hall to the ballroom of Tammany Hall, Democratic Party headquarters, and became a minor figure in New York Democratic politics. But, without question, his late nineteenth-century reputation had nothing to do either with politics or the Crater. It was founded on dance. He made a small fortune with his best-selling *The Art of Dancing Historically (Illustrated), to Which Is Added a Few Hints on Etiquette*, which remains in print today, and a much larger fortune with his dance academy, finally installed at the Lenox Lyceum. It made him the most famous and highly respected dance instructor in America.

As for James Ledlie, Grant directed Meade in December 1864 to relieve him of command, and on January 23, 1865, Ledlie formally resigned his commission. He once again took up his civilian career as a railway engineer and, in the employ of the Union Pacific, participated in the completion of the transcontinental railroad. The hard-drinking Ledlie died at age fifty in 1882.

Henry Pleasants was praised both by the Court of Inquiry and the Joint Committee of Congress for his leadership in planning and excavating the Petersburg mine. Immediately after the Crater battle, on August 1, 1864, Robert Potter recognized his achievement by promoting him to brigade command, and he was brevetted to brigadier on March 13, 1865, in part specifically for his service at Petersburg. After the war, he returned to Pottsville, Pennsylvania, as mining engineer for the Philadelphia and Reading Coal and Iron Company.

The name of one other man caught up in the epic of the Crater appears in no official military record. William Griffith owned the farm through which both the Union and Confederate entrenchment passed and on which the Petersburg mine exploded. He returned to his farm after the war. His house had been burned down. His pasture and fields were ruined. For a year, he was prevented from reclaiming most of his land while Lieutenant Colonel James Moore, U.S. Army, led crews in locating, exhuming, and reburying (in a newly established cemetery southeast of Petersburg) the bodies that had been deposited in mass graves. By the time Moore left, after the second anniversary of the battle, 669 bodies had been recovered. Each was reburied as an "Unknown Soldier," for none could be identified.

Given back his farm at last, Griffith did not return to farming. Instead, he fenced off the Crater, erected a kiosk beside it, marked out carriage and foot paths, and charged visitors 25 cents for the privilege of viewing the site of the explosion close up. After three years of this, Griffith plowed some of his proceeds into building the "Crater Saloon." He did not become wealthy, but he enjoyed a better living than he ever had as a farmer.

Because the Union failed to break through to Petersburg at the Battle of the Crater, the siege dragged on until the end of the war, culminating in the Battle of Five Forks (April 1, 1865) and the final assault on Petersburg (April 2), both of which historians generally count as part of the culminating Appomattox Campaign. Total casualties—blue and gray, killed, wounded, and captured—at the Battle of the Crater were about fifty-six hundred. That was modest compared with the casualty roll many of the war's major battles produced. In the course of the rest of the siege at Petersburg, an additional fifty-eight hundred men were killed, wounded, or captured. Had the Battle of the Crater ended the siege, these men would have been alive, unhurt, and free. Indeed, had the Union broken through to Petersburg, it is likely that Richmond would have fallen quickly afterward and the Army of Northern Virginia would have been forced into an immediate and unfavorable showdown or into fairly rapid starvation for want of supplies. In either case, taking Petersburg would have shortened the war—dramatically.

Just how dramatically is impossible to say. Yet we do know that most of the roughly 1,150,000 killed or wounded in the Civil War fell in seventy-six major battles between April 1861 and April 1865. As of the end of July 1864, when the Battle of the Crater was lost, eight of those seventy-six battles had yet to be fought, and the more than

150,000 men killed or wounded in them were still alive and whole. Whatever the numbers might be, one thing is certain: the butcher's bill tacked to the Union failure at the Battle of the Crater runs far longer than the immediate losses incurred in that single brief and terrible encounter.

Confederate captain William Gordon McCabe memorably called the Crater a "horrid pit," whose scenes were "such as might be fitly portrayed only by the pencil of Dante after he had trod 'nine-circled Hell.'"[16]

It was an apt description—of the Crater and also of war itself, which the Crater symbolized. For what is war (as one of its leading exponents so famously observed) but hell? War is the cauldron in which courage, cowardice, error, sacrifice, humility, arrogance, ignorance, ingenuity, endurance, exhaustion, humanity, and inhumanity are blended in fire to produce heroes, fools, knaves, and men broken or dead. The Crater was the crucible in which all of these attributes were assayed into their most elemental state, the irreducible state Nathan Bedford Forrest—the general William Tecumseh Sherman judged the most dangerous man in the Civil War—evoked when he offered this stark formula: "War means fighting, and fighting means killing."

The Crater was the very distillation of war—and that, surely, is one reason why this comparatively minor battle of brief duration, a "stupendous failure" of little tactical interest, still exerts such a powerful hold on the imagination and the emotions.

The horror of the "horrid pit" seems almost too obvious to point out. It was a place of pain and death and waste. On reflection, however, the sources of the horror run even deeper.

Henry Pleasants, a man suddenly bereaved by personal loss, sought oblivion (or was it salvation?) in war. At a particular moment in a particular corner of that war, he had an idea to end a siege and, perhaps, the war itself. Against ignorance, arrogance, and indifference, he managed to translate his idea into the physical reality of the longest mine in military history.

Ambrose Burnside, hitherto an earnest failure as a military leader, sought to convert the Pleasants mine into the great and decisive victory that had eluded him for so long. He formulated a plan to use black American soldiers in a perilous assault against an enemy dedicated to the enslavement of black Americans. As far as can be known from the written records left to us, Burnside's choice of these troops was pragmatic rather than moral. Because they were black, they had been used by their commanders as common laborers rather than as combat soldiers. They had been kept in the rear. Whereas their white comrades in arms had been physically and emotionally battered by some six weeks of continuous combat, the "colored troops" were fresh and full of fight. Yet even if Burnside's motives were pragmatic, the moral dimension was undeniably present, and the black Americans of Edward Ferrero's Fourth Division surely felt it. They themselves said it made them *men of war*, and anyone else, black or white, could clearly see the moral force of black men fighting against those who would deny them their freedom, their manhood, their humanity.

And yet Ulysses S. Grant and George Gordon Meade, two leading commanders in this war to restore union and end slavery, were somehow unable to see it.

Instead of appreciating the power of moral hope, Grant and Meade recognized only the hazard of moral liability. The black men might win their freedom. But they might also lose their lives. That the men of the Fourth Division were willing to post their lives as collateral against the winning of their freedom counted for nothing. For the white commanders were not willing to let them make this bargain. They were guilty of a cowardice no military tribunal could prosecute, a terrible absence of faith and of hope. And in this grievous lapse, a glorious victory was lost, cast away, with so many lives, into the horrid pit.

Appendix
Order of Battle at the Battle of the Crater

UNITED STATES ARMY
Lieutenant General Ulysses S. Grant, Commander-In-Chief

ARMY OF THE POTOMAC
Major General George Gordon Meade, Commanding
Chief of Artillery: Brigadier General Henry J. Hunt
Chief Engineer: Major James C. Duane
Chief of Staff: Andrew A. Humphreys

IX ARMY CORPS
Major General Ambrose E. Burnside, Commanding
Aide-de-Camp, Lieutenant Colonel James L. Van Buren
Assistant Inspector General, Lieutenant Colonel Charles G. Loring
Chief of Staff, Brigadier General Julius White

FIRST DIVISION
Brigadier General James H. Ledlie
    First Brigade: Brigadier General William Francis Bartlett (P); Lieutenant Colonel Joseph H. Barnes
        21st Massachusetts
        29th Massachusetts
        56th Massachusetts
        57th Massachusetts
        59th Massachusetts
        100th Pennsylvania

    Second Brigade: Colonel Elisha G. Marshall (P); Lieutenant Colonel Gilbert P. Robinson
        3rd Maryland (battalion)

14th New York Heavy Artillery
179th New York
2nd Pennsylvania Provisional Heavy Artillery (112th Pennsylvania Regiment)
Acting Engineers: 35th Massachusetts

SECOND DIVISION
Brigadier General Robert B. Potter
First Brigade: Colonel Zenas R. Bliss
36th Massachusetts
58th Massachusetts
2nd New York Mounted Rifles (dismounted)
51st New York
45th Pennsylvania
48th Pennsylvania
4th Rhode Island

Second Brigade: Brigadier General Simon G. Griffin
31st Maine
32nd Maine
2nd Maryland
6th New Hampshire
9th New Hampshire
11th New Hampshire
17th Vermont
Acting Engineers: 7th Rhode Island

THIRD DIVISION
Brigadier General Orlando B. Willcox
First Brigade: Brigadier General John Hartranft
8th Michigan
27th Michigan
109th New York
13th Ohio Cavalry (dismounted)
51st Pennsylvania
37th Wisconsin
38th Wisconsin (5 companies)
Second Brigade: Colonel William Humphrey
1st Michigan Sharpshooters
2nd Michigan
20th Michigan
24th New York Cavalry (dismounted)
46th New York
60th Ohio
50th Pennsylvania
Acting Engineers: 17th Michigan

FOURTH DIVISION
Brigadier General Edward Ferrero
   First Brigade: Lieutenant Colonel Joshua K. Sigfried
      27th U.S.C.T.
      30th U.S.C.T.
      39th U.S.C.T.
      43rd U.S.C.T.

   Second Brigade: Colonel Henry Goddard Thomas
      19th U.S.C.T.
      23rd U.S.C.T.
      28th U.S.C.T.
      29th U.S.C.T.
      31st U.S.C.T.

   Artillery Brigade: Lieutenant Colonel J. Albert Monroe
      Maine Light, 2nd Battery
      Maine Light, 3rd Battery
      Maine Light, 7th Battery
      Massachusetts Light, 11th Battery
      Massachusetts Light, 14th Battery
      New York Light, 19th Battery
      New York Light, 27th Battery
      New York Light, 34th Battery
      Pennsylvania Light, Battery D
      Vermont Light, 3rd Battery
      Mortar Battery (2nd Penn. Prov. Heavy Artillery)

V CORPS ARTILLERY
   Colonel Charles S. Wainwright
      1st New York Light, Battery B
      1st New York Light, Battery E
      1st New York Light, Battery H
      5th United States, Battery D

VI CORPS ARTILLERY
   Captain William Hexamer
      Maine Light, 4th Battery
      New York Light, 3rd Battery

ARMY OF THE JAMES
   Major General Benjamin Butler, Commanding
      Siege Artillery: Colonel Henry L. Abbot
      1st Connecticut Heavy Artillery

XVIII ARMY CORPS
Major General Edward O. C. Ord, Commanding

X ARMY CORPS (attached to the XVIII Army Corps)
SECOND DIVISION
Brigadier General John W. Turner
First Brigade: Colonel N. Martin Curtis
3rd New York
112th New York
117th New York
142nd New York

Second Brigade: Lieutenant Colonel William B. Coan
47th New York
48th New York
76th Pennsylvania
97th Pennsylvania

Third Brigade: Colonel Louis Bell
13th Indiana (3 companies)
9th Maine
4th New Hampshire
115th New York
169th New York

CONFEDERATE FORCES
ARMY OF NORTHERN VIRGINIA
General Robert E. Lee, Commanding

III CORPS
Major General Ambrose P. Hill, Commanding

RICHARD H. ANDERSON'S DIVISION
Brigadier General William Mahone
Mahone's (Virginia) Brigade: Colonel David Weisiger (W),
Colonel George Thomas Rogers
6th Virginia
12th Virginia
16th Virginia
41st Virginia
61st Virginia

Wilcox (Alabama) Brigade: Colonel John C. C. Sanders
8th Alabama
9th Alabama

10th Alabama
11th Alabama
14th Alabama

Wright's (Georgia) Brigade: Lieutenant Colonel Matthew R. Hall
3rd Georgia
22nd Georgia
48th Georgia
64th Georgia

ARTILLERY, ARMY OF NORTHERN VIRGINIA
Brigadier General William N. Pendleton, Chief of Artillery

I CORPS
Lieutenant Colonel Frank Huger
Haskell's Battalion: Major John C. Haskell
Branch (North Carolina) Battery
Nelson (Virginia) Battery
13th Battalion Virginia Light Artillery: Major Wade Hampton Gibbs (W)
Company A, Otey Battery
Company B, Ringgold Battery
Company C, Davidson's Battery
Mortar battery (manned by men from Otey and Ringgold Batteries)

III CORPS
Colonel Reuben Lindsay Walker
Pegram's Battalion, Lieutenant Colonel William J. Pegram
Crenshaw's (Virginia) Battery
Letcher (Virginia) Light Artillery

DEPARTMENT OF NORTH CAROLINA AND SOUTHERN VIRGINIA
Lieutenant General Pierre G. T. Beauregard, Commanding

JOHNSON'S DIVISION
Major General Bushrod Rust Johnson
Ransom's (North Carolina) Brigade: Colonel Lee M. McAfee
24th North Carolina
25th North Carolina
35th North Carolina
49th North Carolina
56th North Carolina
Elliott's (South Carolina) Brigade: Brigadier General Stephen Elliott (W), Colonel Fitz
William McMaster
17th South Carolina
18th South Carolina

22nd South Carolina
23rd South Carolina
26th South Carolina

Wise's (Virginia) Brigade: Colonel J. Thomas Goode
26th Virginia
34th Virginia
46th Virginia
59th Virginia

HOKE'S DIVISION
Major General Robert F. Hoke
 Clingman's (North Carolina) Brigade: Brigadier General Thomas L. Clingman
  61st North Carolina
 Colquitt's (Georgia) Brigade (assigned to Johnson's Division)
  6th Georgia
  19th Georgia
  23rd Georgia
  27th Georgia
  28th Georgia

ARTILLERY, DEPARTMENT OF SOUTHERN VIRGINIA AND NORTH CAROLINA
Colonel Hilary Pollard Jones, Commanding
Branch's Battalion: Major James C. Coit
  Halifax (Virginia) Battery
  Petersburg (Virginia) Battery

P: became prisoner
W: wounded (survived)

Notes

Prologue; By Direction of the President

1. U.S. War Department, comp. *War of the Rebellion: A Compilation of the Official Records of the Union and Confederate Armies.* 128 vols. (Washington: Government Printing Office, 1880-1901) [hereafter *O.R.*], Series 1 [all references are to Series 1], vol. 40:1, pp. 172-73.
2. Ulysses S. Grant, *Personal Memoirs* (New York: Da Capo, 1982), p. 468.
3. *O.R.*, vol. 40:1, p. 173.
4. Ibid., pp. 174-75.
5. Ibid,, p. 43.

Chapter 1: The Broken Generals

1. William Marvel, *Burnside* (Chapel Hill: University of North Carolina Press, 1991), p. 98.
2. Ibid., p. 114.
3. Ibid., p. 160.
4. Burnside to Halleck, quoted in Alan Axelrod, *Complete Idiot's Guide to the Civil War,* 2nd edition. (Indianapolis: Alpha Books, 2003), p. 167.
5. Grant, *Personal Memoirs,* p. 581.
6. Quoted in "Building the Dimmock Line," http://members.aol.com/siege1864/dimmock.htm. Accessed February 24, 2007.
7. A gabion was a cylindrical basket, anywhere from thirty-three to thirty-six inches high with a diameter of about twenty-four inches, consisting of wooden pickets and thin brushwood rods. Ten to fourteen pickets were set upright in a circular pattern, and the flexible brushwood rods—branches between one-half and one inch thick—were woven around the pickets to form a web. At the top and the bottom, the web was bound with pliable wooden withes, wire, or even heavy twine. The pickets projected four to six inches from the top and the bottom of the web, so that they could be driven into the earth or fastened to horizontal wooden members called fascines or interconnected with other

gabions. The gabions, thus joined and interconnected, were used to create a "revetment"— to reinforce the interior walls of a sloping parapet. They did an extraordinarily effective job of absorbing the impact of small-arms fire, as well as artillery projectiles of all kinds.

8.   A bomb-proof was a trench structure that featured a roof designed to resist or absorb incoming shell impacts and explosions. It usually consisted of a heavy post and beam framework sunken below ground level. The roof incorporated one or more courses of large-diameter timbers, which were in turn covered by four to six feet of tightly tamped soil. Covered ways were passages or roads shielded from incoming fire by sinking them below ground level and building up a parapet on the side facing the enemy. Covered ways connected two or more works across ground that was exposed to enemy fire. They also provided a means of egress for attacking or counterattacking. Troops could sortie out of fortification and be sheltered by the covered way from opposing fire.

9.   Chevaux-de-frise were familiar elements of classic defensive fortifications. They were multiple obstacles, each consisting of a horizontal beam nine to twelve feet long and about a foot in diameter, pierced by two diagonal rows of sharpened lances about two inches in diameter and perhaps ten feet long. Each unit (or, in the French singular, cheval-de-frise) was fitted with eye bolts or hooks and chains to allow it to be linked with another unit in order to form the multiple chevaux-de-frise. The spikes were intended primarily to prevent cavalry attacks, but they were also effective against infantry, which would be slowed down and thereby rendered vulnerable to enemy fire.

10.   Quoted in Axelrod, *Complete Idiot's Guide to the Civil War,* p. 115.

11.   Grant, *Personal Memoirs,* p. 534.

12.   Ibid., pp. 444-45.

13.   Quoted in John Cannan, *The Crater: Burnside's Assault on the Confederate Trenches, July 30, 1864* (New York: Da Capo, 2002), p. 14.

Chapter 2: The Engineer and the Lawyer

1.   Quoted in Cannan, *The Crater,* p. 14.

2.   Quoted in Axelrod, *Complete Idiot's Guide to the Civil War,* p. 230.

3.   Ibid.

4.   Quoted in Jeff Kinard, *The Battle of the Crater* (Fort Worth, Tex.: Ryan Place Publishers, 1995), p. 25.

5.   *O.R.,* vol. 40:2, p. 396.

Chapter 3: The Tunnel

1.   Ibid.

2.   *O.R.,* vol. 40:2, pp. 557-58.

3.   *O.R.,* vol. 40:2, p. 58; my italics.

4.   U.S. Congress, *Report of the Joint Committee on the Conduct of the War, at the Second Session Thirty-Eighth Congress. Army of the Potomac. Battle of Petersburg* (Washington: Government Printing Office, 1865), p. 13; Michael A. Cavanaugh

Notes

and William Marvel, *The Battle of the Crater: "The Horrid Pit,"* 2nd ed. (Lynchburg, Va.: H. E. Howard, 1989), p. 5.
5.   Ibid., p. 2.
6.   Ibid.
7.   Ibid.
8.   Agassiz, George R., ed., *Meade's Headquarters 1863-1865: Letters of Colonel Theodore Lyman* (Boston: Atlantic Monthly Press, 1922), p. 188; Grant, *Personal Memoirs,* p. 581; Douglas Southall Freeman, *Robert E. Lee: A Biography* (New York: Scribner's, 1934), p. 64.
9.   Grant to Henry W. Halleck, quoted in David J.Eicher, *The Longest Night: A Military History of the Civil War* (New York: Simon & Schuster, 2001), p. 723.
10.   *O.R.,* vol. 40:11, pp. 163-64.
11.   Ibid., pp. 557-58.
12.   *Report of the Joint Committee,* pp. 2-3.
13.   Ibid. p. 2.
14.   Quoted in *The National Tribune* (Washington, D.C.), September 4, 1919.
15.   *O.R.,* vol. 40:11, p. 557.
16.   Polybius. *The Histories, with an English Translation by W. R. Paton,* 6 volumes (London, W. Heinemann; New York, G. P. Putnam's Sons, 1922-27), 5, p. 297.
17.   "The Vicksburg Mine" by Andrew Hickenlooper, Brevet Brigadier-General U.S.V. Chief Engineer of the Seventeenth Army Corps, at http://www.civilwarhome.com/vicksburgmine.htm. Accessed February 26, 2007.
18.   Ibid.
19.   Ibid.
20.   Ibid.
21.   Douglas's activities are discussed in Cavanaugh and Marvel, *The Battle of the Crater,* p. 11.
22.   *O.R.,* vol. 40:1, p. 557.
23.   Ibid.

Chapter 4: Men of War
1.   Ibid.
2.   Henry Pleasants to Robert Potter, July 20, 1864, *O.R.,* vol. 40:3, p. 354.
3.   *O.R.,* vol. 4011, p. 136.
4.   Ibid.
5.   Ibid.
6.   Ibid., my italics.
7.   Ibid.
8.   Ibid.
9.   Ibid.
10.   Ibid.
11.   Ibid. p. 59.
12.   Ibid.
13.   Ibid.
14.   Ibid.

15. Ibid.
16. *Report of the Joint Committee,* p. 16.
17. Ibid, pp. 16 and 97; my italics.
18. *O.R.,* vol. 40:1, p. 557.
19. Ibid.
20. Quoted in *The National Tribune* (Washington, D.C.), September 4, 1919.
21. *Report of the Joint Committee,* p. 13.
22. Ibid., p. 14.
23. Ibid.
24. Ibid.
25. Ibid.
26. Ibid.
27. Ibid, p. 15.
28. Ibid.
29. "DEATH OF GEN. FERRERO / A Man Who Achieved Fame in Two Dissimilar Professions. / DANCING MASTER AND SOLDIER / Abandoned a Successful Career in This City and Won High Rank as a Civil War Volunteer," *New York Times,* December 13, 1899, p. 2.
30. Cavanaugh and Marvel, *The Battle of the Crater,* p. 19. It is not likely that all of the "colored troops" of the Fourth Division received special training, and there is evidence that some were not relieved from labor details prior to the assault. Nevertheless, most sources agree that at least a significant number of Fourth Division soldiers were drilled in the wheeling maneuvers contemplated in Burnside's assault plan. Certainly, the officers and men of the Fourth Division were better prepared for the assault than the soldiers of any other unit, even if pre-assault drill had not been universal.

Chapter 5: Battle's Eve

1. *Report of the Joint Committee,* p. 16.
2. Ibid., p. 17.
3. Ibid.
4. *O.R.,* vol. 40:11, p. 46.
5. Ibid.
6. *Report of the Joint Committee,* p. 17.
7. Ibid.
8. Ibid., pp. 17-18.
9. Ibid., p. 18.
10. Ibid.
11. Ibid.
12. Ibid. In his earlier testimony before the army's Court of Inquiry Burnside narrated the episode in somewhat greater detail:

   On Friday forenoon General Willcox and General Potter, two of my division commanders, came to my headquarters, and we talked over the matter of the fight which was to take place on

Saturday morning. I said to one or both of them to this effect: that I had been very much worried and troubled the day before lest General Meade would overrule that part of my plan which contemplated the putting in of the colored troops, but that I hoped nothing further would be heard from it because General Meade had gone to City Point the day before, and the matter was to be referred to General Grant, and that inasmuch as I had not heard from General Meade I took it for granted that he had decided to allow the thing to remain as it was. This I must necessarily give in substance, because my conversations with my division commanders are not guarded. They can be called upon themselves to state what they know about the matter. Soon after that, say 11 o'clock, Generals Meade and Ord came to my headquarters. I am under the impression that I broached the subject myself as to the colored division taking the advance, but whether I did or not he informed me that General Grant coincided with him in opinion, and it was decided that I could not put that division in advance. I felt, and I suppose I expressed and showed, very great disappointment at this announcement, and finally in the conversation which occurred, and to which there are two witnesses here present, I asked General Meade if that decision could not be changed. He said, "No, general, it cannot; it is final, and you must put in your white troops." No doubt in the conversation I gave some of the reasons for not wishing to put the white troops in that I had given at his headquarters, but of that I am not certain. This was the day before the fight. I said to General Meade that that would necessarily change my plan. Now, this conversation either occurred at that time or it occurred at a later hour in the day, say 1 or 2 o'clock, when General Meade returned to my headquarters, because he went off with General Ord for an hour or two, say, and returned to my headquarters. It is not impossible that this conversation occurred in the afternoon instead of in the forenoon of the 29th. (*O.R.*, vol. 40:1, p. 61.)

13. *Report of the Joint Committee,* p. 111.
14. Ibid., p. 18.
15. Ibid.
16. Ibid., p. 9.
17. Ibid.
18. Quoted in Cannan, *The Crater,* p. 49.
19. *Report of the Joint Committee,* p. 18.
20. *O.R.,* vol. 40:1, p. 135.
21. *Report of the Joint Committee,* p. 19.
22. *O.R.,* vol. 40:11, p. 135.
23. Quoted in Cannan, *The Crater,* pp. 51-52.

24. Ibid., p 52.
25. *O.R.*, vol. 40:1, p. 135; *Report of the Joint Committee*, p. 19.
26. *Report of the Joint Committee*, p. 150.

Chapter 6: Sprung
1. Ibid., p. 117.
2. Ibid., p. 114. Pleasants's testimony that he "asked for fuze" and received common blasting fuse again raises the question of just who was responsible for obtaining substandard fuse. Perhaps Pleasants actually failed to specify exactly what he needed. Perhaps, however, he merely omitted that specification from his testimony. Or perhaps he assumed that his request for "fuze" would be understood by ordnance man Henry Hunt in the way that a mining engineer would understand it, as a request for waterproof safety fuse. It is also possible that Pleasants did request safety fuse and that Hunt, for whatever reason, failed to supply it.
3. *O.R.*, vol. 40:1, p. 139.
4. Ibid.
5. Ibid., p. 62.
6. Ibid.
7. Ibid.
8. Ibid., p. 139.
9. Ibid., p. 63.
10. Record of the Court of Inquiry on the Mine Explosion, p. 117.
11. *Report of the Joint Committee*, p. 114. Burnside testified to the Joint Committee that "The fuze material was not furnished in sufficient quantity to run three or four separate fuzes, as was contemplated by the plan. In fact, we had but material enough to run one line of fuze, and that material came to us in small pieces of from ten to fifteen feet in length, and had to be spliced before it was laid." (*Report of the Joint Committee*, p. 19) His explanation that the fuse, supplied in 10- to 15-foot lengths, had to be spliced was accurate, but his observation that there was only enough fuse to run a single line was incorrect. Pleasants ran three parallel lines of fuse.
12. Quoted in Cannan, *The Crater*, pp. 82-83.
13. Quoted in Noah Andre Trudeau, *Last Citadel: Petersburg, Virginia, June 1864–April 1865* (Baton Rouge: Louisiana State University, 1993), p. 109.
14. Quoted in Cannan, *The Crater*, pp. 82-83.
15. Ibid., p. 83.
16. *O.R.*, vol. 40:1 p. 59.
17. Quoted in Cavanaugh and Marvel, *The Battle of the Crater*, p. 40.
18. *National Park Service Historical Handbook: Petersburg National Battlefield*, at http://www.cr.nps.gov/history/online_books/hh/13/hh13f.htm. Accessed February 26, 2007.
19. *O.R.*, vol. 40:1, p. 69.
20. *Report of the Joint Committee*, p. 36; Richards quoted in Cannan, *The Crater*, p. 85.

21.　　*O.R.*, vol. 40:1, p. 558.
22.　　Alabama officer quoted in Trudeau, *Last Citadel*, p. 109; North Carolina artillery adjutant quoted in Cavanaugh and Marvel, *The Battle of the Crater*, p. 40.
23.　　Quoted in Cavanaugh and Marvel, *The Battle of the Crater*, p. 40.
24.　　*O.R.*, vol. 40:1, p. 103.
25.　　Ibid., p. 119.
26.　　Ibid., my italics.
27.　　*O.R.*, vol. 40:1, p. 105.
28.　　Quoted in Cannan, *The Crater*, pp. 89-90.
29.　　Ibid., pp. 91-2.
30.　　Ibid., p. 92.
31.　　*Report of the Joint Committee*, p. 35.
32.　　Ibid.
33.　　Ibid.
34.　　Ibid., p. 36.
35.　　Ibid.
36.　　Quoted in Cannan, *The Crater*, p. 93.

Chapter 7: A Perfect Mob

1.　　*Report of the Joint Committee*, p. 92.
2.　　Quoted in Cannan, *The Crater*, p. 94.
3.　　*Report of the Joint Committee*, p. 92.
4.　　Quoted in Cannan, *The Crater*, p. 95.
5.　　Ibid., p. 103.
6.　　Ibid., pp. 102-3.
7.　　Ibid., p. 99.
8.　　John H. Eicher and David J. Eicher, *Civil War High Commands* (Palo Alto, CA: Stanford University Press, 2001), p. 284.
9.　　*O.R.*, vol. 40:1, p. 101.
10.　　Ibid.
11.　　Ibid., my italics.
12.　　"Brig. Gen. Willcox Dead, He Was a Veteran of the Mexican and Civil Wars and Indian Campaigns," *New York Times*, May 11, 1907, p. 7.
13.　　*O.R.*, vol. 40:1, p. 101.
14.　　Ibid.

Chapter 8: The Ground Blue with Union Dead

1.　　Ibid., p. 140.
2.　　Ibid.
3.　　Ibid., p. 48.
4.　　*O.R.*, vol. 40:1, p. 140.
5.　　Ibid., p. 48.
6.　　Ibid., p. 140.
7.　　Ibid., p. 48.
8.　　Ibid., p. 141.

9.   Quoted in Cannan, *The Crater,* p. 105. Gregg's report of the use of grape shot may or may not have been accurate. Grape shot consisted of a certain number of small iron balls (typically nine), which were either put together between a pair of iron plates or arranged in tiers around an iron pin affixed to an iron tampion, then put into a canvas bag, the balls quilted into place by means of a stout cord. When fired, the balls would separate from the iron plates or the bag, spraying out in a deadly expanding cluster for about one thousand yards. Most authorities believe that canister replaced grape shot during the first year of the war, and some writers claim that grape shot was never used in the Civil War.

10.   Quoted in Cannan, *The Crater,* p. 105.
11.   Ibid., p. 106.
12.   *O.R.,* vol. 40:1, p. 103.
13.   Ibid., p. 118.
14.   Ibid.
15.   Quoted in Cannon, *The Crater,* p. 110.
16.   Ibid., pp. 111-12.
17.   Ibid., p. 112.
18.   Ibid.
19.   Ibid.
20.   *Report of the Joint Committee,* p. 92.
21.   Ibid.
22.   Ibid., pp. 92-93; my italics.
23.   Ibid., p. 93.
24.   Ibid.
25.   *O.R.,* vol. 40:1, p. 119.
26.   *O.R.,* vol. 40:1, p. 92.
27.   Ibid.
28.   Ibid., p. 93.
29.   Quoted in Cannon, *The Crater,* p. 114.
30.   Ibid., p. 115.
31.   Ibid., pp. 115, 116.
32.   Ibid., p. 117.
33.   Ibid.
34.   Ibid., p. 118.
35.   Ibid., p. 119.
36.   Ibid.
37.   Ibid.

Chapter 9: Counterattack
1.   *O.R.,* vol. 40:1, p. 105.
2.   Ibid., p. 194.
3.   Ibid.
4.   Ibid., p. 105.
5.   Quoted in Cavanaugh and Marvel, *The Battle of the Crater,* p. 58.

6. For background on Fort Pillow, see Mark M. Boatner III, *The Civil War Dictionary* (New York: Vintage, 1991), pp. 295-96, and Margaret E. Wagner, Gary W. Gallagher, and Paul Finkelman, eds., *The Library of Congress Civil War Desk Reference* (New York: Simon & Schuster, 2002), pp. 298-99.
7. Confederate atrocities against black soldiers (and their white officers) and black retribution for these are the subjects of George Burkhardt, *Confederate Rage, Yankee Wrath: No Quarter in the Civil War* (Carbondale: Southern Illinois University Press, 2007); the Confederate captain is quoted in Cavanaugh and Marvel, *The Battle of the Crater*, p. 58.
8. Quoted in Cannan, *The Crater*, p. 125.
9. Quoted in Cavanaugh and Marvel, *The Battle of the Crater*, p. 55.
10. Ibid., p. 87.
11. Etheredge quoted in Cannan, *The Crater*, p. 125; Edward A. Pollard, *The Lost Cause* (1866; reprint ed., New York: Gramercy, 1994), p. 537.
12. Quoted in Cavanaugh and Marvel, *The Battle of the Crater*, p. 87.
13. Ibid.
14. Ibid., p. 88.
15. Quoted in Trudeau, *The Last Citadel*, p. 119.
16. *O.R.*, vol. 40:1, p. 103.
17. Quoted in Cavanaugh and Marvel, *The Battle of the Crater*, p. 89.
18. Ibid.
19. Ibid.
20. *O.R.*, vol. 40:1, p. 72.
21. Ibid., p. 141.
22. Ibid.
23. Ibid.
24. Ibid., p. 149.
25. Ibid., p. 151.
26. Ibid., p. 143.
27. Ibid., p. 151, my italics.
28. Ibid., p. 144.
29. Ibid.
30. Ibid.
31. Quoted in Cavanaugh and Marvel, *The Battle of the Crater*, p. 93.

Chapter 10: Put in the Dead Men
1. Quoted in Cavanaugh and Marvel, *The Battle of the Crater*, p. 91.
2. Quoted in Cannan, *The Crater*, p. 133.
3. "That you may have some idea of the attenuated line of General Lee at that time, I will state that when [the Alabama] brigade was withdrawn from the breastworks at the Wilcox farm to be sent to do battle at the Crater, the entire space formerly occupied by [the Virginia, Georgia, and Alabama] brigades was left without soldiers, except a skirmish line consisting of one man every twenty paces." (John C. Featherston, *Battle of the Crater* [1906; reprint ed., Birmingham, AL: The Linn-Henley Research Center of the Birmingham Public Library, 1987], pp. 18-19.)

4.   Quoted in Cavanaugh and Marvel, *The Battle of the Crater,* p. 95.
5.   *O.R.,* vol. 40:1, p. 70.
6.   Ibid.
7.   Ibid., p. 65.
8.   Ibid.
9.   Ibid.
10.   John C. Featherston, *Battle of the Crater* (1906; reprint ed., Birmingham, AL: The Linn-Henley Research Center of the Birmingham Public Library, 1987), p. 19.
11.   Ibid.
12.   Ibid.
13.   Ibid., p. 20.
14.   Ibid.
15.   Ibid.
16.   Ibid.
17.   Ibid.
18.   Ibid., p. 21.
19.   Ibid.
20.   Ibid., p. 22.
21.   Quoted in Cavanaugh and Marvel, *The Battle of the Crater,* p. 98.
22.   Featherston, *Battle of the Crater,* p. 21; Bowley quoted in Cavanaugh and Marvel, *The Battle of the Crater,* p. 99.
23.   Quoted in Trudeau, *Last Citadel,* p. 119.
24.   Ibid.
25.   Featherston, *Battle of the Crater,* p. 21.
26.   Ibid., p. 22.
27.   *O.R.,* vol. 40:1, p. 102.
28.   Ibid.
29.   *O.R.,* vol. 40:1, p. 73.
30.   Quoted in Cavanaugh and Marvel, *The Battle of the Crater,* p. 101.

Chapter 11: A Stupendous Failure
1.   Featherston, *Battle of the Crater,* pp. 22-23.
2.   Pegram to Jenny, Aug. 1, 1864, Virginia Historical Society. Quoted in "No Quarter: Black Flag Warfare, 1863-1865." *North & South,* 10.1 (May 2007): 18.
3.   Featherston, *Battle of the Crater,* p. 23.
4.   *O.R.,* vol. 40:3, p. 687.
5.   Ibid., pp. 654-55.
6.   *O.R.,* vol. 40:3, p. 664.
7.   Ibid.
8.   Featherston, *Battle of the Crater,* p. 23.
9.   *O.R.,* vol. 40:3, pp. 686-87.
10.   Featherston, *Battle of the Crater,* p. 23.
11.   Ibid.
12.   *O.R.,* vol. 40:3, p. 699.
13.   Ibid.

14.   Ibid., p. 691.
15.   Ibid.
16.   Ibid., p. 702.
17.   Ibid.
18.   Ibid.
19.   Ibid., pp. 702-3.
20.   Featherston, *Battle of the Crater,* p. 24.
21.   Ibid.
22.   *O.R.,* vol. 40:3, p. 704.
23.   Ibid., p. 705.
24.   Ibid., p. 691.
25.   Ibid., p. 705.
26.   *O.R.,* vol. 42:2, p. 3.
27.   Ibid., p. 10.
28.   Ibid.
29.   Featherston, *Battle of the Crater,* p. 25.
30.   Quoted in Cavanaugh and Marvel, *The Battle of the Crater,* p. 105.
31.   Grant to Henry W. Halleck, quoted in Eicher, *The Longest Night,* p. 723; Grant, *Personal Memoirs,* p. 468.
32.   *O.R.,* vol. 42:2, p. 18.
33.   Ibid., pp. 24-25.
34.   Ibid., p. 24.

Epilogue: Butcher's Bill
1.   Ibid., p. 59.
2.   Ibid.
3.   Ibid., p. 64.
4.   Ibid., p. 58.
5.   Quoted in Cannan, *The Crater,* pp. 148-49.
6.   Ibid.
7.   *O.R.,* vol. 40:1, p. 128.
8.   Ibid.
9.   Ibid.
10.   Ibid.
11.   Ibid., p. 129.
12.   Ibid.
13.   Ibid.
14.   Marvel, *Burnside,* p. 413.
15.   Marvel, *Burnside,* p. 416; *Report of the Joint Committee,* p. 5. Meade "said he would be satisfied just to have the court of inquiry proceedings published, to counter those of the committee, and eventually the transcripts of both bodies appeared in the same little volume. The dual publication, however, did not constitute the great vindication Meade had hoped it would." (Marvel, *Burnside,* p. 416.)
16.   McCabe is quoted in Cavanaugh and Marvel, *The Battle of the Crater,* on the page facing the title page.

Bibliography

Agassiz, George R., ed., *Meade's Headquarters 1863–1865: Letters of Colonel Theodore Lyman*. Boston: Atlantic Monthly Press, 1922.

Axelrod, Alan. *Complete Idiot's Guide to the Civil War*, 2nd ed. Indianapolis: Alpha Books, 2003.

Blake, Nelson M. *William Mahone of Virginia, Soldier and Political Insurgent*. Richmond: Garrett and Massie, 1935.

Boatner, Mark M., III. *The Civil War Dictionary*. New York: Vintage, 1991.

"Brig. Gen. Willcox Dead, He Was a Veteran of the Mexican and Civil Wars and Indian Campaigns," *New York Times*, May 11, 1907, p. 7.

Burkhardt, George S. *Confederate Rage, Yankee Wrath: No Quarter in the Civil War*. Carbondale: Southern Illinois University Press, 2007.

Cannan, John. *The Crater: Burnside's Assault on the Confederate Trenches, July 30, 1864*. New York: Da Capo, 2002.

Catton, Bruce. *The Army of the Potomac: A Stillness at Appomattox*. New York: Doubleday, 1953.

Cavanaugh, Michael A., and William Marvel. *The Battle of the Crater: "The Horrid Pit,"* 2nd ed. Lynchburg, Va.: H. E. Howard, 1989.

Cullen, Joseph P. "The Siege of Petersburg," *Civil War Times Illustrated*, vol. 9 (August 1970).

Davis, William C. *Death in the Trenches: Grant at Petersburg*. Alexandria, VA: Time-Life Books, 1986.

Eicher, John H., and David J. *Civil War High Commands*. Stanford University Press, 2001.

Eicher, David J. *The Longest Night: A Military History of the Civil War*. New York: Simon & Schuster, 2001.

Featherston, John C. *Battle of the Crater*. 1906; reprint ed., Birmingham, AL: The Linn-Henley Research Center of the Birmingham Public Library, 1987.

Frassanito, William A. *Grant and Lee: The Virginia Campaigns, 1864-1865*. New York: Charles Scribner's Sons, 1983.

Freeman, Douglas Southall. *Robert E. Lee: A Biography*. 4 vols. New York: Charles Scribner's Sons, 1934.

Grant, Ulysses S. *Personal Memoirs*. New York: Da Capo, 1982.

Harrison, W. B. *Petersburg, Virginia, the Cockade City of the Union*. Petersburg: Virginia Printing and Manufacturing, 1909.

Hickenlooper, Andrew. "The Vicksburg Mine by Andrew Hickenlooper, Brevet Brigadier-General U.S.V. Chief Engineer of the Seventeenth Army Corps," at http://www.civilwarhome.com/vicksburgmine.htm. Accessed February 26, 2007.

Hoar, Jay S. *The South's Last Boys in Gray*. Bowling Green, OH: Bowling Green State University Popular Press, 1986.

Howe, Thomas J. *The Petersburg Campaign, Wasted Valor: June 15-18, 1864*. Lynchburg, VA: H. E. Howard, 1988.

Humphreys, Andrew A. *The Virginia Campaigns of '64 and '65*. New York: Charles Scribner's Sons, 1899.

Kinard, Jeff. *The Battle of the Crater*. Fort Worth, TX: Ryan Place Publishers, 1995.

Levin, Kevin M. "'Is Not the Glory Enough to Give Us All a Share?': An Analysis of Competing Memories of the Battle of the Crater," in Aaron Sheehan-Dean, ed., *The View from the Ground: Experiences of Civil War Soldiers* (Lexington: University Press of Kentucky, 2007), pp. 227-248.

Mahone, General William. *The Battle of the Crater*. Petersburg, VA: The Franklin Press, n.d.

Marvel, William. *Burnside*. Chapel Hill: University of North Carolina Press, 1991.

National Park Service. *National Park Service Historical Handbook: Petersburg National Battlefield*, at http://www.cr.nps.gov/history/online_books/hh/13/hh13f.htm. Accessed February 26, 2007.

Pleasants, Henry, Jr. *The Tragedy of the Crater*. Boston: The Christopher Publishing House, 1938.

Pleasants, Henry, Jr., and George H. Straley. *Inferno at Petersburg*. Philadelphia: Chilton Company, 1961.

Pollard, Edward A. *The Lost Cause*. 1866; reprint ed., New York: Gramercy, 1994.

Polybius. *The Histories, with an English Translation by W. R. Paton*, 6 volumes. London, W. Heinemann; New York, G. P. Putnam's Sons, 1922-27.

Sommers, Richard J. *Richmond Redeemed: The Siege of Petersburg*. Garden City, NY: Doubleday, 1981.

Stevenson, Silas, M.D. *Account of the Battle of the Mine or Battle of the Crater in Front of Petersburg, Va. July 30th, 1864*. New Castle, PA: John A. Leathers, Printer, 1914.

Tap, Bruce. *Over Lincoln's Shoulder: The Committee on the Conduct of the War*. Lawrence: University Press of Kansas, 1998.

Trudeau, Noah Andre. *The Last Citadel: Petersburg, Virginia, June 1864-April 1865*. Baton Rouge: Louisiana State University, 1993.

U.S. Congress. *Report of the Joint Committee on the Conduct of the War, at the Second Session Thirty-Eighth Congress. Army of the Potomac. Battle of Petersburg*. Washington: Government Printing Office, 1865.

Bibliography

U.S. War Department, comp. *War of the Rebellion: A Compilation of the Official Records of the Union and Confederate Armies*. 128 vols. Washington: Government Printing Office, 1880-1901.

Wagner, Margaret E., Gary W. Gallagher, and Paul Finkelman, eds., *The Library of Congress Civil War Desk Reference*. New York: Simon & Schuster, 2002.

Index

Acknowledgments

I am very grateful to the team of Keith & Keith: Keith Wallman, the editor who acquired my book for Carroll & Graf, and Keith Poulter, publisher and editor of *North and South: The Official Magazine of the Civil War Society*, who edited my manuscript line by line.

About the Author

Alan Axelrod is the author of three books on the Civil War-*The Complete Idiot's Guide to the Civil War*, first and second editions; *My Brother's Face: Portraits of the Civil War* (with Charles Phillips; reissued in 1998 as *Portraits of the Civil War*); and *The War Between the Spies: A History of Espionage During the American Civil War*. In addition, he has written many volumes of military history and reference, popular history, biography, and general reference, including *Patton: A Biography*, series editor General Wesley K. Clark; *Encyclopedia of the United States Armed Forces*; *America's Wars*; *Congressional Quarterly's American Treaties and Alliances*; and *The Macmillan Dictionary of Military Biography*.

After teaching at the University of Iowa, Lake Forest College, and Furman University he worked as an editor at the Henry Francis du Pont Winterthur Museum (Winterthur, DE), Van Nostrand Reinhold (New York), Abbeville Press (New York), and Turner Publishing, Inc. (Atlanta), a subsidiary of Turner Broadcasting System, Inc. In 1997, he founded The Ian Samuel Group, Inc., a creative services and book-packaging firm, and is its president.

Axelrod has served as consultant to numerous museums and cultural institutions, including the Margaret Woodbury Strong Museum (Rochester, NY), the Airman Memorial Museum (Suitland, MD), and the Henry Francis du Pont Winterthur Museum (Winterthur, DE). He has been a creative consultant for (and on-camera personality in) *The Wild West* television documentary series and *Civil War Journal,* and he served as historical consultant for The Discovery Channel. He lives in Atlanta with his wife, Anita, and son, Ian.